Terry Rudd

VITAL
CONTEMPORARY
ISSUES

THE VITAL ISSUES SERIES

VITAL ISSUES SERIES

VITAL CONTEMPORARY ISSUES

Examining Current Questions & Controversies

ROY B. ZUCK
GENERAL EDITOR

Grand Rapids, MI 49501

Vital Contemporary Issues by Roy B. Zuck, general editor.

Copyright © 1994 by Dallas Theological Seminary.

Published by Kregel Resources, an imprint of Kregel Publications, P.O. Box 2607, Grand Rapids, MI 49501. Kregel Resources provides timely and relevant resources for Christian life and service. Your comments and suggestions are valued.

Cover Design: Sarah Slattery
Book Design: Alan G. Hartman

Library of Congress Cataloging-in-Publication Data
   Roy B. Zuck.
   Vital contemporary issues: examining current
questions and controversies / Roy B. Zuck, gen. ed.
      p.   cm. (Vital Issues Series, vol. 2)
      1. Christian ethics. 2. Church and social problems.
   3. Theology—History—20th century. I. Zuck, Roy B.
   II. Series: Zuck, Roy B. Vital Issues Series.
   BJ1275.V57   1994   241—dc20   94-6931
                                                         CIP

ISBN 0-8254-4071-8 (paperback)

      1 2 3 4 5 Printing / Year 98 97 96 95 94

Printed in the United States of America

Contents

Contributors

J. Kerby Anderson
Executive Vice-president, Probe Ministries, Dallas, Texas

Francis J. Beckwith
Lecturer of Philosophy, University of Nevada, Las Vegas

J. Ronald Blue
President, CAM International, Dallas, Texas

Kenneth D. Boa
Division Director, Search Ministries, Atlanta, Georgia

Thomas R. Edgar
Professor of New Testament Literature and Exegesis,
Capital Bible Seminary, Lanham, Maryland

F. David Farnell
Academic Dean, Southeastern Bible College,
Birmingham, Alabama

Timothy D. Howell
Pastor, Huntersville, North Carolina

J. Carl Laney
Professor of Biblical Literature, Western Conservative
Baptist Seminary, Portland, Oregon

David E. Malick
Assistant Professor of Field Education, Dallas Theological
Seminary, Dallas, Texas

J. P. Moreland
Professor of Philosophy, Talbot School of Theology,
La Mirada, California

W. Gary Phillips
Chairman, Division of Biblical Studies, Bryan College,
Dayton, Tennessee

Preface

Like Siamese twins, ethics and doctrine are closely connected. How we should live and what we should believe are in fact inseparable. The one influences the other.

Issues on both ethical and doctrinal fronts occupy the minds of laypersons and theologians alike. Are there moral absolutes? Is abortion right? Is euthanasia biblical? What about suicide? How should Christians respond to the problems of homosexuality and AIDS?

Doctrinal matters also present challenges for modern-day thinkers. Can people be saved apart from hearing of Christ? Is liberation theology acceptable? What about the Signs and Wonders movement and the sign gifts including prophecy?What does the New Age movement teach?

The chapters in this book, reprinted from *Bibliotheca Sacra*, Dallas Seminary's quarterly theological journal (see page 10), interact with these many practical concerns of life-and-death consequence. The writers discuss the issues in a thoroughgoing manner, presenting arguments on various sides and discussing biblical data helpful in assessing where to stand in relation to these matters of contemporary ethics and doctrine.

ROY B. ZUCK

About *Bibliotheca Sacra*

A flood is rampant—an engulfing deluge of literature far beyond any one person's ability to read it all. Presses continue to churn out thousands of journals and magazines like a roiling, raging river.

Among these numberless publications, one stands tall and singular—*Bibliotheca Sacra*—a strange name (meaning "Sacred Library") but a journal familiar to many pastors, teachers, and Bible students.

How is *Bibliotheca Sacra* unique in the world of publishing? By being the oldest continuously published journal in the Western Hemisphere—1993 marked its 150th anniversary—and by being published by one school for sixty years—1994 marks its diamond anniversary of being released by Dallas Seminary.

Bib Sac, to use its shortened sobriquet, was founded in New York City in 1843 and was purchased by Dallas Theological Seminary in 1934, ten years after the school's founding. The quarterly's one-hundred and fifty year history boasts only nine editors. Through those years it has maintained a vibrant stance of biblical conservatism and a strong commitment to the Scriptures as God's infallible Word.

I am grateful to Kregel Publications for producing a series of volumes, being released this year and next, commemorating both the journal's sesquicentennial (1843–1993) and its diamond anniversary (1934–1994). Each volume in the Kregel *Vital Issues Series* includes carefully selected articles from the thirties to the present—articles of enduring quality, articles by leading evangelicals whose topics are as relevant today as when they were first produced. The chapters have been edited slightly to provide conformity of style. As Dallas Seminary and Kregel Publications jointly commemorate these anniversaries of *Bibliotheca Sacra*, we trust these anthologies will enrich the spiritual lives and Christian ministries of many more readers.

ROY B. ZUCK, EDITOR
Bibliotheca Sacra

For *Bibliotheca Sacra* subscription information, call Dallas Seminary, 1–800–992-0998.

PART 1:

Contemporary Ethical Issues

CHAPTER 1

What Is Behind Morality?

Kenneth D. Boa

T hroughout recorded history mankind has wrestled with a number of fundamental questions. A great variety of social, religious, and philosophical approaches have been used over the centuries in different parts of the world to arrive at meaningful and workable solutions, but most seem to introduce more difficulties than they solve. Three of the most crucial problems that confront man are the metaphysical problem (How do I account for the complexity of the universe and the personality of man?), the epistemological problem (How do I know that I know and how do I distinguish between fact and fantasy?), and the moral problem (What is the basis for morality, and why do all people have moral values?).

This chapter is restricted to a treatment of the moral problem, but it is well to keep in mind that these three problems are related. The way a person approaches one will substantially determine his approach to the others. Also, it should be noted at the outset that philosophy and theology both deal with the same basic questions. They use different terms and often give different answers, but the problems are the same. This is not surprising since philosophers as well as theologians concern themselves with matters of ultimate reality.

Morality Is Universal

Whether a person is a philosopher or a theologian, a poet or a scientist, the experiences he has during his lifetime are qualitatively similar to those of other individuals. In all cultures people have value or moral experiences, aesthetic experiences, and religious experiences. The idea of right versus wrong and good versus bad is firmly entrenched in the human mind, and it is consistently displayed in the human experience. People respond to their experiences of personality, love, and forgiveness, and almost all regard these qualities as superior to impersonality, hatred, and cruelty. Regardless of culture or time in history, everyone has moral inclinations. The norms of morality may vary, but the important thing is that all people believe that some things are right and some things are wrong. A few may object to this, claiming that there is really no such thing as right or wrong, but their objection is hollow. It is hollow because their actions and words betray them every day of their lives. Every time they criticize, complain, or accuse, they are implicitly appealing to some fixed standard of right and wrong. And conversely, every time they approve, applaud, or praise, there is a covert reference to a set of values.

Man's moral experience is so universal that a variation of the ontological argument can be applied as evidence for the existence of a transcendental moral standard. This does not mean, of course, that all people subscribe to a monolithic moral code. There are variations, contradictions, and even absurdities among the ethical codes in various parts of the world. But all too often, the differences and contradictions are emphasized so much that the overwhelming number of similarities is neglected. These similarities are so extensive that they point to a "traditional morality" or "natural law" which has been derived from human experience in all ages and countries. There is, for example, a principle of general beneficence to mankind which is clearly articulated in the moral codes of China, Babylon, Egypt, India, Israel, Rome, and elsewhere. In all societies, the principles of fairness, kindness, and honesty toward other people can be found. Moral codes from cultures around the world emphasize duties toward parents, elders, and ancestors on the one hand, and toward children and posterity on the other. Furthermore, there is a universal admiration of the qualities of munificence, mercy, wisdom, courage, self-control, and patience.

These traditional moral principles make up an ethical standard which has been given various names. In India it has been called the *dharma* or the *rita*. In China it was called the *tao*, the "way" of the universe which should be imitated by man. This *tao* or moral law allows for modifications and developments, and this explains some of the differences among ethical codes. But as C. S. Lewis argues, the development must be from within.[1] One cannot cogently contend for a new ethical code by stepping entirely outside the boundary of traditional morality (the *tao*). If he makes any appeal for the validity of his ethical system, it will necessarily be a masked appeal to those moral principles that are already evident in the *tao*. Philosophers and religious leaders have been able to clarify and bring about advances in the principles of traditional morality, but no one has instituted an entirely new moral value for the world to behold. There is no question that the Golden Rule as set forth by Christ ("Therefore whatever you want others to do for you, do so for them" [Matt. 7:12, NASB) is an advancement over the Silver Rule of Confucius ("What you do not want done to yourself, do not do to others" [*Analects* 15:23]). But it is not a radically new value. As Lewis says, "The human mind has no more power of inventing a new value than of imagining a new primary color, or, indeed, of creating a new sun and a new sky for it to move in."[2]

Many attempts have been made to arrive at new moralities by abandoning traditional values. But those who do so generally eliminate the bulk of these values while clinging tenaciously to the few they have decided to keep. To illustrate, a number of people endeavor to reduce their ethical system to the maxim, "Do your own thing as long as it doesn't interfere with others." Far from being a new morality, however, this would be better described as a severely truncated version of traditional morality. It really represents an arbitrary choice of one maxim from a number of maxims, and there is no logically consistent basis for choosing this particular one and eliminating the rest. It reduces to a subjective (and inadequate) moral code. The same is true for those who scoff at traditional moral values and claim that the only moral imperative people should be concerned about in modern culture is the good of society or the "survival of the species." The only real basis for these moral values is the traditional moral law from which they are derived, and yet this is the very thing these people are attempting to jettison.

But what is the basis for traditional moral law? If these values are based solely on human experiences and subjective feelings, there is a real problem. When people criticize or appeal to moral values, they are appealing to something which in their minds is self-evident and objective. Similarly, Jesus Christ did not institute an entirely new ethical code, even though He did bring about many refinements. Instead, He spoke to those who admitted their sinfulness and disobedience to the already known moral law. These are moral principles which are not limited to Christianity, but which can be found in Babylonian, Chinese, Greek,

Assyrian, and rabbinic texts. If these moral principles were not accepted as self-evident, no one would have sensed his need for the redemption from sin which Jesus was offering.

Certain things must be regarded as given; otherwise nothing can be proved. The given in the area of morality is that something must be good or bad for its own sake. If someone says that the human race should be preserved and that we should be concerned about posterity, another might well ask him why this should be so. It would not require many of these whys before the former is forced to admit that the thing he desires is good because he believes it is good. Each person entertains the concept that some things are objectively right and other things are simply wrong. Even a naturalist who scornfully inveighs against the irrational prohibitions found in the traditional morality has moral values of his own in the background. The process of rationalizing and explaining things away has a definite limit. If it is carried too far, nothing (including explanation itself) will be left.

Thus it can be said that human moral experience points to certain things. It points to a set of transcultural and transtemporal moral values which are held to be self-evidently and objectively true. It shows that this too cannot be entirely overthrown despite many attempts to do so, because no one lives in a moral vacuum. Further, it shows that no one is able to introduce a radically new moral value.

Appeal to an Objective Standard

All this leads to a serious problem. Human moral experience does not account for itself. Instead, it consistently appeals to the existence of some kind of objective standard for its validity. And the objective standard must be external to mankind rather than a subjective fabrication of human minds. This is because man is not a sufficient integration point for himself. Sartre stated that if a finite point does not have an infinite reference point, the finite point is absurd. Man is not his own God. The person who claims that man created God in his own image, for example, runs into real trouble when it comes to moral judgments. In effect, he must reduce moral values to a subjective sentiment produced by cultural conditioning. And if this is so, what basis does he have for being outraged at the cruelties of racial hatred, of violent crime, or even of the Third Reich? Certainly he cannot say that any of these things are wrong or right in any objective and ultimate sense. For by his own admission he has diluted moral values to the level of pure relativism.

Several Approaches to Morality

It is the thesis of this chapter that morality has no genuine validity unless it points to a higher dimension. To support this contention it is necessary to look at the logical implications of several competing approaches. Two ingredients are essential: horizontal self-consistency and vertical fitting of the facts.[3] An ethical system must first be logically consistent; its terms must obey the law of contradiction. Second, it must fit with the facts of the real world. One of the principal facts that it must reckon with is man's cruelty and his egotistic nature. Even if a system provides a consistent basis for moral duty which applies to all men, it must also provide a means of harnessing human desires to carry out this duty. Duty and desire must somehow be merged.

SKEPTICISM

The first basic approach to the problem of ethics is that of total skepticism. There is no rational answer for anything that exists. The universe is meaningless and absurd. Life has no real meaning and death is the greatest absurdity of all. A number of existentialists have arrived at this position, and it is also the theme of many books, plays, and films. According to this viewpoint, there is no basis at all for moral values. Carried far enough on a theoretical level, it would mean that a person could kill or be kind to another person, and it would make no ultimate difference. However, this approach cannot be maintained by anyone on a practical level. No one can be consistent with a position of complete skepticism. There *is* form and order in the world, and people live each day as though this were true whether they admit it or not. They communicate with others in very rational ways and make hundreds of choices which presuppose a consistent and orderly environment.

NATURALISM

Another basic approach to ethics is found in naturalism. Naturalism takes many forms, but all of them assign an impersonal beginning to the universe. The universe and all the phenomena in it are a product of the laws of nature plus time and chance. Naturalism has no place for a personal or supernatural agent originating and sustaining the universe. Consequently the naturalist looks to utility, to instinct, or to reason as his source for moral values.

There are several reasons why this approach is inadequate metaphysically and axiologically. One problem is that it gives no meaning for the particulars of nature and for mankind. Man has no significance or value in an impersonal universe. Such a universe would have no teleological or ordering agency, and it would not account for the complexity observed in living systems. Moreover, it does not explain the personality of man. Personality (including intellect, emotion, and will) is on a higher order than impersonality, and yet the naturalist maintains that it is a product of impersonal, chance factors. Reason and experience consistently show that no effect can be greater than its cause. Personality cannot be derived from an entirely impersonal base.

Man's rational mind is one aspect of his personality. And it is here that naturalism runs into another impasse. Naturalistic theories teach in effect that the human mind is the chance byproduct of an irrational and mindless process. This means that carried to its logical conclusion, the natural evolutionary theory strips away the basis for rationality itself. It reduces human reason to biochemical and electrical mechanisms. Those who argue that man's thoughts can be fully explained as the result of irrational causes are in reality attempting to prove that there are no such things as proofs. It is self-defeating to use human reason to call into question the validity of human reason.

There can be no knowledge unless certain basic things are assumed to be true. All scientists build their work, for example, on at least three presuppositions: (1) the universe is orderly (metaphysical); (2) men will be honest in their research methods and reports (moral); and (3) knowledge is possible (epistemological). All these presuppositions require, *contra* naturalism, a rationality behind the universe.

As stated earlier, the naturalist hopes to find his moral values in utility, in instinct, or in reason. However, none of these is sufficient to generate valid judgments of value. Neither utility (the usefulness of an act for a community) nor instinct can provide a logically consistent basis for one willingly to sacrifice his life for the sake of others. Scientific humanists often speak approvingly about the human instinct for the preservation of the species. They use this instinct as the foundation for the moral imperative that we should live and work for prosperity. But in so doing, they ignore several fatal difficulties. People have a number of instincts or natural desires, but those desires are not all harmonious. They are struggling against one another, vying for attention. The satisfaction of one (e.g., the preservation of the species) can mean the deprivation of others (e.g., the preservation of one's own life). Whence comes the imperative that an instinct like the preservation of humanity should be placed above man's other instincts? There is no real ground for saying that it is more fundamental or basic than the others. Why should a person obey one instinct and not others?

Humans have a natural impulse to preserve their lives and the lives of their children. But this impulse becomes weaker and more abstract the further it is projected into the future. Humans are far more concerned with the well-being of their children and grandchildren than they are with their descendants a thousand years hence. Thus for one to risk his life for the lives of his children for the sake of an abstract posterity has no instinctual foundation at all. Besides this, the sacrifice of one's life would frustrate the satisfaction of every other drive he has.

When all the rhetoric is stripped away, the naturalist's imperative of the preservation of humanity is based not on instinct but on a clandestine reference to an ethical maxim derived from traditional morality.

The same is true of attempts to base morality on pure reason. Reason alone is not sufficient to lead from a statement in the indicative ("this is so") to a statement in the imperative ("this ought to be so," or "we should do this"). It is necessary to assume the ethical from the beginning in order to move from an "is" to an "ought."[4] Even Kant's categorical imperative turns out to be an extension of a traditional moral value.

HUMANISM

The humanist offers another approach. People should be their own lawmakers; they can create their own values. For the humanist, mankind takes the place of God and eliminates the need for a transcendent realm. One option within humanism is individualistic ethics. In this case every person should do "that which is right in his own eyes." This immediately throws us into the danger of solipsism since everything is regarded from one's own experiences, feelings, and desires. This produces anarchy rather than morality. Group ethics is a second option. The problem here is that groups and societies can pursue paths as evil as those followed by any individual. Societies are concerned only for their own good and often try to achieve it at the expense of others. Instead of every person for himself, this is a case of every nation for itself.[5]

The third option within humanism seeks to find universal principles of conduct that transcend personal or group barriers. The brotherhood of all mankind and the need to respect the lives and needs of others are usually mentioned in this connection. As good as this sounds, humanism provides no philosophical basis for values like these. It offers only an impersonal beginning to the universe. People are just byproducts of a slow evolutionary process. All things are in flux and this includes moral values. Since everything is relative, there are no true morals or absolute standards. One is left with changing majority values and arbitrary sociological standards. There is no way of being sure that any of today's cherished ethical values will be valid tomorrow. If an individual is cruel, it is simply part of his nature. Humanism is unable to take an absolute stand against the many examples of genocide in the 20th century because it has no absolutes to which it can appeal. The humanist cannot establish ethical criteria that are universally normative. The humanistic position leads to skepticism not only about moral values, but also about the dignity of mankind. Humanity is just a minute and ephemeral accident in an impersonal and dying cosmos.

PANTHEISM

Instead of deifying mankind, many have opted to deify the universe. This is the pantheistic approach. Pantheism, like naturalism and humanism, is unable to create a foundation for morality. To begin with, the word "pantheism" is misleading because it cashes in on the semantic mysticism involved in the term "theism." It furtively changes the idea of personality found in theism into an impersonal philosophy. To get rid of this improperly used connotative word, Schaeffer has suggested the more accurate appellation, "panevery-thingism."[6] This leads to a tautology: the universe is everything, and everything is the universe.

Pantheism allows no moral categories because what one calls

right and wrong are simply reducible to a part of all that is. There is no ultimate difference between love and hate or between good and evil.

Thus it is evident that the views of skepticism, naturalism, humanism, and pantheism all fall short of providing an adequate basis for moral values. None of them really goes beyond de Sade's dictum, "What is, is right." Because of their relativism, these systems are unable to offer a philosophically valid answer to the question, "Why is murder wrong?" Among the recent plethora of "sophisticated" pornographic films is a film that depicts death by strangulation as a final part of the "love act." Many advocates of the approaches considered thus far would no doubt feel that there is something wrong with a film like this, but can they prove it according to the premises of their systems? What can they really say about the increasing dehumanization of mankind in this technological age? They may criticize wars and racial prejudice and cruelty, but in so doing they are appealing to objective and absolute standards of value that are philosophically inadmissible in their systems. Their own moral experiences continually betray them.

Theism's Approach to Morality

This leads to the next approach to morality: theism. Unlike the other approaches, theism proposes a personal beginning to the universe. Mankind is the product of an intelligent and personal ordering agent rather than an impersonal and mindless cosmos. This means there is a rational mind which in turn produced the human mind. There is a sufficient basis behind human rationality.

In order for the God of theism to have created this universe, He must be infinite as well as personal. He is the Ultimate whose character provides the absolute standard for morality. To speak of true moral values, one must no longer regard the conscience as a byproduct of nature. Rather, it must be derived from a Source that is absolutely moral. Nature itself is not rational or moral but its Creator is.

When people appeal to standards of morality which they believe are objective and absolute, they are living (whether they admit it or not) as though theism were true. Their moral behavior presupposes a transcendent absolute. If God is to be a sufficient integration point for man, He must be infinite, personal, rational, and good. Psalm 19:1–6 and Romans 1:20 say that the creation is able to tell man certain things about the Creator, including His intelligence, His eternal power, and His divine nature. Nevertheless this kind of natural revelation has definite limits. If a person is left only to his religious experiences, he will have little authority to say much more than this about God. Religious experience is interpreted in radically different ways, and the resulting concepts of God are often mutually exclusive.

The Bible, however, claims to be God's authoritative revelation to man. It says that God is not only transcendent; He is also immanent. Instead of being silent, He has communicated to mankind, and He has done so in the realm of spatio-temporal history. The One who created space and time entered into His own creation as the God-Man in order to "give His life a ransom for many" (Mark 10:45). Because of God's revelation, one's concept of God need not be limited to a fabrication of his own mind.

According to the Scriptures the traditional moral values discussed earlier are a result of the *imago Dei* in man. God has implanted the moral law in the human conscience to the extent that those who are honest with themselves must admit that they are unable consistently to live up to the standards they intuitively believe are right. "Indeed, when Gentiles, who do not have the law, do by nature things required by the law, they are a law for themselves, even though they do not have the law, since they show that the requirements of the law are written on their hearts, their consciences also bearing witness, and their thoughts now accusing, now even defending them" (Rom. 2:14–15, NIV). This is why human moral experience leads to certain values that transcend cultural and temporal barriers.

God did not create standards of morality or goodness. Neither does He obey them. Absolute goodness was never created because it is God's eternal character. God revealed His character in the Old and New Testaments, and the God-Man Jesus Christ perfectly lived it. God's character is above the vicissitudes of time and space, which means there is a changeless criterion for right and wrong. This provides an absolute basis for morality.

Nevertheless there is still a problem when one speaks of the goodness of God, and this is the existence of evil in the world. In briefest terms the biblical solution to this problem is that the creature, not God, is responsible for the sin and sorrow of natural and moral evil. Because of the Fall, nature was also cursed. This is the origin of the natural disease-death environment. The Bible speaks of a time when nature, like mankind, will be resurrected from its slavery to corruption (Rom. 8:19–22). Death itself will be overcome. "For since by a man came death, by a man also came the resurrection of the dead. For as in Adam all die, so also in Christ all shall be made alive" (1 Cor. 15:21–22).

Man as he is now is not what he was when God created him. People have not always been cruel. The Scriptures reveal that the human race, in its rebellion against God, changed from its original state of sinlessness to its present condition. There is now a moral discontinuity. Each person knows things about himself that he would not dare tell his closest friend. People cannot even criticize others without condemning themselves because they often find themselves guilty of practicing the same things. Mankind has abused every good gift from God including nature, authority, sex, marriage, food, and wealth.

God created man but He did not cause him to sin. Sin by definition is that which is contrary to the character of God. In order to create a sinful state of affairs God would have to rebel against Himself. Nonetheless many have concluded that God's standard of goodness in the Bible is contrary to man's social standards of goodness. John Stuart Mill held this position. More recently Ayn Rand went a step further and assailed the whole concept of God as "morally evil."[7] However, this ignores the fact that human morality, if it is to have any ultimate validity, must be derived from an absolute, and therefore external, base. Lewis argues for this point:

> There is, to be sure, one glaringly obvious ground for denying that any moral purpose at all is operative in the universe: namely, the actual course of events in all its wasteful cruelty and apparent indifference, or hostility, to life. But then, as I maintain, that is precisely the ground which we cannot use. Unless we judge this waste and cruelty to be real evils we cannot of course condemn the universe for exhibiting them. Unless we take our own standard of goodness to be valid in principle (however fallible our particular applications of it) we cannot mean anything by calling waste and cruelty evils. And unless we take our own standard to be something more than ours, to be in fact an objective principle to which we are responding, we cannot regard that standard as valid. In a word, unless we allow ultimate reality to be moral, we cannot morally condemn it.[8]

If morality is to rise above the subjective sentiments and opinions of finite creatures, there must be an ultimate authority whose eternal character is the essence of goodness, truth, and love.

Two important conclusions follow from all this: (1) God is not responsible for the origin of evil, and (2) His character is the absolute on which morality must be based. The Bible reveals God's character and it also shows that all men have true moral guilt—they fall short of God's standard. However, the Bible also reveals that God Himself has provided a solution to this moral dilemma through the substitutionary work of Christ. He offers release from sin's dominion and provides a way of reconciliation with the holy God.

Christian theism unites duty and desire. The duty consists of a right relationship to God and (consequently) a right relation to others. And Christ gives reason for carrying out this duty. He provides peace, security, joy, and a new quality of life to those who trust in Him. Thus the religious life and the moral life converge in a relationship with Jesus Christ. A genuine Christian does not regard God as an abstract concept or an impersonal Absolute. Instead, the believer desires to lead a life that is pleasing to God (that is, a moral life) as part of his gratitude and love for the God who first loved him. "In this is love, not that we loved God, but that He loved us and sent His Son to be the propitiation for our sins. Beloved, if God so loved us, we also ought to love one another" (1 John 4:10–11). Christians are to love God in response to His love for them, and they are to love each other as a result of their love for God.[9] "We love, because He first loved us. If some one says, 'I love God,' and hates his brother, he is a liar; for the one who does not love his brother whom he has seen, cannot love God whom he has not seen. And this commandment we have from Him, that the one who loves God should love his brother also" (4:19–21).

CHAPTER 2

Biblical Absolutes and Moral Conflicts

Norman L. Geisler

The Christian ethic is an ethic of love. Jesus made it clear that all the Old Testament commandments embodied principles of love (Matt. 22:38–40). The New Testament repeats these moral commandments in the context of grace and enjoins them on Christians believers (cf. Gal. 5:20–21; Rom. 15:8–10).[1] These eternal ethical principles of love are as unchanging as the nature of God on whom they are based, for God is love (1 John 4:16).

Now *in God* there is no conflict among the principles based on His nature, for God is one in nature (Deut. 6:4). And all attributes find their ultimate harmony and unity in the oneness of His nature. However, *in the world* there are conflicts in the commandments of love.[2] There are clashes of moral responsibility and overlapping of duties, as both Scripture and human experience verify. The problem of these conflicting ethical situations is addressed in this chapter. The question is this: What is the Christian's moral responsibility when two or more commands of Scripture appear to be in irresolvable conflict?

The people of God have often faced ethical dilemmas. For example, if it is wrong to kill one's son and it is wrong to disobey God, then what should Abraham have done when God told him to sacrifice Isaac (Gen. 22)? God commanded obedience to the king, but the king commanded the murder of innocent male children. What should the Hebrew midwives have done (Ex. 1)? The Scriptures enjoin obedience to parents but one's parents insist that he not serve God. What is the responsibility of love (Matt. 10:37)? The Bible forbids lying but the lives of God's servants can be saved by intentionally falsifying. What should Rahab have done (Josh. 6)? The queen commanded that all God's prophets be killed. A man defied her and hid one hundred of them. Was Obadiah right (1 Kings 18:13)? The Bible demands obedience to human government (Rom. 13:1–2), but a king ruled that all should worship an idol. Were the three Hebrew children wrong in disobeying the authorities (Dan. 3)?

Besides these biblical examples Christians face many examples of moral conflicts. Should the doctor take the life of the mother or the unborn baby, if both cannot live? Is it right to push someone out of an overcrowded life boat to save others? Should one first save his father or the man who just invented a cancer cure? Is it morally right to return a man's gun to him if he demands it in order to kill his wife? There are several responses one may make to such conflicting ethical situations. The four basic ones will be reviewed here in reference to the Christian biblical ethic of love.

The First Way: There Is Only One Absolute Duty of Love

One way to face the issue is to claim that there is only one absolute duty and so there is really no conflict.[3] It takes two absolutes to have an absolute conflict. If there is only one absolute love norm, then all conflicts are apparent but not real. In each situation there is only one absolute duty, namely, do the most loving thing possible.

Several things are significant about this alternative. First, it is simple. The believer is not overloaded with the baggage of numerous ethical commandments that are many times in conflict with each other. Second, it desires to preserve the absolute nature of love. God is absolute love and the believer is called in each situation to perform the most Godlike (i.e., the most loving) deed. Third, this view is situational in that the action of love takes into consideration varying situations. The general rule is to love, but what this means in particular will be determined by the specific situation.

The situations listed above must each be examined in view of one question: What would have been the most loving thing for them to do? One cannot always be sure in some situations, but he must do his best to discover what is most loving and never do what he does not at least *intend* as the most loving thing he can do in that situation.

How does one know what love means? He discovers it through general ethical principles such as those stated in Scripture. None of these, however, is absolute in itself including those embodied in the Ten Commandments. Each merely contributes to an over-all impression or intuition of love, and this single principle of love is the only thing to be applied to specific conflicting situations. How else, it is contended, could one resolve conflicts between given commandments unless he appeals to some one overall principle to which even these commandments are subject? Each of the Ten Commandments is not an absolute obligation of love. Rather, each is a general principle, spelling out what is usually the loving thing to do. But sometimes love will demand that a man lie or commit adultery or even kill or deny God. For if one could save lives by doing any of these, then surely love would demand that the commandment be broken.

On the surface this view seems attractive, but even in its best form it falls short of a truly Christian love ethic. There are several fatal difficulties. First, there is not just one duty of love; there are many. Jesus said, "Keep my commandments." Even in minimal form Jesus stated at least two, love God and love others, and He indicated that this was merely a "summary" of the "whole" law which is comprised of many specific laws (Rom. 13:8–9). Even these two basic levels come into conflict, as the cases of Abraham and Isaac and obedience to God versus parents demonstrate. As long as the duties of love are on two levels and in various over-lapping areas in a sinful world, there will be conflicts. And it will not do to say there is no absolute duty to love others; Christ commanded the contrary. For what makes the love of one's neighbor an absolute duty is that it comes as a commandment of God based in His very nature as love. To say there is only one duty is to evade the clear statements of Scripture and to ignore the multifaceted relations of ethical relationships to the contrary.

Another serious problem with the one-norm love ethic is that it is too general to be meaningful. It is like having only a summary of a story and being commanded to fill in all the content and details from one's own situations. To tell a man to "love" in all situations without spelling out what this means is like telling him to do "X" or to "zirkle" when he faces a conflict. None of these symbols has any meaning unless it is defined with specific content. On the contrary, the commandments of Christ do spell out the meaning of love for the Christian. Each commandment indicates clearly what love means in a given human relationship. Without these laws the Christian would not know what the absolute obligations of love really are, to say nothing of being able to perform them. He would be left to his own subjective intuitions and guesses.

The Second Way: There Is Always a Third Alternative for Love

A widely held view among Christians, and one which has much more to commend it than the former, is the position that moral conflicts are false dilemmas.[4] In each case there is always a third alternative. One is never forced to do something less than loving, because all the alternatives are not evil. Rahab did not need to lie to save the lives of the spies. God could have preserved her from facing the question or could have delivered the spies from their captors, even if she told the truth. Then too, silence, even to the point of sacrificing one's own life, is always a third possibility. God is faithful to those who are faithful to Him and always "with the temptation [He] will provide the way of escape" (1 Cor. 10:13). God intervened and saved Abraham from having to kill Isaac, and He would do the same for anyone else who is faithful to His commands, as was Abraham.

This view has some obviously appealing features. First, it maintains without compromise the many absolute commands of love in Scripture. There is no evasive attempt to reduce all the many absolute commands of God to a single, virtually meaningless and unusable "love" norm. Second, there is an earnest attempt made to seek third alternatives to breaking any commandment. The assumption is that if God commanded both, then He expects to keep both and He will see to it that they are able to keep His commandments without sinning. All of this is commendable. One can, so to speak, have his "cake" of many absolutes and eat it too, knowing that they never really conflict.

But that is precisely where the problem lies. Are all conflicts merely apparent? Is there always a third way out? The evidence is to the contrary. True, Abraham did not actually kill Isaac, but he did have to *intend to do so*. And Jesus taught morality is a matter of intent (Matt. 5:22, 28). The Hebrew midwives saved the children's lives but they had to disobey God's command to obey government in order to do so. If this was right then at least some commands of God must be suspended on occasion. If so, which ones and on what basis? Surely the ethical principles embodied in the Ten Commandments would be candidates for absolutes. And yet Jesus pointed out real conflicts between the first and fifth commandments. When a parent commands a child to show his love for the family by denying the true God, what third alternative does the child have? It seems overly simplistic and naive to hold, in the face of innumerable cases both within and outside the Bible, that there are never any real conflicts.

A further problem with the third-alternative position has already been implied. Do all commandments have the same force? Are there no higher relationships that take precedence over lower ones? Do all the commandments stand on the same footing? The answer is negative. Jesus spoke of lesser and greater commandments (Matt. 5:19) and of "weightier" matters of the Law (Matt. 23:23). Some things are of higher value than others (1 Cor. 13:13). Indeed love itself comes in degrees of which Jesus called self-sacrifice the "greatest" (John 15:13). So when there is conflict between lesser and greater commands, then one must give way to another. But if this is so, then the position that all the commandments are equally binding on the believer is not so. For when equally binding commands conflict, then the alternatives for this position would necessitate breaking one of the commands. But if one must be broken, then the position is invalidated. For in that case there was a real conflict with no real third alternative.

In addition, this position often leads to legalistic consequences such as were condemned by Jesus. For example to insist that a man's property rights to his gun take precedence over his wife's right to life is an unethical following of the letter of the Law. Such is worse than the Pharisees who insisted on the lesser matters of the Law while neglecting the "weightier" matters (Matt. 23:23), who kept the Sabbath while neglecting justice and mercy.

The Third Way: Perform the Least Nonloving Act

There is another way to maintain an absolute ethic of love without sacrificing the universally binding nature of biblical commands.[5] One may simply admit that there are real conflicts between some absolute commands. Sometimes there is no loving possibility open to a Christian. In this event one must simply do the least nonloving thing available. This is an evil world and tragic moral dilemmas are part of this kind of world. The best one can do is sometimes the least evil possible. This position is popularly called the "lesser of two evils" view. In terms of a Christian ethic of love it contends that when there is no way *not* to break one of the absolute love commandments, then all that remains is to do the least nonloving thing in that situation.

Of course when one breaks a commandment of God, he is guilty. But sin is sometimes unavoidable. The love of God provides forgiveness for those who confess, but the providence of God does not always provide a way to escape sinning. Sometimes there is no third alternative to breaking a commandment. The laws of God are absolute and ought never be broken. But the world is sinful and it is occasionally necessary to break one of God's laws, even for the most godly of believers. When one is confronted with this undesirable conflict, he must decide which is the lesser of the two evils and act accordingly.

Several things commend this view. First, like the previous view, it has the advantage of preserving the absolute nature of biblical commands. There are no exceptions to God's imperatives to love under any circumstance. It is always wrong to lie and to kill, and so forth. If these conflict, then so be it. One must do the lesser evil and lie to save the life. A second advantage is the fact that, unlike the previous position, this view is realistic enough to admit to real conflict situations. There is no special pleading to divine providence to provide miraculous third alternatives and no subtle redefining of terms to escape real dilemmas. There are many absolute commandments and they do sometimes come into irresolvable conflict with each other.

Each of these points would be valuable in an absolute Christian ethic, operating in a real but sinful world. But can one contend for both? Can an ethic be truly Christian if both of these things are so. Three forceful arguments indicate a negative answer. First, is it consistent with the nature of an all-wise, all-loving God to hold a man guilty for doing what was unavoidable? If sometimes a man cannot avoid sinning, but chooses the lesser evil, then God is blaming him for doing what He demands, namely, the least evil. It does not seem consistent with the nature of the God of Scripture to set up absolute but unavoidably conflicting commands and then impute individual guilt to people because they had to break them, even though they did their moral best. Rather, God condemns only those who by His enabling grace could have done otherwise (cf. Matt. 25:26–30).

Second, this view raises a serious problem with regard to the sinlessness of Christ. Christ is the believers' moral example; Christians should act as He acted. Further, they are assured that He is their complete moral example. He faced all the kinds of moral situations believers face. He is "one who in every respect has been tempted as we are, yet without sinning" (Heb. 4:15). But if there are real moral conflicts and Jesus faced them, then sinning was inevitable for Him too. He must have sinned. But the Bible says clearly that He never sinned in word, thought, or deed (2 Cor. 5:22; Heb. 4:15; 1 Pet. 2:22; 1 John 3:5). It follows then, that there are no situations where a lesser evil is called for. A positive good is always possible. Here too, evasiveness will not salvage this position. One might be tempted to appeal to some kind of providential sparing of Christ from these moral dilemmas. But this would be to forsake the lesser of two evils position for the third alternative view. For if God provided third alternatives for Christ, then why not for believers too. Furthermore, if Christ was spared moral dilemmas, then how can He be the believers' example since they face them. Hence, either Christ had irresolvable moral conflicts and sinned, or else He was sinless and there are no situations where the only alternatives are sinful or unloving. God always provides a way for the most loving act to be performed.

A third problem with the "lesser-evil" view arises from its insistence that a person is obligated to do the lesser evil. Since it is a moral obligation and since the action is nevertheless morally wrong, the absurd consequence is that a man is morally obligated to do what is immoral. But this is obviously nonsense to speak of a moral duty to do evil.[6] But if the view retracts the moral duty, then one is left with key ethical situations with no moral imperative. In this case, then, he should be without ethical condemnation and it would no longer be a lesser of two *evils* position. This leads to another position.

The Fourth Way: Subordinate the Lower Laws of Love to the Higher Ones

Love is never caught on the horns of a dilemma. There are levels and spheres of love and one is always higher than another.[7] Each love command is absolute in its area. But when that area overlaps with another area, then the lower responsibility of love should be subordinated to the higher. One's duty to God has priority over his duty to his fellow man when the two conflict. The obligation to save an innocent life is greater than to tell the truth to a murderer, and so on. Each of the absolute commandments of the Bible is absolutely binding on the relationship it specifies. There are no exceptions. Adultery is always wrong as such. Murder is never right as such. Lying is universally culpable in and of itself. However, when one or more of these relationships, which are wrong in themselves, overlaps with another area, then one's duty to the lower may be suspended in view of his responsibility to do the higher. There are no exceptions to absolute commands but there are some exceptions in view of higher priorities of love. There is always a greater good.

This "greater-good" position is distinguishable from the preceding ones.[8] It differs from the "one-norm" position in two important ways. It holds that there are many norms that are absolutely binding as such. There are no exceptions to universal ethical commands. Also because there are many laws defining the nature and areas of love, one has advance information of what love should do in a given situation. Love is not determined by the situation. Rather, love prescribes in advance what must be done in the situation.

This greater love position is different from the other two views as well. In contrast to the third alternative view, it holds that God's commandments do sometimes overlap. There are real moral conflicts in which both laws cannot be followed as one normally would. And in contrast to the lesser-of-evils view this position contends that both alternatives of the dilemma are not wrong. God will not hold a person guilty for doing his best. One way is always the morally right way, namely, following the higher commandment.

The Scriptures give ample illustrations of the principle that higher commands take precedence over lower commands. Jesus said that love for God is more important than love for parents, even though both are commands of God (Matt. 10.37). Peter made it clear that the command to obey human government was not higher than the one to preach the gospel (Acts 4). The Hebrew midwives (Ex. 1) and Daniel's three friends (Dan. 3) were all commended for disobeying human government when it conflicted with a higher ethical command. Abraham's intent to kill Isaac was morally right only because it was put in irresolvable conflict with his direct obedience to God's higher command to obey Him (Gen. 22).[9]

Three things are clear from these and other biblical examples. First, there are real conflicts among God's commands that are personally unavoidable by the individual. Second, a person is morally obligated to follow the highest command when he cannot do both. Third, God does not hold people guilty for following the highest command. Rather, God commends them (cf. Abraham, Hebrew midwives).

This raises one final question, namely, in what sense is this view absolute when it allows that one is not obligated to follow some (lower) ethical laws when they conflict with higher ones? There are three ways in which it may be said that all commands based on God's nature are absolute even though they must sometimes be subordinated to higher ones.[10] First, they are absolutely binding as such on the particular relationship toward which they are directed. Lying as such is always wrong. And in relation to another person's life, it is never right to murder him, and so forth. However, what is absolutely binding *as such* in a simple relation is not necessarily the right course of action in a complex situation where one must decide between two commands *as conflicting*. Second, when there is a conflict, it is an absolutely binding ethical obligation to follow the higher law revealed by God in His Word. Third, implied in the above is the truth that God has established absolutely the very order of commandments based on their proximity to His very nature as holy and loving. In short, some things are more godly and more loving because they are more Godlike. And Scripture is the only true source for knowing precisely the ordering of God's priorities. If we are wrong in ethical judgment, then, it is because as Jesus said, "You do err not knowing the Scriptures" (Matt. 22:29).

A knowledge of the priority of values has two important implications. First, by knowing which commands are higher and which are lower, one knows which "evil" is the greatest good in the more rare irresolvable conflicts. Second, an awareness of divine priorities enables the Christian to distinguish the best from the merely good in the more common everyday choices. For it is not only a *good* to choose the lesser "evil" in unavoidable conflicts, but it is also an *evil* to elect the lesser good when there is no unavoidable conflict. In this latter respect ignorance of the biblical priority of values leaves the Christian vulnerable to the perennial temptation to sacrifice the best on the altar of the good.

CHAPTER 3

The Abortion Epidemic: America's Silent Holocaust

J. Carl Laney

Abortions in recent years have terminated one-third of all pregnancies in America. Since the Supreme Court's decision of 1973 (*Roe vs. Wade*), the annual number of abortions performed in the United States has risen from 1.5 million to "1.6 million or about 4,300 abortions a day."[1] Since 1973 an estimated 30 million[2] unborn babies died in hospitals and abortion clinics throughout America. Nontherapeutic abortion is, in fact, a 20th-century form of birth control. It has become the second most common surgical procedure, circumcision being the first.

Abortion on demand is without question the greatest moral issue facing America today. No other contemporary moral problem in this country results in the deaths of over a million innocent, unborn children each year.

Many Christians today are not sufficiently informed about abortion to form a scripturally based opinion on this issue. Others would like to remain neutral. They do not advocate abortion, but would not prohibit a woman from having one. In an interview on abortion, a California physician stated, "I feel I have the obligation to take care of patients. I don't feel I should enforce my own personal views, especially since I'm not so convinced that [abortion] is ungodly or unbiblical."[3] Still others would identify with the "pro-choice" crusaders who contend that abortion is a right that women must have. They would argue that all other rights—social, economic, political—depend on the fundamental right of a woman to control her own body.[4]

Abortion is a contemporary moral problem that must be addressed scripturally. The purpose of this chapter is to provide sufficient biblical truth and factual data to enable the reader to formulate not only a scriptural view on the abortion issue, but also a plan of action to help end the silent holocaust.

What Is an Abortion?

Abortion is the act of bringing forth young prematurely.[5] A spontaneous abortion is one that takes place naturally—a situation over which the mother has no control. This is often referred to as a miscarriage. An induced abortion, however, is one that is brought about by medical means. In the hospitals and abortion clinics in America the term is used to refer to the destruction of the unborn child in the womb or the extraction of the immature child from the womb in order to end its life. Induced abortion is a violent act that not only destroys the life of the child but also endangers the life of the mother.[6] Several methods of abortion are used.

SUCTION ASPIRATION

Suction aspiration is a procedure used in 80 percent of the abortions up to the 12th week of pregnancy. The mouth of the cervix is dilated. A hollow tube with a knifelike edged tip is inserted into the womb. A suction force 28 times stronger than a vacuum cleaner literally tears the developing baby to pieces and sucks the remains into a container.

DILATION AND CURETTAGE

Dilation and curettage (commonly called D & C) is a procedure that involves dilating the cervix with a series of instruments to allow the insertion of a curetta—loop-shaped knife—into the womb. The instrument is used to scrape the placenta from the uterus and then cut the baby apart. The pieces are then drawn through the cervix. The tiny body must then be reassembled by an attending nurse to make sure no parts remain in the womb to cause infection.

SALINE INJECTION

Saline injection, also known as "salt-poisoning," is an abortion procedure that involves removing some of the amniotic fluid surrounding the baby and replacing it with a toxic, saline solution. The baby then breathes and swallows the solution. In one or two hours the unborn child dies from salt poisoning, dehydration, and hemorrhaging. The mother goes into labor about 24 hours later and delivers a dead (or dying) baby.

HYSTEROTOMY

During the last three months of pregnancy, abortions are performed by hysterotomy, which involves opening the womb surgically and removing the baby as in a cesarean section. However, the purpose of this procedure is to end the infant's life. Instead of being cared for, the baby is wrapped in a blanket, set aside, and allowed to die.

PROSTAGLANDIN

This abortion procedure involves the use of chemicals developed by the Upjohn Pharmaceutical Company. Prostaglandin hormones, injected into the womb or released in a vaginal suppository, cause the uterus to contract and deliver the child prematurely—too young to survive. A saline solution is sometimes injected first, killing the baby before birth, to make the procedure less distressful for the mother and medical staff.

RU 486

RU 486 is a powerful synthetic steroid used to induce abortions between the fifth and seventh weeks of pregnancy. The French pharmaceutical company Roussel-Uclaf sells RU 486 in Britain, France, and Sweden. Ingested in pill form during the early weeks of pregnancy, RU 486 deprives the developing fetus of the vital nutritional hormone progesterone. As a result, the developing child literally starves to death as the nutrient lining of the womb sloughs off. Muscular contractions then cause the dead infant to be expelled from the uterus. RU 486 has no proven use except to kill an unborn child.[7]

Contrary to popular thinking, RU 486 is not the easy, at-home, do-it-yourself technique that pro-abortion groups have been hoping for. The drug is legal in France but is only administered after a woman has signed a document acknowledging its risks. Prolonged heavy bleeding, severe cramps, nausea, diarrhea, headache, skin rash, and vomiting are the usual side effects. The average duration of bleeding is ten days, but it has lasted up to 43 days. In one case surgical intervention was necessary to stop the bleeding. Some women have required blood transfusions as a result of the procedure.[8]

There is concern among some medical authorities about the long-term effects of RU 486. The drug has chemical properties similar to DES, a drug given to women in the 1960s and 1970s to prevent miscarriage. The side effects of that drug did not show up for 20 years.

One of the first actions of President Clinton upon taking office was to roll back the Reagan-Bush restrictions on abortion. One of these actions was to revoke prohibitions on the importation of RU 486 into the United States if the U.S. Food and Drug Administration determines that there is no justification for the prohibition.[9]

The abortion procedures described above are not pleasant. But Christians need to know that when someone exercises "freedom of choice" with regard to abortion, these are the choices involved. It is remarkable that the law protects animals from cruel deaths. A person can kill his dog or cat, but he cannot kill it with cruelty. He would be subject to arrest if he cut off his pet's limbs, dissolved its skin in acid, or starved it to death. Yet the law allows these kinds of atrocities to be carried out against the most defenseless members of the human family.

Do the unborn feel pain during these abortion procedures? Yes, they do. Dr. A. W. Liley, world-renowned professor of fetal physiology at the National Women's Hospital in Auckland, New Zealand, has shown that the unborn child can feel pain and is sensitive to touch, light, heat, and noise as early as 11 weeks after conception.[10] Using closed-circuit television cameras, he has shown that if an unborn child is pricked with a needle, the infant will recoil in pain. But if a beep sounds before the prick, and this is repeated several times, the tiny baby will begin to recoil at the beep in anticipation of the pain he knows will come.

In addition to ending the life of the child, abortion endangers the life of the mother. The popular opinion that abortion is safer than childbirth is absolutely false. Published reports of deaths resulting from legal abortions range from 1.2 to 75 deaths per 100,000 abortions.[11] In the late stages of pregnancy, abortion is far more dangerous than childbirth. Death can result from uterine infection, peritonitis, hemorrhage, perforated uterus, or later tubal pregnancy.[12] Other complications relate to damage done to the cervix, injury to the lining of the womb, and blockage of the fallopian tubes. These include prematurity in subsequent pregnancies, increased miscarriages, and sterility.[13]

What Has Been the Legal Situation?

On January 22, 1973, the United States Supreme Court made a seven-to-two decision on the *Roe vs. Wade* case which virtually established abortion as a constitutional right. The Court granted an absolute right to abortion on demand during the first two trimesters of pregnancy, and an almost unqualified right to abortion for "health reasons" during the third trimester. Such "health reasons," as defined in the *Doe vs. Bolton* case, include the psychological, social, and economic well-being of the mother. Harold O. J. Brown, chairman of the Christian Action Council, has pointed out:

> This places the United States alone among all the civilized nations of the world in permitting abortions at such a late point in pregnancy that the fetus, if born prematurely or by normal Caesarean section at that time, would live. Such late abortions are considered in most nations of the world to be infanticide.[14]

Amazingly, in dealing with the *Roe vs. Wade* case, the Court was unwilling to decide whether an unborn child is fully human, yet they were willing to open the abortion floodgates.[15]

On July 3, 1989, the U.S. Supreme Court upheld in a five-to-four decision a Missouri law restricting abortions. The preamble of the Missouri Act declares that "the life of each human being begins at conception."

The Missouri law (a) bars public employees from assisting in abortions and prohibits abortions from being performed in state hospitals or other publicly owned or leased facilities, (b) prohibits the use of public funds to encourage or counsel a woman to have an abortion not necessary to save her life, and (c) requires that physicians conduct viability tests before performing abortions of 20 or more weeks gestational age.

What Does the Word of God Say?

What does the Bible say about abortion? Does Scripture attribute equal value to the life of an adult and the life of an unborn child? From God's perspective, is an unborn baby a human being? These are questions every Christian must wrestle with in formulating an opinion on the issue of abortion.

THE ABSENCE OF A PROHIBITION AGAINST ABORTION

Since the Bible has no command, "Thou shalt not have an abortion," some Christians have concluded that an induced abortion is not morally wrong or unbiblical. In response to such thinking, Cline states, "The most significant thing about abortion legislation in biblical law is that there is none. It was so unthinkable that an Israelite woman should desire an abortion that there was no need to mention this offense in the criminal code."[16] Why was abortion an unthinkable act for the ancient Israelites? First, children were recognized as a gift or heritage from the Lord (Gen. 33:5; Pss. 113:9; 127:3). Second, God was considered the One who opens the womb and allows conception (Gen. 29:33; 30:22; 1 Sam. 1:19–20). Third, childlessness was thought to be a curse, for the husband's family name could not be carried on (Deut. 25:6; Ruth 4:5). Barrenness meant the extinction of the family name (cf. Jer. 11:10). Induced abortion was so abhorrent to the Israelite mind that it was not necessary to have a specific prohibition to deal with it in the Law. Sufficient was the command, "You shall not murder" (Ex. 20:13).

Interestingly, ancient Assyrian laws attest to the abhorrence of abortion even by heathen nations near Israel. According to those laws, a woman guilty of an abortion was condemned to be impaled on stakes. Even if she lost her life in the abortion procedure, she was still to be impaled as an expression of the community's repudiation of such an abominable practice.[17] What a commentary on the moral decay of the United States that while pagan Assyrians condemned abortion, enlightened "Christian" America has condoned it.

THE MISINTERPRETATION OF EXODUS 21:22–25

Some Christians have concluded from Exodus 21:22–25 that the fetus is merely *potential* human life. They understand the passage to refer to a case of accidental miscarriage. According to this view, a mere fine is levied in the case of an accidental miscarriage, whereas the law of retaliation is applied if the mother is injured or dies. It is concluded that since the punishment for accidentally killing an unborn child is less severe than the punishment for killing an adult, the unborn baby must be considered less than human.[18] Abortion, therefore, according to these persons, does not constitute the termination of "human" life and is not to be viewed as unscriptural.

This approach has two major difficulties—one in the interpretation of the text and the other in the application of the text. The usual Hebrew word for "miscarry" (Gen. 31:38; Ex. 23:26; Job 3:16; Hos. 9:14) is not used in Exodus 21:22. The verb which the New American Standard Bible translates "she has a miscarriage" (literally, "her children come out") is יָצָא which customarily refers in the Old Testament to live births (cf. Gen. 25:26; 38:28–30; Job 3:11; 10:18; Jer. 1:5; 20:18).

On the basis of careful exegesis, Jackson concludes that "Exodus 21:22 must refer to live birth."[19] The late German commentators Keil and Delitzsch agreed that it is better to take Exodus 21:22 as referring not to accidental miscarriage but to premature birth.[20]

It must also be noted that the text itself makes no distinction between harm done to the child and harm done to the mother.[21] In verse 22 two possible situations are contemplated—an accident in which no harm comes to the mother or child and an accident in which the mother or child is injured. The accident without injury results in a mere fine, probably imposed because of the danger to which the mother and child are exposed. In the case of an accident with some injury—to the mother, her child, or both—the law of retaliation is to be applied. The renowned Jewish scholar, Umberto Cassuto, translates the text as meaning premature birth: "But if any mischief happen, that is, if the woman dies or the children die, then you shall give life for life, eye for eye."[22] Frame provides a helpful paraphrase of the text under consideration:

> And if men fight together and hurt a pregnant woman so that her child is born prematurely, yet neither mother or child is harmed, he shall surely be fined, according as the woman's husband shall lay upon him; and he shall pay as the judges determine. But if either mother or child is harmed, then thou shalt give life for life, eye for eye, tooth for tooth, hand for hand, foot for foot, burning for burning, wound for wound, stripe for stripe.[23]

A second difficulty with the "miscarriage" approach to Exodus 21:22–25 is the application of the passage to the abortion issue. Even if it could be successfully demonstrated that the text refers to accidental miscarriage rather than premature birth, it still could not be used to justify abortion. First, the injury is accidental, not intentional as in abortion. Second, though unintentional, the action was considered wrongdoing and punishable by law. Third, while the text may not expressly prohibit abortion, neither does it grant authority to perform abortion.[24]

THE DIVINE INVOLVEMENT IN THE FORMATION OF THE UNBORN

God is active in the event of conception itself (Gen. 29:31–35; 30:17–24; Ruth 4:13; 1 Sam. 1:19–20), and He is also personally involved in the formation and development of the human baby in the mother's womb. God told Jeremiah, "Before I formed you in the womb I knew you, before you were born I set you apart" (Jer. 1:5). The word "formed" (דצר) is used of God's special creation of Adam (Gen. 2:7–8). When used in its secular sense, רצד occurs most frequently in the participial form meaning "potter"—one who forms and fashions a piece of clay into a useful vessel.[25] God fashioned Jeremiah in the womb and also set him apart for his prophetic ministry before his birth. God was actively involved in the life of Jeremiah in his prenatal state.

In the third movement of Psalm 139, David joyfully acknowledged that the Lord intricately wove him together in his mother's womb (vv. 13-16). Here David wrote of God's relationship with him while he was growing and developing before birth. The significance of this psalm is highlighted by Allen:

> The Bible never speaks of fetal life as mere chemical activity, cellular growth, or vague force. Rather, the fetus in the mother's womb is described by the psalmist in vivid pictorial language as being shaped, fashioned, molded, and woven together by the personal activity of God. That is, as God formed Adam from the dust of the ground, so He is actively involved in fashioning the fetus in the womb.[26]

Verse 13 reveals that God, the Master Craftsman, fashioned David into a living person while he was still in his mother's womb. "Yes! You created my inmost self, you knitted me together in my mother's womb" (Ps. 139:13, Ronald Allen).[27] The unborn child is not just a piece of tissue but is a human being with potential for human experience.

In verse 14 David reflected on the fact that he was the product of God's creative actions: "I give public acknowledgment to you that I am awesomely wonderful; full of wonder are Your works, and my soul knows it very well" (Allen). David reflected on the fact that while he was in the womb hidden from the eyes of men, he was never hidden from God: "My bones were never hidden from you when I was being made in secret, and skillfully wrought (as) in the depths of the earth" (v. 15, Allen). The term "skillfully wrought" is used in the participial form in Exodus 26:36 of the one who wove or embroidered the beautifully colored fabric used to screen the doorway of the tabernacle. As this special fabric was intricately and skillfully woven, so David was exquisitely fashioned[28] by God "in the depths of the earth"—a metaphorical reference to his mother's womb.

David then referred to God's watchcare over his "unformed

substance" (NASB), that is, his "embryo."[29] Allen translates, "My embryo—your eyes saw! And in your Book all (my unformed parts) were written; daily they were being fashioned when as yet the whole was not (complete)" (Ps. 139:16). The word "embryo" is a key term in the abortion controversy. In man it refers to the "prefetal product of conception up to the beginning of the third month of pregnancy."[30] David acknowledged that his embryo—from the moment of conception—was under the personal watchcare of God. Concerning the significance of Psalm 139, Ryrie comments, "Even if life in the womb is not the same as it is after birth, it is human life in a certain form. And it is life which God is intimately concerned about."[31] Psalm 139:13–16 is a strong biblical polemic against abortion, for it clearly demonstrates God's personal involvement in the creation, formation, and development of the human baby.[32]

THE HUMANNESS OF THE UNBORN ACCORDING TO SCRIPTURE

According to the Bible, what uniquely distinguishes man from animals is man's creation in the image and likeness of God (Gen. 1:26–27; 5:1; 9:6). Bearing the image of God is the essence of humanness. And though God's image in man was marred at the Fall, it was not erased (cf. 1 Cor. 11:7; James 3:9). If the Bible reveals that the unborn baby is made in the image of God, then it must be concluded that the unborn child is fully human in God's sight.[33] The Protestant Reformers regarded the "image of God" in man as referring to man's immaterial nature as fashioned for rational, moral, and spiritual fellowship with God.[34] Does Scripture reveal that the unborn child possesses these characteristics?

David traced the ongoing of his sin with Bathsheba to his own conception: "Surely I have been a sinner from birth, sinful from the time my mother conceived me" (Ps. 51:5). The "iniquity" (KJV) and "sin" (KJV) referred to here are usually viewed as David's.[35] David is relating his sinfulness to the very inception of his life—before birth. This indicates that the moral law of God was already present and operative in David in his prenatal state. Since Scripture attributes moral guilt to David as an unborn child, a strong likelihood exists that he was human before birth.

Luke 1:41, 44 also point to the humanness of the unborn

child. John the Baptist is said to have "leaped" in Elizabeth's womb "for joy" when Mary's greeting was heard. John's prenatal recognition of the presence of Mary, the mother of the divine Messiah, points to his spiritual and rational capacity in the unborn state. Appropriately, the term used to describe John in his prenatal state is βρέφος ("baby"), the Greek term used for a child before and after birth (cf. Luke 2:12,16; 18:15; 2 Tim. 3:15). Psalm 51:5 and Luke 1:41, 44 reflect the scriptural view that unborn children are spiritual, rational, moral beings. A baby, then, is "in the image of God" in the unborn state. Frame remarks, "There is nothing in Scripture that even remotely suggests that the unborn child is anything less than a human person from the moment of conception."[36]

One other argument that lends support to the humanness of the unborn baby is the traducian view of the origin of the soul. According to the creation theory of the origin of the soul, each human being is created by God and joined to the body at conception, birth, or sometime between. The major objection to this view is that sin must be imputed to each soul after its creation, or else God is creating a sinful being. According to the traducian (from the Latin *traduco*, "to transfer") view, the soul as well as the material part of man is "transferred" by human generation. Thus the whole human race was potentially in Adam. This position is consistent with the scriptural view of the human race as a corporate unity (cf. Acts 17:26; Rom. 5:12). The human race was seminally present in Adam and participated in his original sin (Rom. 5:12; cf. Heb. 7:9–10). The point here is that the soul is present in the unborn child. Since there is moral accountability in the prenatal state, the unborn child must be fully human.

Some feminists have suggested that a distinction between abortion and contraception is inappropriate, for the goal of both is the prevention of an unwanted birth.[37] However, there is a considerable difference between contraception and abortion. Contraception prevents the fertilization of the ovum by the sperm, neither of which alone can generate human life. Abortion, on the other hand, destroys what has already been conceived. In abortion a third party is involved—a unique individual whom God has made. Abortion is an insult to the creative work of God and a transgression against the very image of God in man.

Is Abortion Ever Justifiable?

Is abortion justifiable in the case of rape, incest, or deformity of the unborn child? While these are volatile and emotionally charged issues, they do not focus on the major problem facing America. Abortions in the United States for rape, incest, protection of the mother's life, or voiding of a deformed fetus comprise less than five percent of all abortions.[38] The rest of the abortions being done today are performed mainly for convenience—for purposes of birth control. However, these other difficult issues must be considered.

RAPE

Rape rarely results in pregnancy. A ten-year study in Minnesota showed that no pregnancies resulted from 3,500 cases of forcible rape.[39] Conception can be prevented if the rape victim will seek treatment at a hospital immediately.

But what if a pregnancy should occur? It is a strange sort of justice that allows an innocent child to be killed for the crime of its father. The baby would still be the mother's own flesh and blood, no matter who the father was. Aborting the baby does not end the trauma of the rape; it compounds the sin of the father. One should consider this question: "If you found out today that you were the product of a rape, would you wish that your mother had aborted you?"

INCEST

Just as in the case of rape, special counsel and care is essential for a pregnant victim of incest. But aborting the baby would further jeopardize the physical and emotional well-being of the victim. Abortions performed on young girls are unusually hazardous, and studies show that sterility is as high as 30 percent among women 15 to 17 years of age who have had abortions.[40] As with rape, the child conceived by incest is a family member and should be cared for as such.

PROTECTION

In the abortion controversy, most people think that "protecting the life of the mother" has to do with her physical well-being. Legally, however, the "protection of the mother" may include psychological, social, and economic considerations as well. C. Everett Koop, former Surgeon General of the United

States and a leading pediatric surgeon, has stated, "In my thirty-six years in pediatric surgery I have never known of one instance where the child had to be aborted to save the mother's life."[41] In the rare case where a pregnancy must be abbreviated to protect the life of the mother, the proper procedure would be to give the child extraordinary care with the hopes of bringing it to maturity.

DEFORMITY

By examining a sample of the amniotic fluid in the womb (a process called "amniocentesis"), it is possible for a physician to determine if some deformity or defect is in the unborn child. If this test indicates that the child is deformed, should the child be aborted? When Moses questioned his own ability to speak to Pharaoh, God said, "Who gave man his mouth? Who makes him deaf or dumb? Who gives him sight or makes him blind? Is it not I, the Lord?" (Ex. 4:11). A sovereign God has the rightful authority to make some children "imperfect." These children are special because, as with the man born blind (John 9:3), God can use these handicaps to His glory.

Christians must not minimize the gravity of rape, incest, possible deformity, or danger to the life of the mother due to pregnancy. These infrequent and rather unique situations must be handled with scriptural counsel and loving concern. But situationalism must not govern decision-making in the area of Christian ethics. God is the One who creates life in the womb, and only He has the right to take it (Deut. 32:39; 1 Sam. 2:6).

What Can Christians Do about Abortion?

Christians have a moral and ethical responsibility to do something about abortion (cf. Prov. 24:11–14). Like the prophets of old, evangelical believers must cry out against the social and moral injustices so prevalent today (cf. Isa. 10:1–2; Jer. 2:34–35; Ezek. 22:3; Mic. 3:9–10). Specifically, what can and should believers do about abortion?

INFORMATION

One of the biggest problems in the abortion issue is that most people do not know the facts about abortion. Thus the first thing believers should do is become more informed on this important issue. Literature on abortion from a Christian perspective is available from groups like the Christian Action Council. Most informed Christians will make a decision to be morally opposed to abortion.

PRAYER

Concerned Christians are praying that Congress will pass a "Human Life Bill." Many believers are praying for a Human Life Amendment to the Constitution so that unborn children can receive the same protection as other Americans. Prayer can influence state and national leaders to take a pro-life stand on the abortion issue.

SUPPORT

Christians should know the positions of their political candidates regarding abortion and should support those who share their convictions regarding the value of unborn human life. At the same time, they should not support candidates who favor abortions nor institutions that provide abortion services (e.g., health plans, charity funds, hospitals).

COUNSEL

In counseling someone with an untimely pregnancy, one may help save the life of an unborn baby. Many pregnant mothers need counseling, housing, and help in finding adoptive parents for their babies.

COMPASSION

The more one learns about abortion, the more he or she may become angry. But one must be compassionate in dealing with those who have had abortions. Christians should hate the sin but share Christ's love for the sinner (Rom. 5:8). Many women who have abortions are the victims of exploitation. They are exploited first by men who want sex without responsibility, and then by physicians who are primarily interested in profiting from the lucrative abortion industry. Often those who have had abortions later become the most actively involved advocates for the unborn.

CHAPTER 4

A Critical Appraisal of Theological Arguments for Abortion Rights

Francis J. Beckwith

M any people in the pro-life movement are Christians. They rightly assume that the Bible condemns abortion. How ever, because this biblical assumption has not been, for the most part, defended with great rigor, and those who defend it tend to ignore objections to their exegesis, some people, who claim to be within the Christian tradition, are making an unchallenged defense of abortion rights by appealing to the Scriptures. They argue either that the Bible does not specifically condemn abortion or that the Bible actually supports the pro-choice position. The purpose of this chapter is to respond to those who employ these arguments.

Pro-Choice Argument That the Bible Does Not Specifically Forbid Abortion

Some people, such as Virginia Ramey Mollenkott, claim that "nowhere does the Bible prohibit abortion."[1] This claim is simply untrue if one recognizes that the Bible's statements on some other matters can be used to draw an inference that is consistent with the pro-life position. For instance it is clearly taught in the Bible that murder—the unjustified killing of a human being—is wrong (Ex. 20:13). And it follows logically from this that if the Bible teaches that the unborn are fully human, then it would be morally wrong to kill the unborn. So the real question is whether the Bible teaches that the unborn are fully human, not whether the Bible mentions or directly prohibits abortion. The following passages show that the Bible clearly teaches the full humanity of the unborn, though it is not an exhaustive list.[2]

PERSONAL LANGUAGE IS APPLIED TO THE CONCEPTUS

A number of passages in the Bible apply personal language to the unborn from conception. Genesis 4:1 reads, "Now the man had relations with his wife Eve, and she conceived and gave birth to Cain." Commenting in this passage, Davis has observed that "the writer's interest in Cain extends back beyond his birth, to his conception. That is when his personal history begins. The individual conceived and the individual born are one and the same, namely, Cain." What follows from this is that Cain's "conception, birth, and postnatal life form a natural continuum, with the God of the covenant involved at every stage."[3]

Job said, "Let the day perish on which I was to be born, and the night which said, 'A boy [לֶבֶר] is conceived'" (Job 3:3). This passage connects the individual born with the individual conceived. "Job traces his personal history back beyond his birth to the night of conception. The process of conception is described by the biblical writer in personal terms. There is no abstract language of the 'product of conception,' but the concrete language of humanity."[4] It is interesting to note that the Hebrew word translated "boy" is specifically applied to the unborn, although it is usually used to describe postnatal humans and is usually translated "male," "man," or "husband" (see Pss. 34:8; 52:7; 94:12; Prov. 6:34).

Another passage, Psalm 51:5, states, "Behold, I was brought forth in iniquity, and in sin my mother conceived me." This verse too indicates that one's existence begins with conception.

THE UNBORN ARE CALLED "CHILDREN"

The Bible refers to the unborn in the same way it refers to infants and young children. In Luke 1:41, 44 the word "baby" (brevf)oïs applied to the unborn: "And it came about that when Elizabeth heard Mary's greeting, the baby leaped in her womb; and Elizabeth was filled with the Holy Spirit. . . . 'For behold, when the sound of your greeting reached my ears, the baby leaped in my womb for joy.'" Compare this with Luke 2:12, 16 where the infant Jesus is called a "baby" (brevf)o "'And this will be a sign for you: you will find a baby wrapped in cloths, and lying in a manger.' . . . And they came in haste and found their way to Mary and Joseph, and the baby as He lay in the manger."

THE UNBORN ARE KNOWN BY GOD IN A PERSONAL WAY

A number of biblical passages are clear on this point. "For thou didst form my inward parts; Thou didst weave me in my mother's womb. I will give thanks to Thee, for I am fearfully and wonderfully made; wonderful are Thy works, and my soul knows it very well. My frame was not hidden from Thee, when I was made in secret, and skillfully wrought in the depths of the earth. Thine eyes have seen my unformed substance; and in Thy book they were all written, the days that were ordained for me, when as yet there was not one of them" (Ps. 139:13–16).

"Listen to Me, O islands, and pay attention, you peoples from afar. The Lord called Me from the womb; from the body of My mother He named Me" (Isa. 49:1).

"Before I formed you in the womb I knew you, and before you were born I consecrated you; I have appointed you a prophet to the nations" (Jer. 1:5).

"Then the angel of the Lord appeared to the woman, and said to her, 'Behold now, you are barren and have borne no children, but shall conceive and give birth to a son.' . . . Then the woman came and told her husband, saying, 'A man of God came to me and his appearance was like the appearance of the angel of God, very awesome. . . . But he said to me, "Behold, you shall conceive and give birth to a son, and now you shall not drink wine or strong drink nor eat any unclean thing, for the boy shall be a Nazirite to God *from the womb to the day of his death*"'" (Judg. 13:3, 6–7, italics added).

Some authors, including Robert Wennberg,[6] have questioned the use of many of these passages to establish the full humanity of the unborn. Though he makes valid points concerning some passages, which should provoke pro-lifers to clarify their exegesis, Wennberg tries to rob the right-to-lifer's biblical case of its strength by a hermeneutical sleight-of-hand. First, concerning those passages that use personal language to describe the unborn, Wennberg writes that "such references designate individuals not only before birth but before conception . . . and so they are not really to the point."[7] One problem with this criticism is that it is not applicable to all such passages, for some do speak of personal existence beginning at conception (e.g., Gen. 4:1 and Job 3:3).

Another problem is that these passages do not claim that the persons in question existed before their conception, but rather, that God knew them or had plans for them before conception. This is certainly possible for an eternal God, who knows all things simultaneously (Job 28:24; Ps. 147:5; Isa. 41:21–24; 46:10) and is not bound by time or space (Ps. 90:2; Isa. 40:28; 43:12b–13; 57:15a), since He is the Creator of time and space (Acts 17:25; Col. 1:16–17; Heb. 11:3; Rev. 4:11). That is, it is possible for him to know every person before he or she is conceived. Such foreknowledge prior to conception cannot be cited to explain away conception as the beginning of personal existence. Nor can God's foreknowledge rightly be used to explain away personal existence being attributed to prenatal life when certain passages specifically state that a certain individual either has personally existed from conception (e.g., Gen. 4:1) or has personally existed before birth (e.g., Jer. 1:5; Ps. 139:13–16; Luke 1:41–44). Moreover, the word "conception," or "to conceive," implies a genesis or a beginning, such as when one says, "This is the finest idea he ever conceived." Hence when the Bible speaks of God knowing a person before his conception, it is making an epistemological claim (a knowledge claim), not an ontological claim (a being claim). In light of these clarifications, the burden of proof is on Wennberg to show why the more simple and natural interpretation of the above passages should be given up.

Wennberg puts forth a second argument.

> Extending our examination, it would be a mistake to argue that since it was David who was being *formed* [or "brought forth" in NASB] in his mother's womb (Ps. 51:5) it must therefore have been David *the person* who was in his mother's womb. That would be to confuse "formation/ creation" of a thing with the "completion/existence" of that thing. The fact is that an entity can be on the way to becoming a particular thing without it being that thing. It is quite natural for us to refer to what is in the process of becoming (the zygote or fetus in a Semite woman's womb) in terms of what it will eventually become (a King David), but we are not then speaking with technical accuracy. If a butterfly is being formed in a cocoon, it does not follow that there is a butterfly there (rather than a caterpillar or something betwixt or between).[8]

In essence, Wennberg is arguing that one cannot cite passages such as Psalm 51:5 to show that the unborn are fully human, since such passages are only saying that the person in question is "being formed," not that the human being in the womb has become that person. There are several problems with this argument. First, even if Wennberg's interpretation of passages such as Psalm 51:5 were correct, he would still have to deal with other passages, such as some of the ones already cited, which clearly state that individual personal existence begins at conception (e.g., Gen. 4:1).

Second, Wennberg commits the hermeneutical fallacy that James Sire calls "world-view confusion."[9] This fallacy "occurs whenever a reader of Scripture fails to interpret the Bible within the intellectual and broadly cultural framework of the Bible itself and uses instead a foreign frame of reference."[10] Wennberg's distinction between person and human being is an invention of some contemporary philosophers who argue that a human being becomes a person at some stage in his or her development. Since it is doubtful that the authors of the Psalms were cognizant of such a distinction, Wennberg is reading back into David's assertion a foreign world view.

Third, the passage does say that "in sin my mother conceived me." This clearly indicates that David's personal existence can be traced back to conception, since he asserts that he was conceived. And if this is the case, then it seems natural to interpret the first half of Psalm 51:5 ("I was brought forth" or "I was being formed") as describing the subsequent physical development of David in the womb, which continues after birth into infancy, childhood, adolescence, and adulthood. Wennberg is correct in saying that "if a butterfly is being formed in a cocoon, it does not follow that there is a butterfly there (rather than a caterpillar or something betwixt or between)." But the insect that is becoming the butterfly is still the same insect that was once a caterpillar and will be a butterfly. In the same way the being at conception is the same person who will become the infant, the child, the adolescent, the adult. It is clear that passages such as Psalm 51:5 describe a person who is in the process of becoming, not a thing that is in the process of becoming a person.

Concerning the Bible and abortion, the following can be concluded: Just as the Bible does not forbid murdering people with submachine guns, the Bible does not forbid abortion. But since one can infer that murdering persons with submachine guns is wrong from the fact that the Bible forbids murdering in general, one can also infer that the Bible teaches that abortion is not justified from the fact that the Bible refers to unborn human beings as persons and forbids the murdering of persons in general. If one were to accept the principle that whatever the Bible does not specifically forbid is permissible, one would be in the horrible position of sanctioning everything from slavery to nuclear warfare to computer vandalism. Hence the question is not whether the Bible specifically forbids abortion, but whether the unborn are treated as persons. If they are, then we can infer that abortion is morally wrong.

Pro-Choice Argument from God's Granting of Free Moral Agency

Mollenkott argues that because God created mankind as free moral agents, to use public policy to make abortion illegal would be to rob the pregnant woman of the opportunity to be a responsible moral agent.[11] Mollenkott's argument can be stated as follows:

1. God created humans as free moral agents.
2. Any public policy that limits free moral agency is against God's will.
3. Public policy forbidding abortion would limit the free moral agency of the pregnant woman.
4. Therefore forbidding abortion is against God's will.

The problem with this argument lies with the second premise. It does not seem obvious that "any public policy that limits free moral agency is against God's will." For example laws against drunk driving, murdering, smoking crack, robbery, and child-molesting are all intended to limit free moral agency, yet it seems counter-intuitive, not to mention unbiblical, to assert that God does not approve of these laws. And such laws are instituted because the acts they are intended to limit often obstruct the free agency of other persons (e.g., a person killed by a drunk driver is prevented from exercising his free agency). Hence it would seem consistent with biblical faith to say that God probably approves of a public policy that seeks to maintain a just and orderly society by limiting some free moral agency (e.g., drunk driving, murdering, etc.), which in the long run increases free moral agency for a greater number (fewer people will be killed by dunk drivers and murderers, and hence there will be a greater number who will be able to act as free moral agents).

In fact Mollenkott herself advocates a public policy that limits the free moral agency of those who do not believe it is their moral obligation to use their tax dollars to help the poor pay for abortions. She believes that "if Christians truly care about justice for women, they will work to assure the availability of legal, medically safe abortion services for those who need them including the public funding without which the impoverished women cannot exert their creative responsibility."[12]

It seems clear that Mollenkott must assume that the unborn are not fully human in order for her argument from free agency to work. Thus she begs the question. For only if the act of abortion does not limit the free agency of another (i.e., no one else is harmed besides the actor) would a law forbidding abortions unjustly limit free moral agency. Hence if the unborn are fully human, a public policy forbidding abortions would not be against the will of God, as Mollenkott defines it.

Pro-Choice Argument from Exodus 21:22–25

This is a theological argument popular among some biblical scholars. It can be put in the following outline:

1. In Exodus 21:22–25 a person who accidentally kills a pregnant woman is given the death penalty.
2. In Exodus 21:22–25, a person who accidentally kills an unborn human is only fined for the crime.
3. Therefore Exodus 21:22–25 teaches both that the pregnant woman is of greater value than the unborn human she carries and that the unborn human does not have the status of a person.
4. Therefore abortion is justified.

This argument can be criticized on three counts. First, assuming that the pro-choicer's interpretation of Exodus 21:22–25 is correct, does it logically follow that abortion-on-demand is morally justified? After all, the passage is saying that the unborn are worth something. In stark contrast, contemporary pro-choicers seem to be saying that the unborn are worth only the value their mothers place on them. Therefore this Exodus passage does not seem to support the subjectively grounded value of the unborn assumed by the pro-choice movement.

Furthermore even if the pro-choicer's interpretation of this passage is correct, the passage in question is not teaching that the pregnant woman can willfully kill the human contents of her womb. It is merely teaching that there is a lesser penalty than for accidentally killing the mother. To move from this truth to the conclusion that abortion-on-demand is justified is a non sequitur.[13] So saying that the unborn are not worth as much as the born does not justify the contemporary practice of abortion-on-demand.

Second, one can also raise the more general hermeneutical question, as Montgomery has pointed out, as to whether a statement of penalty in the legislation God gave to ancient Israel ought to establish the context of interpretation for the total biblical attitude to the value of the unborn child (including not only specific and non-phenomenological Old Testament assertions such as Ps. 51:5, but the general New Testament valuation of the [*brephos*], as illustrated especially in Luke 1:41, 44).[14]

Montgomery then asks, "Should a passage such as Exodus 21 properly outweigh the analogy of the Incarnation itself, in which God became man at the moment when 'conception by the Holy Ghost' occurred—not at a later time as the universally condemned and heretical adoptionists alleged?"[15] Montgomery's point is that if pro-choicers were correct in their interpretation of Exodus 21, they still would have to deal with the grander context of Scripture itself, which does seem in other texts to treat the unborn as persons.

Third, it can be shown that premise two of this argument is false or at least that there is no scholarly consensus that it is true. In the Revised Standard Version, Exodus 21:22–25 reads as follows: "When men strive together, and hurt a woman with child, so that there is a miscarriage, and yet no harm follows, the one who hurt her shall be fined, according as the woman's husband shall lay upon him; and he shall pay as the judges determine. If any harm follows, then you shall give life for life, eye for eye, tooth for tooth, hand for hand, foot for foot, burn for burn, wound for wound, stripe for stripe."

The ambiguity of this passage is sufficient to divide commentators into two camps. One camp holds that the passage teaches that the woman and the unborn have different values.[16] According to this group, the passage is saying that if the unborn is accidentally killed, there is only a fine, but if the pregnant woman is accidentally killed, it is a much more serious offense. Therefore the death of the unborn is not considered the same as the death of a person. Some translations, such as the Jerusalem Bible, interpret the verse in this way: "If, when men come to blows, they hurt a woman who is pregnant and she suffers a miscarriage, though she does not die of it, the man responsible must pay the compensation demanded of him by the woman's master; he shall hand it over, after arbitration. But should she die, you shall give life for life, eye for eye, tooth for tooth, hand for hand, foot for foot, burn for burn, wound for wound, strike for strike."

This interpretation, however, has been called into question by many critics.[17] They argue that the Jerusalem Bible translation and others like it (e.g., TEV) are a mistranslation and that the passage is saying (in the Hebrew) that the mother and the unborn are to receive equal judicial treatment, that is, the mother and the unborn are both covered by the *lex talionis* (the law of retribution). Cassuto offers this interpretation:

> The statute commences, *And when men strive together*, etc., in order to give an example of accidental injury to a pregnant woman, and . . . the law presents the case realistically. Details follow: *and* they *hurt* unintentionally *a woman with child*—the sense is, that one of the combatants, whichever of them it be (for this reason the verb translated "and they hurt" is in the plural) is responsible—*and her children come forth* (i.e., there is a miscarriage) on account of the hurt she suffers (irrespective of the nature of the fetus, be it male or female, one or two; hence here, too, there is a generic plural as in the case of the verb "they hurt"), *but no mischief happens*—that is, the woman and the children do not die—the one who hurt her *shall surely be punished* by a fine, *according as the woman's husband shall lay*—impose—*upon him*, having regard to the extent of the injuries and the special circumstances of the accident; *and he* who caused the hurt shall pay the amount of the fine to the woman's husband *with judges*, in accordance with the decision of the court that will confirm the husband's claim and compel the offender to pay compensation, for it is impossible to leave the determination of the amount of the fine to the husband, and, on the other hand, it is not with the husband's power to compel the assailant to pay if he refuses. But if *any mischief happen*, that is, if the woman dies or the children die, *then you shall give life for life*, eye for eye, etc.: you, O judge (or you, O Israel, through the judge who represents you) shall adopt the principle of "life for life," etc.[18]

Archer points out that a major reason Cassuto's rendering is an appropriate interpretation is that the portion of the Hebrew translated in the New American Standard Bible as "so that she has a miscarriage" does not necessarily entail the death of the unborn, but can also mean the expulsion of a premature infant from his or her mother's womb regardless of whether the expulsion results in death.[19] Hence Exodus 21:22–25 is saying that if the incident in question results in only a premature birth, the perpetrator should be fined. However, if "harm follows" (i.e., if either the mother or the child is injured or killed), the same should be inflicted on the perpetrator.

In summary, since the interpretation of Exodus 21:22–25 is at best divided,[20] and since the Bible's larger context teaches that the unborn are persons (as argued earlier), it seems rather foolish for the pro-choice advocate to put all his ideological eggs into one dubious biblical basket.[21]

Pro-Choice Argument from Numbers 5:11–31

This passage is quoted in a tract published by Episcopalians for Religious Freedom, "A Pro-Choice Bible Study."[22] It is from the New English Bible translation.

"When a married woman . . . is unfaithful to her husband, and has sexual intercourse with another man . . . and the crime is undetected . . . but when . . . a fit of jealousy comes over a husband which causes him to suspect his wife . . . the husband shall bring his wife to the Priest. . . . He [the priest] shall take clean water in an earthenware vessel, and shall take dust from the floor of the Tabernacle and add it to the water. He shall set the woman before the Lord, uncover her head . . . shall . . . put the woman on oath and to say to her, '. . . may the Lord make an example of you . . . by bringing upon you *miscarriage and untimely birth* [abortion]; and this water that brings out the truth shall enter your body, bringing upon you *miscarriage and untimely birth.*' The woman shall respond, 'Amen, Amen.' . . After this he shall make the woman drink the water. If she has been unfaithful to her husband [and] when the priest makes her drink the water that brings out the truth . . . she will suffer a *miscarriage or untimely birth.* . . . But if the woman has not let herself become defiled and is pure . . . she will bear her child [italics added]."

The author of "A Pro-Choice Bible Study" claims that this passage proves that "*a planned abortion* is in the Bible as part of God's law given to Moses." He interprets the passage to mean that the request for abortion "comes from a husband, and his wife must agree to drink a potion prepared by a Hebrew priest. If the woman has been unfaithful, God initiates an abortion. This passage illustrates the direct intention of both potential parents plus a holy man to cause a miscarriage, an abortion."[23]

There are several problems with this interpretation. First, even if the passage were saying that abortion is justified in circumstances of infidelity, the passage is also saying that it is the Lord who brings on her "miscarriage and untimely birth," not the priest, the husband, or the wife. Therefore the passage supports not abortion on demand by a human being, but only abortion by God for adultery.

Second, nothing in the passage is saying that the unborn human is not fully human. If execution by God makes one nonhuman, then the residents of Sodom and Gomorrah and others killed by God were not human.

Third, it is peculiar that someone defending women's rights would cite a passage in which a husband who suspects his wife of having committed adultery is granted the right to take her to a priest who administers a drug and then prays that God cause an abortion if the pregnancy was the result of adultery. This is certainly not pro-choice. One can hardly imagine that this approach to female infidelity would be welcomed with opened arms by contemporary feminists.

Fourth, there is good reason to suppose that the translation from which this passage is quoted (the New English Bible) is not accurate. The Jerusalem Bible translates "miscarriage and untimely birth" as "making your thigh shrivel and your body swell." The New American Standard Bible says, "making your thigh waste away and your abdomen swell." Other translations are similar: "make thy thigh to rot, and thy belly to swell" (KJV); "make thy thigh to fall away, and thy body to swell" (ASB); "May he cause your genital organs to shrink and your stomach to swell up" (TEV); "he causes your thigh to waste away and your abdomen to swell" (NIV). An alternative reading in the NIV states: "causes you to have a miscarrying womb and barrenness."

All these translations seem to be saying that if the wife had committed adultery, her sexual organs will become useless, thus resulting in a miscarrying womb and barrenness. But if she did not commit adultery, she "will be able to have children" (Num. 5:28b, NIV).[24] This seems to be the most natural interpretation of this passage, since Numbers 5:11–31 is a test for a woman's adultery if her husband is unsure of her fidelity, not a test for a pregnancy, which may or may not result from adultery. Since a vast majority of adulterous unions do not result in pregnancy, a test for adultery that procured an abortion would not be a very good test. For what good would such an adultery test be if the wife had committed adultery and yet did not become pregnant? Thus it makes sense to reject the New English Bible translation.

Pro-Choice Argument from "Breath"

Some people argue that since Adam became a living soul when God "breathed into his nostrils the breath of life" (Gen. 2:7), birth is the time at which a child becomes a living being, since it is at this time that it begins to "breathe." There are at least two problems with this argument.[25] First, it is simply false to say that the unborn from conception do not breathe in a true biological sense. As Davis points out, "While breathing in the usual sense does not begin until birth, the process of *respiration* in the more technical biological sense of the transfer of oxygen from the environment of the living organism occurs from the time of conception." Thus it is "in the *mode* but not the *fact* of this oxygen transfer which changes at birth."[26] Therefore the "breath of life" exists from the moment of conception.

Second, there is no analogy between the creation of the first man, Adam, which was a unique historical event, and the ordinary birth of a child. As Brown points out, "if God took inanimate matter and made a man from it, as Genesis 2:7 seems to be saying, then obviously what He created was not a human being until it was given life. But the fetus is not 'inanimate matter.' It is already alive. And it is already human." Therefore "to apply Genesis 2:7 to human beings who were carried for nine months in a mother's womb before birth is clearly ridiculous. This argument is seldom used by people who take Scripture seriously."[27]

Miscellaneous Pro-Choice Arguments

Since the following passages and arguments are weak biblical defenses of the pro-choice position, the critiques of them will be brief. Almost all of them come from "A Pro-Choice Bible Study."

ARGUMENT FROM PSALM 51:5

David wrote, "Behold, I was brought forth in iniquity, and in sin my mother conceived me." Strangely enough, as already noted, this passage is also used to defend the pro-life position. In any event, the pro-choicer argues that since David could not have been an actual sinner because he had yet to actually sin, David was only a potential sinner. This is because he was only a potential person.

There are several problems with this argument. First, it does not address the fact that Psalm 51:5 does clearly state that it was David who came into existence at conception. Second, even if this passage were claiming that the unborn are potential sinners, this would still imply that the unborn are actual human persons, since only actual persons can be potential sinners, just as only actual persons can be potential violinists, philosophers, basketball players, or deli managers. And third, the passage is not saying that David, as a zygote, performed a sin, but rather, that he was conceived a sinner by virtue of being Adam's descendant. That is to say, Adam's sin nature is passed on to all who share his human nature. But this supports the pro-life position, for, as Geisler points out, "the very fact that humans are declared sinners from conception reveals that they are human, that is, part of the fallen human race. It is only by virtue of being part of the Adamic human race that we are conceived in sin (see Rom. 5:12)."[28]

ARGUMENT FROM PSALM 139:13, 16a

The passage reads, "For Thou didst form my inward parts; Thou didst weave me in my mother's womb. . . . Thine eyes have seen my unformed substance." The pro-choice advocate argues that since this passage says that the unborn is still being "weaved" and is "unformed," it is therefore not fully human.

The interpretation faces at least two problems. First, "'unformed' (v. 16) does not mean unhuman any more than deformed does."[29] Far from casting aspersion on the unborn's full humanness, Psalm 139 eloquently describes God's creative activity in prenatal human development, thus implying the full humanness of the unborn from the moment of conception. For in human development, "unformed" is a relational term which implies a lack a person may have in relation to a more advanced state of his development. That is to say, a pre-embryo is "unformed" in relation to an embryo, an embryo is "unformed" in relation to a fetus, a fetus is "unformed" in relation to an infant, an infant is "unformed" in relation to an adolescent, and an adolescent is "unformed" in relation to an adult. So it does not follow that since one is "unformed," one is therefore not fully human.

Second, it is poor hermeneutics to quote this passage in isolation from other statements about the unborn found in both the Book of Psalms (e.g., Ps. 51:5) and the rest of the Bible, which speak of personal human existence beginning from conception (e.g., Gen. 4:1), or refer to the unborn by personal pronouns (e.g., Jer. 1:5), or apply terms to the unborn which are used of postnatal children (e.g., Luke 1:41, 44; cf. 2:12, 16).

ARGUMENT FROM PSALM 139:16b

The second part of Psalm 139:16 is sometimes used to deny the unborn's full humanness: "And in thy book they were all written, the days that were ordained for me, when as yet there was not one of them." Pro-choice advocates argue that this passage is saying that while in the womb David's life had not yet begun ("When as yet there was not one of them"). The problem, however, with this interpretation is that the text does not say that the days of David's life excluded his prenatal existence. The passage is simply saying that all of David's days were ordained and written in "Thy book." And since God has known everything from all eternity, it follows that God knew of David's days "when as yet there was not one of them." These words must refer to the time before his conception, since Psalm 51:5 states that David's beginning can be traced back to his conception and Psalm 139 gives a detailed account of God's personal interaction with the development of the prenatal David.

ARGUMENT FROM JOB 10:18–19

This passage reads, "Why then hast Thou brought me out of the womb? Would that I had died and no eye had seen me! I should have been as though I had not been, carried from womb to tomb." The author of the tract "A Pro-Choice Bible Study" interprets this passage to mean that "Job did not consider the prenatal period as an existence."[30] This interpretation is totally unjustified for two important reasons. First, the passage is saying just the opposite: one does exist prenatally. Job said that if he had not been born it would be "as though" he "had not been." He was not saying that if he had not been born he would never have existed, only that it would be as though he had never existed. People speak this way all the time. For example a disenchanted husband may say that his wife treats him as though they were not married, but he is still married to her. In the same way, when Job claimed that if he had been stillborn it would be as though he had never existed, he still existed. One cannot use "as though" unless one "is."

Second, as already noted, Job 3:3 affirms the personhood of the conceptus: "Let the day perish on which I was to be born, and the night which said, 'A boy is conceived.'" Therefore Job 3:3 and 10:18–19 support the pro-life position.

ARGUMENT FROM ECCLESIASTES 11:5

This verse reads, "You do not know the path of the wind and how bones are formed in the womb of the pregnant woman [or, 'how the spirit comes to the bones of a woman with child,' RSV], so you do not know the activity of God who makes all things." The author of "A Pro-Choice Bible Study" claims that "the writer of Ecclesiastes admonishes the Bible reader not to speculate about how or when the spirit of the child arrives. It could be presumptuous to claim that life begins at conception, which the Bible refuses to do."[31]

There are several problems with the pro-choice interpretation of this verse. First, it is way off the mark. The verse is not speaking against Bible students speculating about when the spirit of a child arrives. The verse makes no mention of *when*. Instead it says that one does not know *how* the "bones are formed in the womb of the pregnant woman." It does not follow from one's ignorance of the mechanism by which the soul or spirit is given by God that he does not know when this occurs. That a person may not know *how* his mind works (and it is still a mystery to the scientific community) does not mean he cannot know *when* his mind is working. Though one does not know how God brings human persons into existence, one does know when personhood begins, since so many other biblical passages clearly indicate that full humanness begins at conception.

Second, even if the pro-choice interpretation of Ecclesiastes 11:5 were correct, the verse does not support abortion on demand. For certainly abortion could still be a serious moral wrong even if the unborn entity were not fully human during the entire nine months of pregnancy. Furthermore the pro-choicer is admitting that the verse is teaching that the spirit of the child arrives sometime before birth (after all, the woman is said to be "with child," RSV). Hence the pro-choice view of this verse does not support the pro-choicer's own position.

Third, if this verse were really claiming that one does not know when the unborn becomes fully human, then it would be just as presumptuous to deny that life begins at conception (i.e., the pro-choice position) as it would be to affirm that life begins at conception. Therefore even with a so-called "pro-choice" interpretation, this verse could still be used as a pro-life proof text: Since one does not know when life begins, one should not kill the unborn entity, for it is a real possibility that if one performs an abortion one is committing a homicide. It is legal negligence to perform an act in which one does not know whether one is harming another (e.g., demolishing a building without checking to see if anyone is inside).

ARGUMENT FROM 1 CORINTHIANS 15:46

This verse states, "However, the spiritual is not first, but the natural; then the spiritual." Pro-choicers who use this verse argue that the physical reality of the unborn precedes its spiritual endowment. In this view, before a certain point of time in gestation, the unborn does not possess a spirit and hence it is not a person. The problem with this interpretation is that the verse has nothing even remotely to do with embryology or human development. The context is clearly referring to human salvation. As the verses before and after verse 46 reveal, Paul was contrasting the first Adam with the second Adam, Jesus: "So also it is written, 'the first man, Adam, became a living soul.' The last Adam became a life-giving spirit. However, the spiritual is not first, but the natural; then the spiritual. The first man is from the earth, earthy; the second man is from heaven. As is the earthy, so also are those who are earthy; and as is the heavenly, so also are those who are heavenly. And just as we have borne the image of the earthy, we shall also bear the image of the heavenly" (1 Cor. 15:45–49).

ARGUMENT FROM THE FACT THAT GOD CALLS BELIEVERS BY NAME

Since the Bible teaches that "God calls us by name" (Isa. 43:1, 7; Rev. 3:5; Luke 10:20), and "a child is ready to be named at birth because the sex is only then normally known" (Gen. 29:31–35; Eccl. 6:4),[32] pro-choice advocates conclude that one is not fully human until birth.

This argument is factually and logically absurd. First, none of the verses cited establishes the pro-choice position. Second, it does not follow from not being named that one is not fully human. For it would still be wrong for a parent to murder her one-year-old even if she had not given the child a name. Third, it does not follow that because something is named it is human. Some parents have named their miscarried children. Will the pro-choicers who deny the full humanity of such beings now concede that they were human? If a person were to name his pet hamster Margaret Sanger, would that make the hamster human? Fourth, since it is now known that gender is genetically determined from conception, and that it is possible in principle to know the gender of one's unborn child a few days after conception, is it now wrong to abort the offspring of parents who name them long before their birth? Fifth, though it is true that God "calls us by name," it does not follow that one who is not named by another human, such as a parent, does not have a name known only to God. For if this were the case, then unnamed newborns, infants, and adults would not be human. Sixth, Isaiah 49:1 states that God has indeed called people by name from the womb even before they were named by their parents: "Listen to Me, O islands, and pay attention, you peoples from afar. The Lord called Me from the womb; from the body of My mother He named Me."

ARGUMENT FROM THE FACT THAT EVERY PERSON
LIVES UNDER GOD'S CARE FROM THE TIME OF BIRTH

This argument states that since both the psalmist and the Prophet Isaiah taught (Pss. 22:9–10; 58:3; 71:6; Isa. 49:5) that "every person lives under God's care from the time of birth, instead of conception,"[33] full humanness does not begin until birth.

This is a strange argument. None of the passages cited supports the pro-choice position on abortion. In fact they all lend support to the pro-life position. Psalm 22:10 says that "from my mother's womb you have been my God" (JB). Psalm 58:3 merely asserts that "wicked men . . . have been in error since birth" (JB). This hardly proves that these "men" had no prenatal existence. One can certainly use the word "since" in reference to a thing's attribute, such as "being in error," when the thing in question existed before acquiring that attribute. For example, if a person says he has weighed 180 pounds since 1988, it implies that he existed at another weight before 1988.

Psalm 71:6a ("I have relied on you since I was born," JB) can be understood along the same lines as Psalm 58:3. Psalm 71:5 says, "Yahweh, I have trusted you since my youth" (JB), and the second part of verse 6 states, "You have been my portion from my mother's womb" (JB). If the psalmist is claiming in the first part of verse 6 that there was no prenatal existence, then in verse 5 he is claiming that there is no preadolescent existence. But the second part of verse 6 is affirming prenatal existence. Therefore verse 6 supports not the pro-choice position, but the pro-life view.

Isaiah 49:5a reads, "And now Yahweh has spoken, he who

formed me in the womb to be his servant, to bring Jacob back to him, to gather Israel to him" (JB). Since being "formed in the womb" is consistent with, and lends support to, personhood beginning from conception, it is incredible that this passage is cited in defense of the pro-choice position.

ARGUMENT THAT LIFE BEGINS WHEN BLOOD COMES INTO EXISTENCE

Since certain biblical passages teach that "life is in the blood" (Gen. 9:4; Lev. 17:11, 14; Deut. 12:23), and since "embryologists have determined that blood cells do not develop until 20 days after fertilization," therefore, pro-choice advocates argue "life" does not arrive "until three weeks after conception."[34]

Aside from the fact that these passages do not support abortion on demand for the entire nine months of pregnancy, there is a fundamental problem with the use of these verses to establish the pro-choicer's conclusion. Not one refers to unborn humans; they all refer to mammals at a stage in their development when blood is a necessary condition for their mortal existence. The pre-20-day-old embryo, however, is a mammal and in particular is a living human being who does not need blood as a necessary condition for his existence. It does not follow from the fact that blood is a necessary condition for the existence of post-20-day-old humans that pre-20-day-old humans are not fully human.

Conclusion

This chapter has critically analyzed the major biblical and theological arguments for abortion rights, concluding that none of them is logically compelling. In fact it seems that the Bible points toward the opposite conclusion: almost all abortions are acts of unjustified homicide. But one should not conclude from this that Christian pro-lifers do not have good secular arguments they may use in order to persuade those who do not share their faith. In fact this writer has presented such arguments in detail elsewhere.[35] It should not be forgotten that a long and rich tradition in Christian church history, extending back to the early church fathers, has been against the practice of abortion.[36] This fact solidifies the pro-life interpretation of Scripture defended in this chapter. That to say, since the early church fathers were so close to the writing of the New Testament, it is reasonable to say that there is a presumption in favor of their interpretation of Scripture and their application of what they believed the Bible teaches on ethics. The church fathers could have been wrong, but the burden of proof is on those who would bring this accusation against them.[37]

CHAPTER 5

Euthanasia: A Biblical Appraisal

J. Kerby Anderson

Pastors and physicians alike agonize over the ethics of euthanasia. Is it moral to withhold medical treatment from a terminally ill patient? Is it ever right to "pull the plug" on a patient? These are only two of the many ethical questions surrounding the practice of euthanasia.

The term "euthanasia" was coined (in its currently prominent sense) by historian W. E. H. Lecky in 1869. Derived from the Greek for "happy death" or "good death," the term "euthanasia" traditionally conveyed the idea of keeping terminally ill patients free from pain in their last days. Unfortunately in recent years it has come to mean many other things.

This change in definition is well illustrated by the standard dictionary definition of euthanasia used in most courts. Webster's Dictionary provides two definitions: (1) "an easy death or means of inducing one" and (2) "the act or practice of painlessly putting to death persons suffering from incurable conditions or diseases."[1]

This definition immediately reflects the problem with a discussion of euthanasia. Euthanasia means different things to different people. Most lay people once assumed the focus was merely on what can properly be called "palliative care," which includes attempts by doctors and nurses to ease pain in terminal patients, but does not justify "inducing death." But to many people today, euthanasia includes not just a passive management of pain but an active termination of a suffering patient's life by a second party.

Thus crucial to any discussion of euthanasia is a proper definition of the various forms of euthanasia. Under this broader definition of euthanasia are some practices that can be justified from a biblical perspective while many others are clearly immoral and even criminal in nature.

Forms of Euthanasia

Ethical and medical discussions of euthanasia frequently include various forms of treatment or lack of treatment that fall under the general term "euthanasia." Four categories of euthanasia are frequently discussed in the medical literature.

1. Voluntary, passive euthanasia. This form of euthanasia assumes that medical personnel, at the patient's request, will merely allow nature to take its course. In the past, passive euthanasia meant that the physician did nothing to hasten death but did provide care, comfort, and counsel to dying patients.[2]

2. Voluntary, active euthanasia. This means that the physician, by request, hastens death by taking some active means (e.g., lethal injection). This raises the controversial issue of whether nonmedical personnel such as a spouse or friend would be permitted to end the suffering of another.[3]

3. Involuntary, passive euthanasia. This assumes that the patient has not expressed a willingness to die or cannot do so. The medical personnel do not go to any extraordinary measures to save the patient but they often withhold food (by removing nasogastric tubes), antibiotics, or life-support systems (respirator).

4. Involuntary, active euthanasia. This begins to blur into genocide. The physician does something active to hasten death, regardless of the patient's wishes, for humanitarian reasons, economic considerations, or genetic justifications.

Analysis of Different Forms of Euthanasia

An analysis of the moral questions in each form of euthanasia needs to be made. Each form has its own unique set of issues.

VOLUNTARY, PASSIVE EUTHANASIA

This is not truly euthanasia in the modern sense. In these situations it is assumed that death is imminent and inevitable. At this point the medical personnel's attention turns from curing the disease to making the patient as comfortable as possible. Further medical treatment to prolong life becomes pointless and an entirely different medical strategy is implemented.

This medical strategy is frequently referred to as palliative care. The prime focus is on alleviating pain, while not actually curing the patient.

Medications that deaden pain but do not dim consciousness can be administered. Medical personnel can give the patient the so-called Brompton's cocktail, which is made of morphine, cocaine, alcohol, syrup, and chloroform water in order to deaden pain but allow conscious activity.

Certain patients can even be released to hospices where they can spend their last days with family and friends rather than in a clinical hospital setting. The hospice program provides a coordinated program of doctors, nurses, and special consultants who help the dying patient and his family through their time of struggle.

But even this form of euthanasia is not without its controversy. Many physicians are reluctant to discontinue medical efforts to cure terminal patients. Their reluctance is not so much driven by a belief that they will be successful as it is by their concern about possible malpractice suits from the family. Patients who are ready "to go to be with the Lord" may find themselves at odds with doctors fearful they may have to prove in a court of law that they did "all they could" for the patient.

Stepping into this legal/ethical dilemma has been the President's Commission for the Study of Ethical Problems in Medicine. The Commission came to the following conclusions concerning terminally ill patients.[4] (1) The Commission stated that a terminally ill patient generally should have the right to choose to die without interference from lawyers, legislators, or bureaucrats. (2) The Commission believes that patients suffering loss of consciousness should have the type of care that is dictated largely by their families' wishes. (3) Resuscitation need not always be attempted on a hospitalized patient whose heart stops. Patients likely to suffer cardiac arrest should be informed before the operation and allowed to decide in advance for or against resuscitation. (4) Patients should have greater rights to give instructions in advance of becoming incapacitated. They should have the right to appoint a proxy to carry out their wishes.

These conclusions of the President's Commission have provided the basis for revision of state laws governing medical care of the terminally ill. In general they provide doctors with greater latitude in making decisions concerning dying patients. But they do raise significant questions for Christians.

First, is there such a thing as a "right to die"? From the Christian perspective, this is certainly questionable (as discussed later in this chapter under Biblical Analysis). But it also raises important legal questions never addressed by the founders of this country nor by modern courts. While the Declaration of Independence does recognize a "right to life," it does not recognize (nor even assume) a "right to die."

Second, the conclusions suggest that a patient's decisions about life and death can be done by proxy. In most cases this has been done through a legal instrument known as "the living will" or through a "durable power of attorney" (DPOA).

Presently 35 states allow individuals to draw up a legal document known as a "living will," in which they specify their desires regarding medical treatment if they become terminally ill and incompetent. A DPOA gives a third party, or proxy, power to make decisions on behalf of the patient. In the past these covered only financial decisions, but court precedents have extended these to cover health-care decisions as well.

The fundamental problem with these proxy arrangements is that they are usually based on some "quality of life" standard. Yet a Christian perspective on human life sees all life as sacred and given by God. Decisions about life and death should be governed by a "sanctity of life" standard rather than by a "quality of life" standard.

VOLUNTARY, ACTIVE EUTHANASIA

This implies that something is done to hasten death. This raises both moral and legal questions. Does active euthanasia constitute an act of murder or assisted suicide? Or is it merely a compassionate act of mercy-killing?

It is helpful to distinguish between mercy-killing and what could be called mercy-dying. Taking a human life is not the same as allowing nature to take its course by allowing a terminal patient to die. The former is immoral (and perhaps even criminal), while the latter is not.

However, drawing a sharp line between these two categories is not as easy as it used to be. Modern medical technology has significantly blurred the line between hastening death and allowing nature to take its course.

Certain analgesics, for example, not only ease pain, but can also shorten a patient's life (by affecting respiration). An artificial heart will continue to beat even after the patient has died and therefore must be turned off by the doctor. So the distinction between actively promoting death and passively allowing nature to take its course is sometimes difficult to determine in practice. But this fundamental distinction between life-taking and death-permitting is still an important philosophical distinction.

Another concern with active euthanasia is that it eliminates the possibility for recovery. While this should be obvious, somehow this problem is frequently ignored in the euthanasia debate. Terminating a human life eliminates all possibility of recovery, while passively ceasing extraordinary means may not. Miraculous recovery from a bleak prognosis sometimes occurs. A doctor who prescribes active euthanasia for a patient may unwittingly prevent a possible recovery he did not anticipate.

A further concern with this so-called voluntary, active euthanasia is that these decisions might not always be freely made. The possibility for coercion is always present. A few years ago Richard D. Lamm, former governor of Colorado, said that elderly, terminally ill patients have "a duty to die and get out of the way." Though those words were reported somewhat out of context, they nonetheless illustrate the pressure many elderly feel from hospital personnel.

Former Surgeon General C. Everett Koop has said that proponents of active euthanasia "have gotten across to a whole segment of the elderly population that somehow because they are living, they are depriving someone else of a prior right to resources. That is a most reprehensible thing." He added

> When I was doing research for *Whatever Happened to the Human Race?*, I went to nursing homes and talked to people who felt that pressure. Old people were apologizing to me for using a bed, for being alive, for taking medication, because they "knew" somebody else deserved it more. I think that's pitiful.[5]

INVOLUNTARY, PASSIVE EUTHANASIA

In this form of euthanasia, an act of omission, medical personnel do not go to any extraordinary measures to save the patient. This can be a morally acceptable omission when dealing with terminal patients.

Unfortunately this omission often includes actions that are

more accurately described as active euthanasia. Withholding food (by removing nasogastric tubes), antibiotics, or life-support procedures (respirator) is much more than passive euthanasia. As already mentioned, candidates for euthanasia have been known to make miraculous recoveries, but such a possibility is eliminated when a patient is starved to death.

Sometimes, however, decisions must be made about "pulling the plug." A comatose patient without any brain wave activity (a flat EEG, electroencephalogram) should be removed from life-support systems. But in other situations a comatose patient might recover. These difficult decisions should be left up to the neurophysiologist who can evaluate a patient's prognosis. But in general one may assume that the patient will recover and therefore life-support systems should be continued, thus placing the burden of proof on those who wish to "pull the plug."

Motives behind involuntary euthanasia are frequently mixed. Are the medical personnel recommending euthanasia because of bed shortages or depleted medical facilities? Or are they suggesting euthanasia out of a compassionate concern for the patient? Is a son, for example, agreeing to euthanasia out of concern for his mother's well-being or out of a desire to gain her inheritance?

The mixed motives behind these decisions are not easy to sort out, and they add further moral and legal questions to the medical landscape. Motives are clearer when nature is allowed to take its course and agonizing decisions are not thrust on the patient or family about when to "pull the plug."

INVOLUNTARY, ACTIVE EUTHANASIA

In this form a second party makes decisions about whether active measures should be taken to end a life. Foundational to this discussion is an erosion of the doctrine of the sanctity of life. But ever since the Supreme Court ruled in 1973 in *Roe v. Wade* that the life of unborn babies could be terminated for reasons of convenience, the slide down society's slippery slope has continued.

The progression was inevitable. Once society begins to devalue the life of an unborn child, it is but a small step to begin to do the same with a child that has been born. Abortion slides naturally into infanticide and eventually into euthanasia. In the past few years doctors have allowed a number of so-called "Baby Does" to die (either by failing to perform lifesaving operations or else by failing to feed the infants). And governmental attempts to prevent such practices have been overruled by the courts.[6]

Once society becomes conformed to a "quality of life" standard for infants, it will more willingly accept the same standard for the elderly. As C. Everett Koop has said, "Nothing surprises me anymore. My great concern is that there will be 10,000 Grandma Does for every Baby Doe."[7]

Once human life is devalued, all sorts of actions defined as "euthanasia" can be justified. This is precisely what happened in Nazi Germany and can happen in this country as well. Ethicist Yale Kamisar provides this descriptive progression of events:

> Miss Voluntary Euthanasia is not likely to be going it alone for very long. Many of her admirers . . . would be neither surprised nor distressed to see her joined by Miss Euthanize the Congenital Idiots and Miss Euthanize the Permanently Insane and Miss Euthanize the Senile Dementia. And these lasses whether or not they themselves constitute a "parade of horrors" certainly make excellent majorettes for such a parade.[8]

Biblical Analysis

Foundational to a biblical perspective on euthanasia is a proper understanding of the sanctity of human life. For centuries Western culture in general and Christians in particular have believed in the sanctity of human life. Unfortunately this view is beginning to erode into a "quality of life" standard. Before, the disabled, retarded, and infirm were seen as having a special place in God's world; but today many medical personnel judge a person's fitness for life on the basis of a perceived quality of life or lack of such quality.

No longer is life seen as sacred and worthy of being saved. Now patients are evaluated and lifesaving treatment is frequently denied based on a subjective and arbitrary standard for the supposed quality of life. If a life is not judged worthy to be lived any longer, people feel obliged to end that life.

Western society must return to the fundamental belief that because human beings are created in the image of God (Gen. 1:27; 5:1–2), all human life is sacred. Society must not place an arbitrary standard of quality above God's absolute standard of human value and worth. This does not mean that people will no longer need to make difficult decisions about treatment and care, but it does mean that these decisions will be guided by an objective, absolute standard of human worth.

Another foundational principle involves a biblical view of life-taking. The Bible specifically condemns murder (Ex. 20:13), and this would surely include active forms of euthanasia in which another person (doctor, nurse, or friend) hastens death in a patient. While there are situations described in Scripture in which life-taking may be permitted (e.g., self-defense or a just war), euthanasia should not be included with any of these established biblical categories. Active euthanasia, like murder, involves premeditated intent and therefore should be condemned as immoral and even criminal.

Christians should also reject the attempt by the modern euthanasia movement to promote a so-called "right to die." Secular society's attempt to establish this "right to die" is wrong for two reasons. First, giving a person a right to die is tantamount to promoting suicide, and suicide is condemned in the Bible. Man is forbidden to murder and that includes murder of oneself. Moreover, Christians are commanded to love others as they love themselves (Matt. 22:39; Eph. 5:29). Implicit in the command is an assumption of self-love as well as love for others.

Suicide, however, is hardly an example of self-love. It is perhaps the clearest example of self-hate. Suicide is also usually a selfish act. People kill themselves to get away from pain and problems, often leaving those problems to friends and family members who must pick up the pieces when the one who committed suicide is gone.

Second, this so-called "right to die" denies God the opportunity to work sovereignly within a shattered life and bring glory to Himself. When Joni Eareckson Tada realized that she would be spending the rest of her life as a quadriplegic, she asked in despair, "Why can't they just let me die?" When her friend Diana, trying to provide comfort, said to her, "The past is dead, Joni; you're alive," Joni responded, "Am I? This isn't living."[9]

But through God's grace Joni's despair gave way to her firm conviction that even her accident was within God's plan for her life. Now she shares with the world her firm conviction that "suffering gets us ready for heaven."[10]

Another foundational principle is a biblical view of death. Modern medicine defines death primarily as a biological event; yet Scripture defines death as a spiritual event that has biological consequences. Death, according to the Bible, occurs when the spirit leaves the body (Eccl. 12:7; James 2:26).

Unfortunately this does not offer much by way of clinical diagnosis for medical personnel. But it does suggest that a rigorous medical definition for death be used. A comatose patient may not be conscious, but from both a medical and biblical perspective he is very much alive and treatment should be continued unless crucial vital signs and brain activity have ceased.

On the other hand Christians must also reject the notion that everything must be done to save life at all costs. Believers, knowing that to be at home in the body is to be away from the Lord (2 Cor. 5:6), long for the time when they will be absent from the body and at home with the Lord (2 Cor. 5:8). Death is gain for Christians (Phil. 1:21). Therefore they need not be so tied to this earth that they perform futile operations just to extend life a few more hours or days.

In a patient's last days, everything possible should be done to alleviate physical and emotional pain. Giving drugs to a patient to relieve pain is morally justifiable. Proverbs 31:6 says, "Give strong drink to him who is perishing, and wine to him whose life is bitter." As previously mentioned, some analgesics have the secondary effect of shortening life. But these should be permitted since the primary purpose is to relieve pain, even though they may secondarily shorten life.

Moreover, believers should provide counsel and spiritual care to dying patients (Gal. 6:2). Frequently emotional needs can be met both in the patient and in the family. Such times of grief also provide opportunities for witnessing. Those suffering loss are often more open to the gospel than at any other time.

Difficult philosophical and biblical questions are certain to continue swirling around the issue of euthanasia. But in the midst of these confusing issues should be the objective, absolute standards of Scripture, which provide guidance for the hard choices of providing care to terminally ill patients.

CHAPTER 6

The Morality of Suicide: Issues and Options

J. P. Moreland

On December 2, 1982, 62-year-old Barney Clark became the first human to receive a permanent artificial heart. In addition he was given a key that could be used to turn off his compressor, if he wanted to die. One of the physicians, Dr. Willem Kolff, justified the key by stating that if Clark suffered and felt that life was not enjoyable or worth enduring anymore, he had the right to end his life. Clark never used the key. He died 15 weeks after the operation.

This case illustrates the growing importance of ethical reflection regarding suicide. Today it is the 10th leading cause of death in the general population, and the suicide rate is on the rise in groups ranging from teenagers to the elderly. The purpose of this chapter is to clarify important issues and options involved in the ethical aspects of suicide.

It is crucial that pastors and other Christian leaders understand how these issues are being argued, apart from reference to the biblical text. This will enable the Christian community to argue in a pluralistic culture for positions consistent with the Bible and to understand how others are framing the debate. This chapter focuses on three issues: the definition of suicide, the moral justifiability of suicide, and moral problems involved in paternalist state intervention to prevent people coercively from committing suicide.

The Definition of Suicide

Before discussing the morality of suicide, two preliminary issues must be examined. First is whether the term "suicide" should be used in a purely conceptual, descriptive manner or in a normative, evaluative manner. Second is the need to define suicide to show how suicidal acts differ from other self-destructive acts.

IS SUICIDE A DESCRIPTIVE OR AN EVALUATIVE TERM?

Should suicide be defined in a purely conceptual, descriptive manner or in normative, evaluative terms? Suppose one person said suicide is sometimes morally permissible and another said suicide is always wrong. It would be possible for these two people to agree over substantive moral issues regarding suicide and differ merely in their definition of what counts as suicide. For example two people could agree that a Jehovah's Witness who refuses a blood transfusion (see case six discussed a few paragraphs later) was morally justified in his action, one arguing that it was a morally justifiable suicide, the other that it was not a suicide at all but a case of martyrdom. Thus definitions are important in clarifying where agreement and disagreement lie in a moral discussion.

Beauchamp and Childress have argued that one should opt for a stipulative definition of suicide, which is conceptual, descriptive, and nonevaluative.[1] The definition they propose is this: An act is a suicide if and only if one intentionally terminates one's own life, no matter what the conditions or precise nature of the intention or the causal route to death. Their argument for this stipulative definition is that an ordinary language definition is evaluative and carries with it an attitude of disapproval. If an act is a suicide, many say, then it is wrong. But, according to Beauchamp and Childress, this prejudices one's understanding of suicide and removes objectivity from the conceptualizing of the term. If an act of self-caused death is morally appropriate, one should hesitate to label it a suicide because of the evaluative nature of the term.

Hauerwas has argued against Beauchamp and Childress, claiming that the evaluative use of moral terms is preferable to mere stipulative, descriptive uses.[2] Hauerwas points out that the idea of a normatively "uncorrupted" definition of suicide distorts the very grammar of the term. He agrees that the definition of suicide itself cannot settle how and why suicide applies to certain kinds of behavior and not to others. But this is because the use of moral terms of appraisal like "suicide" derives from broad world view considerations of the culture in question. Within one's world view a person finds the factual and moral beliefs that are necessary to make judgments about when a range of life-ending behavior is morally inappropriate. So the way one understands "suicide" already incorporates moral judgments and factual beliefs about the world in general.

In this writer's judgment, Hauerwas is right. By their nature, moral terms are evaluative, they are intended to guide behavior, and the normative component of a moral term derives its applicability from world view considerations of the community that uses the term to praise or blame behavior. Thus an "uncorrupted" definition fails to weight properly the evaluative component of the term "suicide," and it would be revisionary in nature and could therefore affect the way the morality of specific behaviors is perceived.

WHAT IS SUICIDE?

When an ethical term is being defined, a proposed definition should explain the ordinary language intuitions of people of good will regarding clear and borderline cases of what to count as acts of suicide. Thus cases are important guides in defining ethical terms.

Examination of cases. The following cases may be noted:

1. An elderly man, despairing of life, leaves a note behind and jumps off a bridge.
2. A soldier captured in war takes a capsule in order to avoid a torturous death and to hide secrets from the enemy.
3. A truck driver, foreseeing his own death, drives off a bridge to avoid hitting children playing in the road.
4. A hospitalized cancer patient with six months to live shoots himself in order to save his family from unneeded psychological and financial suffering.
5. A terminally ill patient, realizing death is imminent, requests that she not be resuscitated again if another heart failure occurs.
6. A Jehovah's Witness refuses a simple blood transfusion for religious reasons and subsequently dies for lack of blood.

Case one above (the elderly man jumping off the bridge) is clearly a case of suicide. Suicide clearly involves at least a person's death and that person's involvement in his or her own death. In a suicide a person must willingly bring about his or her own death. This insight is expressed in what might be called the standard definition of suicide: a suicidal act involves the intentional termination of one's own life. But this definition needs clarification in light of the other cases listed.

Consider first the matter of intention. Some understand intention to be the notion that a person has the power to avoid a foreseen death, and yet willingly and knowingly chooses not to do so. On this view, all six cases above would be suicides. But most people would not agree with this usage because they say cases two, three, and five do not appear to be suicides at all.

A different understanding of intention defines it in terms of what someone is trying to do. The intent of an act specifies what the act itself is, and an intent can be clarified by the reasons or motives for doing the act. For example in the truck driver case above, the ultimate intent of the act seems to be the sacrificial preservation of the life of others. In this case the truck driver did not desire to die, but permitted his own death to accomplish an act of life-saving. This second sense of "intent" seems more in keeping with the common usage of "suicide," so it is to be preferred to the first sense.

Case two raises the issue of coercion. The soldier terminated his own life because he knew he would be killed by means of prolonged torture and because he did not wish to reveal his country's secrets. Some have argued that this is not an example of suicide because it involves (a) coercion and (b) other-directed and not self-directed motivation. If the soldier were not under coercion but terminated his life anyway, this would most likely be classified as a suicide. Thus if an act is coerced, it probably does not count as a suicide.

What about self-destructive acts for the sake of others such as cases two and three? Some hold that these are not suicides because they involve other-directed and not self-directed motivation. These are sacrificial acts, not suicides. Here death is not desired, but one's own life is taken for the sake of others.

Some philosophers add the stipulation that other-directed acts are suicidal if they are done for animals or nonpersonal states of affairs (e.g., wealth). Thus case four is an act of self-destruction for others (a cancer patient shoots himself to save others economic and psychological distress) and should be classified as a suicide because it is not done to save the lives of others, but to realize a nonpersonal state of affairs.

The Jehovah's Witness case could be treated similarly. If God does command that no blood be taken and if a blood transfusion violates this command, then refusing a blood transfusion would be not a suicide but a sacrificial act of martyrdom. An important issue in this case is whether the Jehovah's Witness interpretation of Scripture is accurate. Most biblical scholars do not think so and thus would have a factual problem with case six. What about a Buddhist monk who sets fire to himself in protest of a war? Some would argue that this is not a suicide because it is self-sacrifice for the lives of others. Beauchamp disagrees and believes that such an act is suicidal because the monk himself directly and intentionally causes the life-threatening condition (the fire) that brings on the death.[3] According to Beauchamp, most people would judge such an act as suicidal and this shows that usage turns on the fact that the agent creates the conditions for death, not on the notions of sacrifice or martyrdom.

But even if one grants that the monk's act is a suicide, all that follows is that there are different ways an act counts as suicidal, and in addition to the issue of self-motivation versus other-motivation, there is also the issue of direct causation of death. It would seem then that all things being equal, an act of martyrdom or sacrifice for the lives of others is not a suicide.

However, Beauchamp's point does raise the issue of direct causation and active means used by the individual. This writer considers case four a suicide but not case five. If a sick but non-terminal person died as a result of refusing to eat or take medication, that would be considered a suicide. These insights indicate that a self-destructive act is a suicide if the person is nonterminal and death is intentionally and directly caused as a means to some other end. In case five death is foreseen, but not directly and intentionally caused. Thus this is an example of passive euthanasia. In case four, however, death is directly and intentionally caused by a gunshot, and this is what makes the act a suicide.

A proposed definition of suicide. From these deliberations about the cases listed above, fundamental intuitions about suicide, embedded in ordinary language, become clearer. On the basis of these deliberations the following definition of suicide can be formulated: An act is a suicide if and only if a person intentionally and/or directly causes his or her own death as an ultimate end in itself or as a means to another end (e.g., pain relief), through acting (e.g., taking a pill) or refraining from acting (e.g., refusing to eat) when that act is not coerced and is not done sacrificially for the lives of other persons or in obedience to God.[4]

This attempt to define suicide does not mean that all nonsuicidal acts of self-destruction are considered morally permissible.

For example a daredevil, foolishly performing an unnecessarily risky stunt for money or fame, jumps to his death. Such acts can be wrong for several reasons: they harm others (e.g., loved ones left behind) by removing a member of the community, they manifest a disrespect for human life, they can contribute to similar acts, and so on.

Is Suicide Moral?

Before discussing different views regarding the morality of suicide, two preliminary points should be made. First, this discussion of the morality of suicide focuses on the morality of a suicidal act done by a rational, competent decision-maker. Such a person can effectively deliberate about and understand different courses of action and the ends they accomplish, as well as different means to accomplish those ends.

Second, some ethicists argue that the subjective and objective aspects of the morality of suicide should be distinguished. The former refers to the guilt incurred by the person who commits suicide; the latter refers to the morality of suicide considered objectively as an act in itself. The idea behind this distinction is that some persons may commit suicide who are in such a state of distress (e.g., they are severely depressed, acting on false information, etc.) that their act may be objectively wrong but the individuals themselves may not be blameworthy. The act may be called a serious mistake, but excusable.

However, this distinction is a questionable one, since in such cases it could be claimed that the person was not acting rationally and since it is not clear how an act can be at once morally wrong but not blameworthy. Perhaps the act is not blameworthy in the weak sense that one can easily understand and empathize with it. But the act would still be morally blameworthy if it is a morally wrong act, and it is the moral sense of blameworthy that is of chief interest in ethics. In any case the focus here is on the "objective" side of the morality of suicide: Can a suicidal act as such be morally justifiable when it is done by a rational, competent decision-maker?

THE LIBERAL VIEW: SUICIDE AS SUCH CAN BE MORALLY
    JUSTIFIABLE

The first view is a liberal approach to suicide. Advocates of this approach hold that an act of suicide may be morally justifiable even if that act does some harm to others, provided that the act does not do *substantial damage* to others and that it is in keeping with the individual liberty of the agent. Even if a person has some duty to others, say, family members, the suicide can still be morally acceptable provided the distress to others caused by the suicide does not outweigh the distress to the person who refrains from committing suicide. No person is obligated to undergo extreme distress in order to save others from a smaller amount of distress.

There are two major approaches to the morality of suicide within the liberal camp: the utilitarian approach and the autonomy approach. These views are not necessarily mutually exclusive.

The liberal utilitarian position. Brandt defines suicide as the intentional termination of one's own life and argues against the view that suicide is always immoral.[5] It may be appropriate, he says, to take one's own life to avoid catastrophic hospital expenses in a terminal illness and thus meet one's obligation to one's family. It may also be the case that a person may maximize his or her long-range welfare by bringing about death.

A person who is contemplating suicide is making a choice between "world-courses"—a world-course that includes his immediate suicide and several possible world-courses that contain his death at a later point. These alternatives are to be understood as world-courses, Brandt says, not as future life-courses which refer only to the alternatives for the individual alone. This is because one's suicide or failure to commit suicide impacts the rest of the world, and the morality of suicide must take into account the welfare of all relevant parties, not just the welfare of the person contemplating suicide.

A prospective suicidal person must attempt to take into account all the relevant information, including all his own short-term and long-term desires. Brandt argues that though one can never be certain of all these factors, he must not let this fact stand in his way. A prospective suicidal person should compare the world-course containing his suicide with the *best* alternative. If the former world-course maximizes utility, all things being considered, then it would be rational and morally justifiable to commit suicide.

Among the problems regarded as good and sufficient reasons for suicide are these: painful, terminal illness; some event that has made a person feel ashamed or lose his prestige and status;

reduction from affluence to poverty; the loss of a limb or of physical beauty; the loss of sexual capacity; some event that makes it seem impossible to achieve things deemed important; loss of a loved one; disappointment in love; and the infirmities of increasing age. If a person experiences these or other serious blows to his prospect for happiness, he may be justified in suicide if such an act maximizes the net amount of utility compared to alternative acts. In cases of morally justifiable suicide, others are morally obligated to assist in executing the decision, says Brandt, if the person needs help.

The liberal autonomy position. A second liberal approach to the morality of suicide is the autonomy position. Major advocates of this view are Beauchamp and Childress.[6] They state that persons should be allowed to be self-determining agents who make their own evaluations and choices when their own interests are at stake. If a person is a competent, rational decision-maker, he has a right to determine his own destiny even if others believe that a course of action would be harmful to the individual.

The principle of beneficence states that a person should seek to benefit others and himself, and the principle of nonmaleficence expresses the duty not to harm others or oneself. In a case of rational suicide, there may be a conflict of duties between autonomy on the one hand, and beneficence and nonmaleficence on the other hand. In such cases autonomy should take precedence over other moral considerations. Disrespect is shown to individuals and the principle of autonomy is violated if the right to commit suicide is denied when, in their considered judgment, they ought to do so and no serious adverse consequences for others would result (such consequences do not necessarily present overriding grounds for opposing suicide).

The autonomy view is consistent with both a utilitarian ethic and a deontological ethic. If the autonomy view is utilitarian, then the principle of autonomy is justified on the grounds that accepting this principle maximizes utility compared to rejecting autonomy and acting on alternative rules. In this case the autonomy view becomes a way of expressing a utilitarian approach to the question of suicide.

If the autonomy view is deontological, then it becomes an alternative to the utilitarian approach. Here autonomy is seen as an expression of an intrinsic duty to respect persons and the priority of autonomy vis-à-vis beneficence and nonmaleficence becomes an attempt to emphasize individual liberty and quality-of-life considerations regarding suicide.

THE CONSERVATIVE VIEW: SUICIDE AS SUCH IS NOT MORALLY JUSTIFIABLE

The conservative view holds that suicide as such is not morally justifiable. A number of reasons have been offered for this view: It violates one's sanctity-of-life duty to respect oneself as an end and not a means; it violates a natural law principle that man's very nature is such that he has an inclination to continue in existence and he has a moral duty to act in keeping with that nature; it violates man's duty to God as the Giver and ultimate Owner of life; and it violates one's duty to one's community by injuring that community in some way.

According to Hauerwas, an ethics of autonomy (where the principle of autonomy overrides all other moral considerations) implies that suicide is not only rational, but also that it is a moral right.[7] This shows, Hauerwas says, how inadequate a minimalistic ethic of autonomy and a nonnaturalistic view of rationality really is as an overall approach to morality, suicide included. An ethics of autonomy has an insufficient view of the good life—the life of the virtuous person and community that each person ought to seek. As a result an ethics of autonomy fails to explain why anyone should decide to keep on living in the face of difficulties.

First, Hauerwas argues that the basic reason suicide is wrong is that life is a gift bestowed by a gracious Creator. While there are other reasons against suicide, any account of suicide must consider the rational support given for the factual belief that human lives are gifts from God. Because life is a gift, man is obligated to his Creator to live. Living is an obligation in that man is to go on living even when he is far from figuring out why things happen as they do. This obligation expresses the rational belief that God gives purpose to life in the midst of hardships.

Second, Hauerwas states man should not commit suicide because of his duty to others in the community. People should not be viewed as atomistic individuals who are loosely connected to others. Rather, people live in systems. A person's existence depends on his and others' lives in community. Their willingness to live in the face of pain, boredom, and suffering is (a) a moral service to one another; (b) a sign that life can be endured; (c) an opportunity to teach others how to die, how to face life, how to live well, and how a wise person understands the connection between happiness and evil (e.g., one does not obtain joy or live a good life only when he avoids hardship, but when he learns to live with it); and (d) a way of refusing to give the community a morally unhelpful memory of the person who committed suicide, which could hurt those left behind in their attempt to live well as individuals and in community with others. An act of suicide signals the failure of the community to be present to care for the suicidal person in his time of need, and it signals the person's lack of care for the community.

Third, Hauerwas argues that suicide is inconsistent with the very nature of medicine, especially the authority of medicine. Medicine is not to be defined merely as a technological field. The authority of medicine is not just that of a technologically skilled group of people. It is the authority of a virtuous profession wherein people in a community signal the virtue of being present for one another in time of need. The medical professional expresses his or her commitment to be present to heal or to care for the weak and sick when care cannot be reciprocated. The sick person signals his or her desire to place trust in the community's representative, the medical personnel, and allow the community to care for that person in time of need. Suicide signals a break in this value to be present for one another in time of need, and thus suicide is inconsistent with the presuppositions that make medicine itself intelligible.

ASSESSMENT OF THE VIEWS

Broad world view considerations. The debate about suicide clearly surfaces two fundamentally different sets of presuppositions about how to approach broad issues such as the purpose of life, the nature of morality, community, medicine, and persons, and the ultimate ownership of life. Thus the debate about suicide is difficult to separate from broad world view considerations. What is the good life, what is the point of life, and how does one's answer to these questions inform one's perspective about the nature and purpose of suffering? Is life sacred? Should life be treated as a gift? Is utilitarianism a better approach to ethics or is a deontological view a better approach? Is a quality-of-life or a sanctity-of-life approach to suicide preferable? Should persons be ultimately viewed atomistically, as individuals, or should they equally and irreducibly be seen as members of a community to which they are responsible? Is medicine to be understood along the traditional lines as presented by Hauerwas, or should it be seen as a contractual arrangement between patient and physician wherein medical goods and services are obtained so long as the patient wishes to have them?

The liberal and conservative views tend to answer these questions differently. Their competing views on the morality of suicide express deep differences on these basic, world view questions. It is beyond the scope of this chapter to attempt a broad analysis and evaluation of these different outlooks, apart from some brief, specific considerations to be offered shortly. One's view about the morality of suicide is an expression of one's general world view. It is here that a Judeo-Christian world view becomes especially precious and relevant.

The statements of the liberal and conservative views above have already presented some of the specific arguments relevant to assessing these positions. Further, the arguments against the liberal views function as arguments for the conservative view. Therefore the following pages focus directly on criticisms of the liberal position. These criticisms show that the liberal view is morally inadequate and the conservative view is to be preferred.

Criticisms of the liberal utilitarian view. First, the liberal, utilitarian view is problematic because of the difficulties inherent in utilitarianism in general (e.g., the failure to treat people as ends in themselves and the failure to recognize the fact that some moral rules are intrinsically right). Further, if a utilitarian justification is offered for a specific act of suicide, then that justification proves too much; it does not merely make the act of suicide permissible, it makes it morally obligatory. Why? Because one is morally obligated to maximize utility, and if an act of suicide maximizes utility, then it would be morally obligatory. But any view which makes a suicide obligatory is wrong.

Utilitarians respond to this argument in two ways. First, they argue that under certain circumstances, a rule requiring suicide would not be morally wrong. Deontological ethicists argue that this rule would dehumanize persons by treating them as a means to an end and by elevating a quality-of-life standard above a sanctity-of-life standard. It should be clear that one's evaluation of this debate will turn on one's opinion regarding the relative merits of utilitarianism versus deontological ethics and quality of life versus sanctity of life.

Second, utilitarians argue that a rule requiring suicide in certain circumstances might turn out to be wrong because adopting such a rule may itself fail to maximize utility. Deontologists respond by pointing out that utilitarians cannot rule out the possibility that such a rule may maximize utility and in any case the moral impermissibility of a rule requiring suicide is not grounded in utility considerations but in the moral inappropriateness of requiring someone to treat himself or herself as a means to an end.

Criticisms of the liberal autonomy view. Other criticisms can be raised against the autonomy model which apply to the utilitarian model as well. For one thing, the liberal view in both forms violates a person's duty to himself or herself. This has been expressed in at least five ways.

1. To take one's own life is to deny its intrinsic value and dignity. It is to assume wrongly that man is the originator and therefore the controller of his life.
2. Some have offered a natural law argument to the effect that everything, human nature in particular, is naturally inclined to perpetuate itself in existence. In response, it has been pointed out that suicidal persons do not have this inclination to continue existing. But this response fails to recognize that the notion of inclination used in natural law arguments is not to be understood as a psychological preference for life, but as a normative, natural urge grounded in one's nature as a human being.
3. Suicide is wrong because it involves the direct, intentional killing of human life. Such an act treats persons, who have intrinsic value, as means to ends.
4. Suicide is also a self-refuting act, for it is an act of freedom that destroys future acts of freedom; it is an affirmation of being that negates being; it serves a human good (e.g., a painless state) by violating other, more basic human goods (e.g., life itself) as a means to that end; it is an act of morality that gives up on all other moral responsibilities and rejects the moral way of life.[8]
5. Suicide runs the risk of being an inappropriate way of entering life after death. Even if one does not believe in life after death, such a state is possible and perhaps rea-

sonable in light of arguments that can be raised in support of it. Either way, it is unwise to risk entering life after death in a morally improper way.

As Hauerwas has pointed out, the autonomy model fails to capture the importance of community, the traditional understanding of medicine as a morally authoritative vocational expression of the community's respect for life, and a virtuous understanding of the good life and suffering. Suicide fails to explain adequately why anyone should continue to live when he no longer wishes to, and thus it is inappropriate from a moral point of view.

Paternalism and Suicide Intervention

GENERAL STATEMENT OF THE VIEWS

Is it justifiable for some agent of the state coercively to prevent a suicide or to compel a competent adult to take life-saving medical treatment? Opinions differ on this question. The libertarian view opposes such paternalistic interventions because they are considered a violation of individual liberty, patient autonomy, and the respect for persons that presents an obligation to respect the wishes and desires of competent, adult decision-makers (provided of course that no overriding harm is done to others). According to this view people have a right to commit suicide.

The second view, the beneficence model, is generally in favor of such interventions to keep the person from serious and irrevocable harm. Society has a duty to prevent people from harming themselves in acts of suicide.

IMPORTANT DEFINITIONS

Paternalism is the refusal to accept and go along with a person's wishes, choices, and actions for that person's own benefit. Paternalism is rooted in the idea that the community as represented, say, in a physician, has better insight into what is good for a patient than does the patient, and thus can do what is medically good for the patient even if it is not judged good by the patient's own value system.

Strong paternalism involves overriding the competent, rational wishes, choices, and actions of another. Individual liberty is overridden because of benefit to the person, even though that person is not impaired as a decision-maker. *Weak paternalism* involves acting in the best interests of a person who is impaired as an actor or as a decision-maker. There is little disagreement that weak paternalism is morally justifiable. In fact most ethicists do not see it as paternalism at all, because it involves acting or deciding for a person who is incapable of doing so. Often such interventions eventually restore patient autonomy and liberty.[9]

The principle of *respect for persons* requires that persons be treated as ends in themselves and never as a means only. Respect is shown for the intrinsic worth and dignity of a person. The principle of *autonomy* requires that individuals should respect the self-determination of others by not doing for them what they would not want done to themselves and doing for others what they would wish done to themselves. The principle of *beneficence* says that people have a duty to benefit others and to act in their best interests. Beneficence comes in degrees: one ought not inflict harm on others, one ought to prevent harm, one ought to remove harm, and one ought to do good.

EXPOSITION AND EVALUATION OF THE VIEWS

The libertarian view. According to Engelhardt, in the present secular society moral pluralism must prevail.[10] Individual communities may share a substantive vision of the good life (and the good death), but a peaceable secular state must remain pluralistic and must respect rights that preserve individual liberty. Peace is maintained only by respecting the principle of autonomy as the supreme moral principle. Autonomy prevails in every situation, provided of course, that autonomous actions do not do overriding harm to others. Beneficence is important, says Engelhardt, in that it gives content to different individual or community visions of the good life. Thus beneficence preserves autonomy.

Regarding suicide, a rational, competent decision-maker has the autonomous right to refuse life-saving treatment or to commit suicide without interference. Further, such individuals have a right to be assisted in suicide by others. In a peaceable, secular state, it is wrong to interfere with the moral authority expressed in free choices of individuals or those who assist them in refusing treatment or in committing suicide. In such a state autonomy reigns supreme and paternalistic interventions are unjustifiable.[11]

Several strengths have been claimed for the libertarian view. First, it is important to respect the principle of autonomy, individual rights, and the privacy of individuals, and the libertarian view attempts to express this respect. Second, respecting the autonomy of a person can be part of what is needed to cure that person, so violations of patient autonomy can do harm. However, when it comes to suicide, this point is not applicable. Third, the libertarian view is a reaction to class dominance, and in a pluralistic society, legal moralism (liberty is limited to prevent a person from acting immorally) can easily be an oppressive tool in the hands of an elite. Forcing someone to live against his or her own will can be oppressive and fails to respect persons, so the argument goes, by failing to honor his self-determination.

In spite of these strengths, a number of weaknesses in the libertarian view have been surfaced. First, this view easily degenerates into an inordinate individualism that fosters, under the guise of respect for autonomy, disinterest in the plight of others and premature abandonment of a patient in time of need. Honoring autonomy is not always the best way to respect a person, especially when he is autonomously choosing to disrespect himself in a serious way. Suicide is a serious act of disrespect for oneself, even when chosen autonomously, and so honoring a suicide disrespects a person. Freedom is not a bare, formal principle. People are free to do what they *ought* to do, they are not entitled to do anything they *want* to do, and suicide violates the sanctity of life.

Second, the libertarian view fails to recognize that decision-making is an interpersonal process. The physician-patient relationship, the family-individual relationship, and other important relational systems (e.g., friendships) should be part of decision-making. Usually when a person is contemplating suicide, the others in that person's system will argue against it out of respect for the sanctity of life and the desire not to lose the suicidal person. Admittedly this may not be true in all cases. But the libertarian model does seem to individualize decision-making inordinately and fails to guard adequately against hasty decisions that may not be morally justifiable.

A third, related point is that the libertarian view, in its retreat to private morality, treats people as atomistic individuals. Thus it fails to come to grips with the common good, the nature of community and how community constitutes part of what it is to be a person, and the community's interests in preserving the sanctity of life.

This atomistic view of individuals also distorts the patient-physician relationship by viewing it as an autonomous contractual agreement for the exchange of services that both parties enter freely. But the patient-physician relationship is a commitment between unequal parties (the patient needs healing) which must be present in order to heal. This involves altruistic, but authoritative beneficence on the part of the physician, and trust on the part of the patient. This model can be abused, but it does seem to capture the real nature of the patient-physician relationship. The physician is committed to healing, and suicide is an act against that commitment.

Fourth, as Callahan has pointed out, the libertarian view expresses a minimalistic ethic (one may morally act in any way he chooses if he does not harm others).[12] The libertarian view, as a minimalistic ethic, has a number of features that make it barren and inadequate as a social ethic. It confuses a useful principle for government regulation with the broader requirements of the moral life; it inappropriately draws a sharp line between the public and private spheres with different standards for each; it has a shriveled notion of public-private morality in its reduction of interpersonal, moral obligations to a simple honoring of those agreements people have freely and voluntarily entered; it fails to account for the moral importance of communal life, the common good, and shared values; and it tends to view all interventions into autonomous adult decision-making in a negative light.[13]

Fifth, the libertarian view utilizes the wrong notion of rationality. On this view, rationality is nonnormative rationality: the ability to understand options and their consequences, formulate means to ends, and so on. Such a view of rationality in morality tends to reduce substantive ethics to procedural ethics: one arrives at a morally correct outcome if he uses the correct procedure in reaching that outcome. In the case of suicide, if a rational procedure was followed in the deliberation process, the choice of suicide is correct.

A more adequate view of rationality is a normative one: One is morally rational if one has the ability (perhaps through the cultivation of virtue) to gain insight into what is morally true and good. This view of rationality emphasizes the substantive aspects of ethics. It is true that men of good will frequently differ over what is in fact morally true and good. But the solution to this is an emphasis on argumentation and virtue, not a retreat to nonnormative rationality and procedural ethics. The libertarian view does the latter and for that reason is inadequate.

The beneficence view. Advocates of the beneficence view are more sympathetic to the legitimacy of limiting individual liberty, including the right to commit suicide, in order to (a) benefit the individual and prevent him or her from serious and irrevocable harm, (b) preserve the common good and the community's interest in the sanctity of life, and (c) preserve the beneficent, healing, covenantal model of medicine.

It may be best to view the libertarian-beneficence debate as a continuum, with the former emphasizing quality of life, individual autonomy, and nonnormative rationality, and the latter emphasizing sanctity of life, beneficence, the common good, and normative rationality. Not all advocates of the libertarian view would sanction every act of rational suicide and not all advocates of the beneficence model would hold that a line is never crossed where a person should be permitted to commit suicide. Some advocates of the beneficence model hold that all acts of suicide require intervention, while others would severely limit the permissibility of suicide but agree that in some rare and extreme cases it may be allowed.

Two main advocates of the beneficence model are Edmund Pellegrino and David Thomasma.[14] They argue that autonomy should not always win in medical conflicts and that in general, beneficence should be ranked higher than autonomy. This ranking is grounded in a virtue approach to ethics, which involves respecting the sanctity of life, the traditional view of the physician as a beneficent healer, and the common good.

Pellegrino and Thomasma express their views about suicide in the context of the Elizabeth Bouvia case. In 1983 Elizabeth Bouvia, a twenty-six-year-old who was virtually quadriplegic, dependent on others for her bodily functions, and suffering from intense pain, entered a California hospital and stated that she wanted to starve to death. A lower court rejected her petition and authorized involuntary tube feedings. In April 1986 the California Supreme Court granted removal of a nasogastric feeding tube from Bouvia on the grounds that she was a rational, competent decision-maker and that her request was in keeping with patient autonomy and privacy.

Pellegrino and Thomasma agree that a competent person has a moral right to refuse life-sustaining systems, but assisted suicide is clearly wrong and once a feeding tube was given Bouvia, its removal was wrong because it involved a clear intent to bring about death. By contrast other advocates of the beneficence model would not agree that Bouvia had a moral right to refuse life-sustaining treatment. Thus advocates of this view are more conservative than those of the libertarian view, but differ over the right to refuse life-sustaining treatment for a nondying patient.

Summary

The morality of suicide clearly surfaces how broad world view considerations are important for understanding and evaluating different moral positions. In the final analysis one's approach to suicide is determined largely by the world view one brings to the issue. Christian leaders should study the general arguments involved in suicide and other ethical issues of broad cultural concern. When they do, they will be in a better position to discuss the issues while being sensitive to the secular, pluralistic nature of the culture. Also they will have excellent opportunities to present the gospel of Christ at intellectually appropriate places in the discussion.

CHAPTER 7

The Condemnation of
Homosexuality in Romans 1:26–27

David E. Malick

In the past several decades waves of moral and ethical issues have broken on the shores of Western civilization, often leaving those expected to answer the sound of the surf dazed by the multitude of approaches and solutions to the problems. Homosexuality, and especially the question of its validity as a practice for Christians, is one such breaker.

The pervasiveness of this issue is especially evident in the United States and Great Britain. In 1948 the Kinsey Institute Report changed general attitudes toward homosexuality and heterosexuality. Instead of viewing those practices as polar opposites, people were led to view everyone on a continuum between exclusive heterosexuality and exclusive homosexuality. The report also affirmed that between 5 and 10 percent of the population is exclusively or primarily homosexual in orientation.[1] Stott reported that "in Britain the Sexual Offenses Act of 1967 declared that a homosexual act performed between consenting adults over 21 in private should no longer be a criminal offense."[2] Likewise Logan notes that in 1973 the American Bar Association called for the repeal of all laws categorizing homosexual activity between consenting adults in private as a crime.[3] Also Socarides reports,

> On December 14, 1973, the Board of Trustees of the American Psychiatric Association, meeting in Washington, D.C., eliminated homosexuality from its official Diagnostic and Statistical Manual. In essence and by direct implication this action officially declared homosexuality a normal form of sexual life. Henceforth, the only "disturbed homosexual" would be one who was disturbed because he was homosexual. He would be considered neurotic only if "unhappy."[4]

Clearly the social cry of the West has been one of reevaluation with respect to the legality, if not the morality, of homosexuality.[5]

This wave of questioning has since been sympathetically set in motion in the discipline of theology.

Pittenger supports homosexuality from a "theological basis" in four ways. (1) He says love is the dominant quality by which one measures all human activity.[6] (2) He asserts that since between 10 and 15 percent of the human race is homosexual, there must be theological relevance for these people.[7] (3) He relegates specific Old Testament and New Testament passages either to cultural nonrelevance or to a lack of truth and thus a lack of authority.[8] (4) He insists that the variety in God's creation allows for variety in mankind as they express love toward other men and women.[9]

From these early splashes of permissive arguments the dike seems to have been broken by authors who not only speak in broad general terms but also invoke considerable Hellenistic cultural and linguistic arguments against any specific scriptural prohibitions of homosexuality.[10] These questions have particularly focused on the Pauline texts of Romans 1:26–27; 1 Corinthians 6:9; and 1 Timothy 1:10 since these alone are the New Testament prohibitions against homosexuality. Therefore it is necessary to examine Paul's rationale for condemning homosexuality in light of contemporary arguments for its validity as a practice for Christians.

The focus of this chapter is on Paul's condemnation of homosexual activity in Romans 1:26–27. Contemporary arguments are examined in light of historical, lexical, cultural, and contextual exegesis to demonstrate that Paul actually did condemn homosexual activity for all mankind and especially in the church.

A Critique of Contemporary Views

A plethora of explanations have been applied to the Apostle Paul's discussion of homosexual activity in Romans 1:26–27 in an attempt to ease or even erase any relevance to present-day expressions of erotic, same-sex relationships. Some accuse Paul of imposing Jewish customs and rules on his readers. Others affirm that Paul was not presenting homosexuality as sinful but as punishment for idolatrous sin. But the most permissive view suggests that Paul was referring to abuse within the genus of healthy homosexuality. Those advocating this view affirm that he was addressing *perverted* homosexuality, either as unnatural homosexuality by heterosexuals, homosexuality combined with idolatry or with temple prostitution, or pederasty (men having relations with boys).

VIEW ONE: AN IMPOSITION OF JEWISH CUSTOMS AND RULES

Scanzoni and Mollenkott wrote that in Romans 1:26–27 "it is doubtful that Paul is speaking of nature in the sense of custom, unless he is referring to a violation of Jewish custom and law."[11] Their point is that since homosexuality was an accepted part of the social custom in the Greek and Roman world, Paul must have been imposing his Jewish custom on his readers.

Scroggs also suggests that Paul's knowledge of Greek homosexuality was less than extensive. "What he 'knew' probably originated from the rumor mills of the day, particularly perhaps from Jewish suspicions about Gentile activities."[12]

These affirmations, however, are full of presuppositions and exegetical oversights, as the following discussion reveals.

Paul's cultural setting. It is true that Jewish culture opposed homosexuality. The Jews' Scriptures did,[13] and their extrabiblical sources did.[14] However, Paul was not merely imposing Jewish custom onto the Greek and Roman world.

Paul demonstrated extensive awareness of Greek culture, having been born and educated in Tarsus in the region of Cilicia, one of the three centers of Greek culture in his day (Acts 21:39).[15] As Blaiklock has commented, "He could talk and think like a Greek and quote his native Cilician poets to the intellectuals of Athens. He could write strong Greek in closely argued documents."[16] Paul was hardly an isolated Jew in a Greek world, and would thus be well aware of the homosexual activities of his time without depending on "Jewish rumor mills."[17]

Specific terms in Romans 1. In sharp contrast to the notion that in Romans Paul was speaking only of Jewish culture are the very terms he used—terms that reach back into the creation account of Genesis 1 and 2 rather than Hellenistic Judaism.

Φύσικος and φύσις ("nature") refer to one's constitution as given by God the Creator.[18] When Peter compared the false prophets to "unreasoning animals, born as creatures of instinct [γεγεννημένα φυσικὰ] to be captured" (2 Peter 2:12), he was referring not to Jewish tradition or heritage but to a natural constitution as established by God in the creation of animals. Also Romans 1:26 bears the idea of a natural constitution as established by God in the creation of the human race.[19] Θύσις may have the figurative sense of a natural endowment or condition inherited from one's ancestors, as in Romans 2:27.[20] However, there is also the literal sense of a physical naturalness that is beyond heritage and is based on creation. Paul clearly used the term this way in 1 Corinthians 11:14 when he referred to "nature" as an argument for head coverings.[21] In Romans 11 Paul wrote of the branches of an olive tree that are "natural" (κατὰ φύσιν, v. 21) and of the tree itself which is "by nature [κατὰ φύσιν] a wild olive tree" (v. 24) and has had branches grafted into it contrary to nature (παρὰ φύσιν).[22] Therefore Cranfield rightly observes that in Romans 1:26 φύσικος means "in accordance with the intention of the Creator" and παρὰ φύσιν means "contrary to the intention of the Creator."[23] "The decisive factor in Paul's use of [φύσις] is his biblical doctrine of creation. It denotes that order which is manifest in God's creation and which men have no excuse for failing to recognize and respect (cf. vv. 19 and 20)."[24]

῾Αι θήλειαι αὐτῶν ("their women," v. 26) and οἱ ἄρσενες ("the men," v. 27) are terms chosen by Paul to highlight the created order of male and female rather than other connotations which might be communicated through γυνή and ἀνήρ. It is significant that the Septuagint uses ἄρσην and θῆλυς in referring to the creation of humankind as "male and female." When Jesus discussed divorce, He spoke of God's created order in Genesis 1:27, and both Matthew 19:4 and Mark 10:6 use ἄρσην and θῆλυς to refer to male and female. Also in Paul's first epistle, he used these terms to define men and women as polar opposites in the race (Gal. 3:28). Therefore these words for men and women do not refer to the cultural heritage of marriage but to the "natural" expression of mankind as seen in God's creation.

Other terms in Romans 1:23 draw the reader's attention to creation rather than to Hellenistic Judaism. Paul's reference to the unsaved exchanging the glory of the incorruptible God "for an image" alludes to the creation account in Genesis 1:26 ("Let us make man in Our image, according to Our likeness").[25] The emphasis is on the fall of the race from God's design (Rom. 1:18–22), and from the worship of God (v. 23). Also the words "of birds and fourfooted animals and crawling creatures" (v. 23) are reminiscent of "the birds of the sky and over the cattle and over all the earth" in Genesis 1:26. This emphasizes the creation account and thereby the fall of the race from God's design and from the natural, moral pattern of God for sexual expression (Rom. 1:24–27) and social interactions (vv. 28–32).[26]

Therefore the terms of the passage show that Paul's discussion was based not on Jewish customs and rules but on the Hebrew creation account.

The argument of the passage. Another argument opposing the view that Paul described merely a cultural heritage in Romans 1:26–27 is the logical progression of thought in 1:18–3:20. Paul's thesis is that all mankind is condemned and needs God's righteousness, including the unrighteous who reject God (1:18–32), the moralists in their hypocrisy (2:1–16), and Jews who trust in the external aspects of their religion (2:17–3:8). Paul then validated this from Scripture by affirming that all are under sin (3:9–19). Paul did not even address Judaism until 2:17. Up to that point he was simply speaking to the natural man on the basis of general revelation and reason from the vantage point of creation.

Therefore there seems to be no hard evidence to indicate that in Romans 1 Paul addressed homosexual activity from the perspective of Jewish customs and rules that no longer apply today. On the contrary, Paul addressed same-sex relations from the transcultural perspective of God's created order.

VIEW TWO: HOMOSEXUALITY IS PUNISHMENT FOR IDOLATROUS SIN

Bartlett affirms that Paul did not present homosexuality as sinful in itself but as a punishment for sin.[27] He then builds on this supposed observation with the following line of reasoning:

> Those who really want to be "pauline" [*sic*] in their understanding of homosexual practices today would have to argue that people who engage in homosexual acts are being punished by God for their idolatry. One wonders whether people who engage in homosexual practices have been more idolatrous than heterosexual people. Turning it around, one wonders why, given the pervasive idolatry in which most of us live, more of us have not been "punished" by burning with homosexual lust.[28]

This view poses three problems. (1) Bartlett assumes that this punishment has no relationship to sin, (2) he intimates that Paul's argument is not true for today since more people are not "punished" even though this is not the only consequence of idolatry (cf. the added vice-list in Rom. 1:28–32), and (3) he misses the significant point that Romans 1:18–32 is not a description of the pattern of individuals today who act out homosexuality, but is a description of the movement of mankind historically. Each individual's experience may be different, but the result—homosexuality—is still an evil perversion of nature.

The punishment is related to the sin. Paul's discussion of homosexuality does pertain to the consequence of idolatry.[29] But does that mean that no moral kinship exists between the sin and its consequence? One answer, though debated, is that in 1 Corinthians 6:9 and 1 Timothy 1:10 Paul clearly identified homosexuality as a sin. However, Romans 1 also indicates that the punishment for sin was a handing over of mankind to sin.

The strongest support for this observation is in the use of the phrase "God gave them over" (παρέδωκεν αὐτοὺς ὁ Θεός) in Romans 1:24, 26, and 28.[30] Johnson discusses three views of this term: (1) the permissive sense, which means God passively permitted men to fall into retributive consequences (however, the active force of παρέδωκεν argues against this);[31] (2) the privative sense, which means God withdrew His restraining hand from evil (however, this too misses the active sense of the verb),[32] and (3) the active judicial sense, meaning that God actively gave men over to retributive vengeance. This third sense is the idea in Paul's writings elsewhere (Rom. 4:25; 6:17; 8:32; 1 Cor. 5:5; 1 Tim. 1:20; cf. Acts 7:42). As Johnson says, "Both the Romans and Acts passages describe the act of God as a penal infliction of retribution, the expression of an essential attribute of God's nature and being and it is thoroughly consistent with His holiness."[33] And Hays wrote, "God's judgment allows the irony of sin to play itself out; the creature's original impulse towards self-glorification ends in self-destruction. The refusal to acknowledge God as creator ends in blind distortion of the creation."[34]

The reversal of the created order in worship (Rom. 1:21–23, 25) is reflected in a reversal of the created order in sexuality. Both are instances of overturning God's design and are thus evil by nature. This is emphasized by the term "exchanged," which links rebellion against God with the consequences of that rebellion.[35] Also the words "degrading passions" (πάθη ἀτιμίας) in verse 26 and "committing indecent acts" (τὴν ἀσχημοσύνην κατεργαζόμενοι) in verse 27 describe the sinfulness of the punishment.

Therefore a strong correlation exists with respect to the sin and the retributive consequence which by nature is also sin.

A reference to mankind. The argument that this must be the experience of each individual disregards the fact that Romans 1:18–32 refers to the fall of the human race and not each individual's private experience. The sweep of the passage highlights the movement of the race of mankind in general rather than that of any particular person. Four facts support this view. (1) God's wrath is against all ungodliness and unrighteousness of "men" (ἀνθρώπων, v. 18). (2) General revelation has been available to mankind since creation (vv. 19–20). (3) "Men" (all the verbs and pronouns are plural) rejected this revelation by worshiping creation rather than the Creator (vv. 21–23). (4) "Therefore" (διὸ, v. 24) God gave "them" (again the pronouns are plural) over as a race to their lusts (vv. 24–31). This does not mean that every individual must have passed through this pattern for the passage to have any bearing on him. Rather, the practice of homosexuality is an expression of God's giving mankind over to its fallen desires. Paul was simply saying that the roots of homosexuality are in the turning of the race from God. It is unnatural within God's creation (vv. 26–27), as this is a judgment on the unnatural way in which the race turned from the revelation of God.

Therefore each person need not be an idolater for this passage to have relevance to him. Also all idolaters need not experience this particular form of judgment; many other consequences are listed in verses 28–32.[36]

VIEW THREE: PAUL WAS ADDRESSING PERVERTED
HOMOSEXUALITY

Another contemporary view of Romans 1:26–27 is that Paul was discussing the practice of homosexuality by heterosexuals and not present-day expressions of love by true homosexuals. Boswell is one of the strongest proponents of this view. He wrote, "The persons Paul condemns are manifestly not homosexual: what he derogates are homosexual acts committed by apparently heterosexual persons."[37] He adds, "It is in fact unlikely that many Jews of his day recognized such a distinction [between gay persons with a permanent homosexual preference, and heterosexual persons], but it is quite apparent that—whether or not he was aware of their existence—Paul did not discuss gay *persons* but only homosexual *acts* committed by heterosexual persons."[38]

A variant of view three is that Paul viewed pederasty as an abuse. The strongest proponent of this interpretation is Scroggs.[39] He defines all Hellenistic homosexuality as pederasty and then says that Paul's discussion of παρὰ φύσιν is a reference to pederasty.[40]

Homosexual activity by heterosexuals. Some have argued against the hetero-homo perversion view on the basis of the words "degrading passions" (πάθη ἀτιμίας) and "committing indecent acts" (τὴν ἀσχημοσύνην κατεργαζόμενοι),[41] but these words could support either view since those affirming "homosexuality by heterosexuals" would agree that this is a "dishonorable passion" and an "indecent act."

However, Romans 1:18–32 refers to humanity's downward movement away from God and thus away from morality as well. The permissive argument presupposes that homosexuality is a "natural" practice rather than a perversion of God's design of heterosexual relationships in marriage. However, the passage teaches otherwise. There is a movement from heterosexuality to homosexuality in Romans 1:26–27, and according to the rest of Paul's argument, this is a movement away from godliness. Having moved from the knowledge of God, the human race has also moved from God's natural, moral pattern for sexual expression (vv. 24–27) and social interaction (vv. 28–32). Therefore it is improper to limit this one expression to a particular immoral expression of an otherwise acceptable practice referred to as "natural homosexuality." Homosexuality is no more godly, and thus is no more "natural," than any of the other evils mentioned.

Another evidence that homosexuality in general is in view as a movement away from God's design and thus from godliness is that, as stated earlier, the word παρέδωκεν (He "gave them over," vv. 24, 26, 28) is not simply permissive or even privative but is descriptive of a judicial act of God giving men over to judgment for turning from the Creator. While this condemnation is not enough in itself to prove that Paul was addressing homosexuality in general rather than "homosexuality by heterosexuals," it adds to the overall argument that Paul was describing the movement of humanity away from the Creator and thus from God's created order of heterosexuality. Therefore homosexuality is not another proper expression of sexual relationships but is a perversion of God's created order. Homosexuality in itself (and not homosexual acts by heterosexuals) is the talionic expression of judgment against man's movement from the Creator.

As noted earlier, Boswell claims that Paul did not discuss gay persons but only homosexual acts (with the idea that no one in Paul's day distinguished between those who were inwardly gay and those who were simply carrying out homosexual acts).[42] However, if Paul did not make such a distinction himself, how can it be maintained that Romans 1:26–27 strictly observes the distinction?[43]

Therefore the movement in Romans 1:26–27 from heterosexuality to homosexuality does not mean a perversion of same-sex relations but instead refers to an exchange of the created order (heterosexuality) for a talionic perversion (homosexuality).

Pederasty. As mentioned, Scroggs approaches the New Testament passages on homosexuality with his conclusions already drawn before he even examines the material.

> In all three of the passages the material is expressed in very traditional terms, that of Greco-Roman and/or Hellenistic Jewish cultures. Thus not only is the New Testament church uninterested in the topic, it has nothing new to say about it. The passage in Romans may on the surface seem to be an exception to this judgment, but in the final analysis I do not think such a claim can be substantiated.[44]

Scroggs then proposes that Paul was opposing the practice of pederasty.[45] Four observations point up the fallacy of this view.

First, even if pederasty were the dominant expression of homosexuality, Paul's argument in Romans 1 need not be limited by the cultural expression of sin in his day since it is related to the creation account.[46] Because Paul linked his argument to creation, and thus to God's design for sexual fulfillment in monogamous, heterosexual marriage, any movement away from that standard is sinful. Therefore since homosexual relationships are a departure from heterosexual relations, homosexuality is wrong. If Paul's awareness of homosexuality was primarily that of pederasty, that need not mean that the application of his words must likewise be limited to pederasty rather than to mutual adult-adult relations.

Second, many of the terms Paul used in Romans 1 allow for more than pederasty. They support a much more general idea of homosexuality including adult-adult mutuality. (1) Paul wrote of "males with males" (ἄρσενες ἐν ἄρσεσιν, v. 27); he did not refer to men with boys as did Plato.[47] (2) In verse 27 Paul compared male homosexuality to lesbianism (ὁμοίως, "likewise"). Lesbianism was usually understood to be between mutual adults, thereby arguing for adult-adult actions, not adult-child actions. (3) The phrase "natural use [or 'function'] of the woman" (τὴν φυσικὴν χρῆσιν τῆς θηλείας) in verse 27 describes the activity of adults rather than adult-child behavior. (4) The phrases "toward one another" (εἰς ἀλλήλους), "men with men" (ἄρσενες ἐν ἄρσεσιν), and "their error" (τῆς πλάνης αὐτων) describe reciprocal activity with adults.

Third, in Hellenistic literature the phrases κατὰ φύσιν and παρὰ φύσιν do not necessarily describe pederastic relationships. Plato used them to describe natural (normal) and unnatural (abnormal) sexual relations and nothing more.[48]

Fourth, a major flaw in the argument that Paul was limiting his discussion to pederasty is that he also discussed homosexual acts by women. Even Olson notes this.

> It seems strange that Paul begins with a brief reference to women. Pederasty, by definition involves only men. And not only does the Old Testament never prohibit female homosexual activity, but secular Greco-Roman literature hardly even acknowledges its existence. If there were some kinds of female activity at this time, they were not well known—and almost never discussed. Given present resources, it's almost impossible to know what kind of female homosexuality Paul had in mind.[49]

Olson does later explain Paul's inclusion of women as an attempt by Paul to be comprehensive in his theological statement, but in doing so he accuses Paul of speaking figuratively with his inclusion of women as he supposedly did in Romans 2:1 when he accused "Jews" of doing the same things as the Gentiles.[50] The problem here is that Paul had not come to his discussion of the Jews (cf. 2:17). In verse 1 he was still discussing Gentiles or mankind as a whole (note ὦ ἄνθρωπε, in v. 1), though he was referring there to "moralists" among the Gentiles. Also αὐτὰ in 2:1 refers to the practices mentioned in 1:27–32 which include more than homosexuality.

Olson also suggests that Paul may "have had some specific kind of destructive female homosexual behavior in mind, something unmentioned in other literature of the period."[51] In response it is interesting to note that in order to avoid the view that Paul was addressing homosexuality in general, Olson had to call this "destructive female homosexual behavior." Also if Paul spoke about female homosexuality whereas the literature of his day did not, why was he not able to speak about male homosexuality in a similar way? One must assume that pederasty is a case of special pleading that ignores the very terms and arguments of the passage placing the perversion against the norm of God's created order.[52] Therefore the view that Paul was discussing pederasty in Romans 1:26–27 breaks on the rocks of logical and exegetical reasoning.

Conclusion

A contextual and exegetical examination of Romans 1:26–27 reveals that attempts by some contemporary writers to do away with Paul's prohibitions against present-day same-sex relations are false. Paul did not impose Jewish customs and rules on his readers; instead he addressed same-sex relations from the trans-cultural perspective of God's created order. God's punishment for sin is rooted in a sinful reversal of the created order. Nor was homosexuality simply a sin practiced by idolaters in Paul's day; it was a distorting consequence of the fall of the human race in the Garden of Eden. Neither did Paul describe homosexual acts by heterosexuals. Instead he wrote that homosexual activity was an exchange of the created order (heterosexuality) for a talionic perversion (homosexuality), which is never presented in Scripture as an acceptable norm for sexuality. Also Hellenistic pederasty does not fully account for the terms and logic of Romans 1:26–27 which refers to adult-adult mutuality. Therefore it is clear that in Romans 1:26–27 Paul condemned homosexuality as a perversion of God's design for human sexual relations.

CHAPTER 8

The Church and the AIDS Crisis

Timothy D. Howell

AIDS—an acronym for Acquired Immune Deficiency Syndrome—is a problem not just for a certain segment of society. It is a problem everyone must face. The number of persons diagnosed with the dreaded disease is increasing annually. Experts estimate that one million Americans are infected with the AIDS virus at the present time. Kübler-Ross has pointedly challenged the public by asking, "How many more wars, epidemics, famines, or other tragedies do we humans need before we open our minds, hearts, and ears and finally believe that whatever happens to our fellowmen happens to us?"[1] Another health expert, Reed Tuckson, Commissioner of Public Health for the District of Columbia, has stated, "I am convinced that when the history of this time is written, it will best be characterized by how we as a society responded to the multiple challenges presented to us by AIDS."[2]

Most sectors of society are grappling with this crisis. Unfortunately Christians have not always led the way in facing difficult issues. It is easier to say AIDS is a divine judgment or that it happens only to a limited group of sinners. Kübler-Ross presents a challenge: "Since we can no longer deny that AIDS is a life-threatening illness that will eventually involve millions of people and decimate large portions of our human population, it is our choice to grow and learn from it, to either help the people with this dread disease or abandon them."[3] The church can no longer avoid the problem of AIDS or pretend it is not the church's concern. The church has the opportunity to respond to those diagnosed with AIDS by sharing God's love.

> Just as Americans have been known to be a death-denying people, so it has become quite obvious that we also attempt to deny AIDS, to pretend it is none of our business! We hear weekly, from thousands of pulpits, "Love thy neighbor," but when it comes to putting that into practice we quickly add a few conditions. And it is those who preach the loudest who have shown the poorest records in their care and compassion.[4]

Background Information on AIDS

AIDS was first reported in the United States in June 1981. In the 10–year period from 1981 to 1991 almost 180,000 persons in the United States have been afflicted with AIDS, according to the Federal Center for Disease Control in Atlanta.[5] AIDS is a disease that undermines the body's immune system, making a person susceptible to infections and diseases not generally life-threatening to one with a normal immune system. AIDS can also cause disorders in the central nervous system.

AIDS is caused by a virus known as Human Immunodeficiency Virus (HIV). Infection with this virus normally destroys certain white blood cells, which results in the individual's severely diminished ability to combat infection. A person can be infected with HIV for years without developing symptoms of AIDS. The Center for Disease Control in Atlanta says that more than one million people in the United States are infected with HIV,[6] and in February 1992 the World Health Organization estimated between 10 million and 12 million adults and one million children worldwide have HIV.[7]

THE THREE STAGES OF AIDS

Doctors know of three stages of the deadly disease: (1) Asymptomatic Carrier State. In this stage the individual is infected with the virus but shows no detectable signs or symptoms. Though there are no visible signs of infection, the HIV carrier can infect others through body fluids and secretions. (2) AIDS-Related Complex. In this stage an infected individual begins to have symptoms of HIV infection, such as persistent fever, weight loss, diarrhea, swelling of the lymph nodes, and chronic fatigue. (3) Fully Developed AIDS. The Center for Disease Control has defined an AIDS patient as one who has HIV infection and one or more "opportunistic" diseases in the absence of all other known causes of immune system deficiency. The most frequently occurring opportunistic diseases during this terminal stage include various forms of cancer, pneumonia, or fungal infections.[8] Early treatment with certain drugs delays the progression through these three stages, but no cure has been found.

THE TRANSMISSION OF AIDS

The HIV virus is spread by sexual discharge (contact of infected sexual discharges with mucous membranes, which happens in vaginal and/or anal intercourse or in oral-genital sex), injection of infected blood with blood or blood products either by intravenous or intramuscular needles, or perinatal transmission, in which an infected mother passes HIV to her fetus during pregnancy, labor, or delivery. About 70 percent of the cases are transmitted by contact with infected sexual discharges, and about 25 percent are conveyed by needle-sharing drug users.[9]

Studies have confirmed that the AIDS virus is not spread by sneezing, coughing, breathing, hugging, or using the same toilet facilities.[10] Yet Masters, Johnson, and Kolodny warn of the risk if the virus continues to infect individuals throughout society.

> There is no way of quantifying the magnitude of this risk at present. But even if it is now very small, as the prevalence of HIV infection in the general population mounts, the risk of infection from nonsexual, non-drug abuse, nontransfusion contact with blood will mount too. It makes for a scary situation.[11]

In a study published in 1987 most AIDS patients were found to be homosexual/bisexual males (66 percent), 61 percent were whites compared with 24 percent blacks and 14 percent Hispanics; and 47 percent were between 30 and 39 years of age.[12]

Though presently no cure exists for AIDS, scientists have learned a great deal about it over the past few years. More is known about AIDS than about many other diseases that have been studied for longer periods of time. The basic problem confronting scientists is why the antibodies produced by the body to fight the AIDS virus are not able to destroy that virus. As former Surgeon General C. Everett Koop has aptly cautioned, "The most certain way to avoid getting the AIDS virus and to control the AIDS epidemic in the United States is for individuals to avoid promiscuous sexual practices, to maintain faithful monogamous sexual relationships and to avoid injecting illegal drugs."[13]

THE EMOTIONAL EXPERIENCE OF AIDS

For people dying with the AIDS virus, the pain and suffering are traumatic. The emotional problems faced by AIDS patients include feelings of hopelessness, helplessness, abandonment, loneliness, anger toward oneself and God, personal rejection, and loss of physical and emotional strength, dignity, mental ability and/or memory, friends and family members, and income.

Questions patients with AIDS normally ask are these: How do I tell my family I have AIDS? What about my career now that I have AIDS? How can I face dying and death? Many AIDS patients search as never before for the meaning of life as they face the prospect of death.

REACTIONS TOWARD AIDS

Kübler-Ross has penned, "If we are not careful the emergence of the AIDS epidemic will continue to polarize the population: a split between those who offer to help, and those who judge, label, and denigrate those afflicted."[14] In 1987 President Ronald Reagan appointed a Commission on the AIDS Epidemic, a group of 13 people who after studying the epidemic and its related problems made 597 recomendations. Admiral James Watkins, chairman of the commission, commented on the reactions of the public to the work of the commission: "A society [with AIDS] is somewhat abhorrent to us. Sexual promiscuity comes to the fore, and we don't like that. So why do you want to be sensitive to those individuals?"[15]

Many people react to the problem of AIDS with fear or anger or with the tendency to place a high level of blame on AIDS patients. Others tend to evidence lack of concern or compassion.

While chairing the President's Commission on the AIDS Epidemic, Watkins visited many cities in the United States and interviewed hundreds of people. At first, he admitted, he felt little compassion for those suffering from the disease. Yet, as he viewed the cities, slums, and sickly, he felt a surge of new-found compassion and understanding. His statement is a profound realization of where many people are who have never had to confront AIDS personally.

> I had no idea of the link between what is now defined as the "underclass" in our nation and AIDS. It was an emotional experience for me because I did not realize the suffering, the agony, the rejection, the denial we're building [in] that underclass now. We're moving them in separate ways. We've got to save the next generation now![16]

Some clergy and church members have reacted to the epidemic with alarm. Believing that AIDS is a judgment by God on the homosexual community, many Christians have shown lack of concern for and a bias against AIDS patients. However, the AIDS crisis provides an unusual opportunity for the church to communicate the unconditional nature of God's love and the ultimate hope found in Christ Jesus. One pastor recommends that all clergy encourage the people in their congregations to pray for AIDS patients and their wholeness, provide hope for AIDS patients, promote the formation of AIDS ministry teams, seek to win AIDS patients to Christ, and minister to the families of those suffering with AIDS.[17]

When Jesus encountered individuals who were suffering from leprosy, the most dreaded disease of His day, He joined in their suffering by associating with them, He communicated His love and mercy to them, and He exemplified God's power in His healing touch.

RESEARCH ON CHURCH ATTITUDES TOWARD AIDS

In 1988 this author distributed a questionnaire to several churches in Rockingham County, North Carolina. The questionnaire was designed to measure attitudes of church members toward AIDS and those who have contracted the disease. Approximately 250 questionnaires were distributed to the churches, and 190 were completed. The respondents include 83 males and 107 females, with a median age of 41.

The questionnaire included 20 questions with five possible responses to each question: strongly disagree, disagree, don't know, agree, and strongly agree. The responses were as follows:

	Disagree	Don't Know	Agree
1. A person who is an AIDS carrier should be allowed to attend our church.	8%	9%	84%
2. The church membership should be told if a person with AIDS is attending the church services.	44%	11%	45%
3. Children with AIDS should be allowed to attend Sunday school but should be kept in a separate class.	64%	13%	23%
4. Parents should be told if a student who has AIDS is in their child's Sunday school class.	25%	11%	64%

5. If I had a student in my Sunday school class with AIDS, I would treat that person as I treat all other students in my class.   5%   13%   82%

6. AIDS should be a major concern to the Christian community.   5%   5%   90%

7. I feel that AIDS is a direct punishment by God for sinful behavior.   42%   21%   37%

8. The local church should have a policy for dealing with persons who have AIDS.   35%   21%   44%

9. I feel that the AIDS issue is blown out of proportion in the news media.   55%   11%   34%

10. All active cases of AIDS should be quarantined.
                                        52%   21%   27%

11. I believe that abstinence should be encouraged among our young people.   3%   3%   94%

12. I believe that AIDS is primarily a homosexual disease.
                                        38%   6%   56%

13. A new convert who is infected with AIDS should not be allowed to join the church.   77%   12%   11%

14. I believe that AIDS can be transmitted through casual contact.   63%   21%   16%

15. If a member of my church is diagnosed with AIDS, I question his or her lifestyle.   41%   18%   41%

16. I believe God will protect all innocent children and adults from contracting the AIDS virus. 71%   15%   14%

17. Christians do not have to worry about the AIDS virus if they have a moral lifestyle.   65%   8%   27%

18. Monogamous marriage partners cannot contract the AIDS virus.   68%   13%   19%

19. If a person with the AIDS virus becomes a Christian, God will heal him of the disease.   66%   29%   4%

20.
    I do not believe a person with AIDS can be a Christian.
        89%   6%   5%

The areas where highest agreement was expressed were items 1, 5, 6, and 11. Items where disagreement was highest were 3, 13, 14, and 16–20. Four areas where at least one-fifth of the respondents said they did not know were 7, 8, 10, 14, and 19. The areas where there was a balance between disagreement and agreement were items 2, 7, 8, and 15.

Guidelines for Churches in Making Policies Concerning AIDS

Churches must ask hard questions about AIDS before the epidemic catches them off guard. Churches must face the possibility of AIDS-infected persons being in their congregations. How should churches react to such individuals? What attitudes should Christians have toward people with AIDS and the family members of AIDS patients?

The following recommendations are given to help churches formulate policy statements pertaining to AIDS. Hopefully these points will help stimulate discussion by church leaders as they devise AIDS-related policies.

1. Church leaders should appoint individuals who can be prepared to minister to terminally ill people in the church family. This group could be called, for example, "Compassion Unlimited."
2. The pastoral staff should teach the congregation biblical truths on illness, disease, and death.
3. The compassionate nature of Christ's ministry toward the ill, diseased, and handicapped needs to be modeled through preaching, teaching, and ministry groups in the church.
4. Sex education should be taught from a theological perspective, promoting abstinence before marriage, the true nature of love, and the value of appropriate relationships.

5. Lifestyles condoned by the non-Christian culture, such as premarital sex, homosexuality, and adultery must be labeled as sins, as indicated in the Scriptures.

6. The teaching and actions of church leaders should reflect a high regard for the monogamous, heterosexual family unit in society.

7. The church should react toward people with AIDS as Christ reacted in His ministry on earth to seriously ill people.

8. The church should offer hope to those suffering with AIDS in light of Christ's preaching the good news and helping the diseased at the same time.

9. Support groups should be established for the benefit of those suffering with AIDS and for their families. These groups can help the suffering deal with grief, giving hope through Christ and befriending the patients in their suffering and loneliness.

10. The pastoral staff and others should teach what the Bible says about sickness and disease in a sin-fallen world, to combat alarmist views and harsh judgments by believers toward those with AIDS.

11. Any teaching or preaching on God's judgment in light of the AIDS crisis should center on the work of Christ on behalf of sinners, based on God's love and grace.

12. Confidentiality should be a privilege for any victim or family suffering with AIDS in the church. So far as possible church leaders should work with the victim or family in deciding who in the congregation should be told that an individual has AIDS.

13. Since the church should be a place where all people are accepted, those suffering with AIDS should not be turned away from the services or activities of the church family.

14. When it becomes known to the church leaders that a child with AIDS is attending Sunday school, the leaders should confer with the child's parents and doctor on the extent of probable contagion to other students. If there is danger of contagion, proper arrangements should be made for the infected student.

15. Information about an AIDS-infected child should be known only to the pastoral staff and teachers and should not be released to the class or congregation.

16. Special arrangements should be made for children who are neurologically handicapped, who lack control of bodily secretions, who have uncoverable oozing lesions, who display unusual aggressive behavior such as biting, in short, whose behavior or symptoms may be a hazard to others, regardless of whether AIDS is causing the problem.

17. The church should offer options for parents of a nursery-age child infected with AIDS (e.g., a special nursery with a registered nurse may be provided, or a registered nurse may be sent to the home to care for the baby during church services), keeping in mind the danger that so-called healthy children can be to one whose immune system is not adequately protected from infection.

18. The churches should keep a file of public health information and programs on AIDS.[18]

19. Church leaders should select a special committee to develop and monitor changes in the church's AIDS policies as additional medical information on AIDS becomes available.

20. If a church member contracts the AIDS virus, church leaders should recommend the following steps: regular monitoring of the person's medical condition, counseling for the victim and his or her family, and joining a support group dealing with AIDS.

21. The church should start a prayer team that prays on behalf of AIDS patients and their families.

22. Church members should be encouraged to offer help to families during the illness of an AIDS-infected relative and after his or her death.

Conclusion

Like a monster, AIDS is attacking society and the church. The attack on the church is not so much physical as it is ethical. How the church responds to this crisis is a test of its love and compassion for sinners. For most AIDS patients the hardest part of the disease is the fear and rejection they receive. Christians have a great opportunity to show the compassion of Christ at a time when it is most needed. Premature judgment by Christians against AIDS victims is sometimes based on a lack of factual data, both medically and theologically.

It is true that a majority of AIDS victims have or have had

homosexual lifestyles. And it is true that the Bible teaches that homosexuality is a sinful way of life. Yet one must not hastily assume that AIDS is God's specific judgment on every AIDS-infected person.

"It is more difficult to state with assurance just how and when God acts in judgment, or just how and when 'acts of God' are acts of God. At the least, the Bible is clear that God's judging ways are inscrutable to us, and that we are not to participate in final judgment of sin."[19] Compassion needs to replace condemnation, thereby reflecting Christ's own ministry and love.

PART 2:

Contemporary Doctrinal Issues

CHAPTER 9

Evangelical Pluralism: A Singular Problem

W. Gary Phillips

T wo traditional teachings—direct faith in Jesus Christ as the only means of salvation and the understanding of hell as a place of eternal torment—have historically disturbed non-Christians as unworthy doctrines. Further, the point at which these two teachings coalesce most sharply is the destiny of those who have never heard. How could a just and loving God consign to eternal torment those whose providential circumstances prevented them from hearing?

This is not simply an abstract problem in theodicy, occupying the speculations of armchair theologians. The question of those in other religions—particularly those who have not heard the gospel—tugs deeply at one's emotions.

This challenge to theodicy is compounded when one reflects on the concept of absolute justice. People often (incorrectly) assume fairness may be approached inductively; surely it is a matter of common sense to examine all variables and then state what is or is not "fair." But the issue of inductive justice is not decided so easily. Can absolute justice be determined inductively? Should one even try? This writer argues that the answer to both questions is no. The purposes of this chapter are to present these issues within the broader context of pluralistic options and to present and evaluate some current evangelical views on pluralism in relation to the question of the destiny of the untold.

The Options of Pluralism and the Question of Truth

Over the years theologians of differing persuasions have answered the questions of religious pluralism in a variety of ways.[1] These approaches to world religions may be grouped in three categories.

> *Inclusivism* says there is only one true religion through which salvation may be obtained (the religion of the inclusivist). But God may impute salvation to the sincere worshipper [*sic*] of false gods. Although those in other religions may refuse to partake from (or not know about) the proper religious diet, God will not let them starve.
>
> *Exclusivism* maintains that there is one God, and that other truth-claims which conflict with the religion of the exclusivist are therefore false. All other positions lead to spiritual anorexia.
>
> *Universalism* says (positively) all worldviews can be valid avenues of salvation and (negatively) exclusivism is wrong. Because all religions are equally true, we should toss all religious truth claims into one huge melting-pot and enjoy religious stew. The undergirding assumption of universalism is that we have no access to ultimate reality for deciding which worldview is true. We are left with diversity but no unity, relatives but no absolutes.[2]

Logically (and theologically) prior to the question of God's justice in dealing with those who for various reasons never embrace Christ is the question of the nature of truth. A pluralistic approach to religions is "frequently grounded in a relativism about revelation, truth and the goal of human life which is uncongenial to most interpretations of the Christian message."[3]

Is truth absolute or is it relative? If truth is relative, then the Bible's claim that Jesus died on the cross, and the Koran's claim that Jesus did not die on the cross,[4] can both be true. Furthermore exclusivism would necessarily be false; one might attain salvation through any number of (mutually contradictory) avenues.[5]

Aristotle's law of noncontradiction,[6] foundational for the concept of absolute truth, has fallen on hard times. In direct parallel, exclusivist religions—such as Islam and Christianity—have not fared well in modern pluralistic society. One may venture to say, "This is true," so long as one does not add, "Therefore that is false." However, Clark states that "the law of [non]contradiction means that each word, to have a meaning, must also not mean something."[7] McGrath observes, "To allow 'relevance' or 'openness' to be given greater weight than truth, is, quite simply, a mark of intellectual shallowness and moral irresponsibility."[8]

To function in daily life, one must assume that truth is absolute (apparently the "truth" of an oncoming train motivates speculative relativists and absolutists alike to move out of the way). Likewise such absolutism is tolerated as acceptable and coherent in the discipline of analytical philosophy. However (and inconsistently), the concept of absolute truth seems to grate on modern ears when applied to spiritual truth-claims. The same relativist

who moves away from an oncoming train expresses moral out-
rage when evangelicals assert the absolutist claim that Jesus is
the Way, the Truth, and the Life. Relativism is intolerant of
what it perceives as intolerance.

Thus it comes as no surprise that conservative evangelicals
have traditionally been *persona non grata* as participants in pluralistic dialogue, for as Gros observes, "in such a scheme inter-
religious dialogue can only go on either by brackcting one's call
to mission or by using dialogue as a means to conversion in
Christ, a motive often interpreted as ulterior by the dialogue
partner."[9] However, recent publications within the evangelical
camps reveal alarming trends.

Recent Evangelical Developments

The increasingly pluralistic world has recently caused a number of evangelicals to reexamine truth-claims previously held as
unquestionable. Some evangelical scholars have departed from
former positions, and there is serious dissension within
evangelicalism over the issue of religious pluralism.

In 1988 Sanders wrote a detailed essay, entitled "Is Belief in
Christ Necessary for Salvation?"[10] The next year Osburn's article,
"Those Who Have Never Heard: Have They No Hope?"[11] was
published. Both writers maintain that there is redemptive hope
for the untold through both general revelation and special revelation (oral tradition, dreams, visions, etc.).

Soon after Osburn's article appeared, the 1989 annual meeting of the Evangelical Theological Society was held in San Diego,
California. Both plenary and parallel sessions dealt with the problems of religious pluralism. Pinnock commended Osburn's essay
and recommended a "lenient" view toward the untold, as well as
toward sincere devotees of other religions.[12] Sanders offered verbal support in a plenary session. Discussion was intense and not
always clear. Meanwhile Christian leaders from Asia and Africa
watched closely as the American evangelicals debated. Asian
theologian Bong Ro said, "We are looking to you, the American
church, to make a clear statement on the uniqueness of Christ [as
the epistemological basis for salvation]. Frankly, we are fighting
a battle for it in Asia."[13]

The Evangelical Theological Society meetings in 1990 and
1991 continued the discussion. In 1990 this writer wrote an essay interacting with the positions put forth by Osburn, Pinnock,

and Sanders.[14] In 1992 this writer participated in the annual Wheaton Theology Conference,[15] presented some of the points discussed later in this article, and engaged in a brief public dialogue with John Sanders.

Recently evangelicals have written four significant books dealing with this issue: Harold Netland, *Dissonant Voices* (Grand Rapids: Eerdmans, 1991), William Crockett and James Sigountos, eds., *Through No Fault of Their Own?* (Grand Rapids: Baker, 1991); John Sanders, *No Other Name* (Grand Rapids: Eerdmans, 1992); and Clark Pinnock, *A Wideness in God's Mercy* (Grand Rapids: Zondervan, 1992). These books demonstrate that within evangelical circles a significant shift is occurring regarding the fate of those in other religions. The reader can expect to see much more discussion and dialogue arising in the future from the issues now being debated. The views presented in the four books cited above need to be examined carefully.

Three Salvific Propositions

In evangelical circles the confrontation related to pluralism is between inclusivists and exclusivists. Historically evangelical exclusivists have insisted that Jesus Christ is both the ontological and the epistemological basis of salvation. Those who die without placing faith in Christ in this life—whether they have heard and rejected Christ, or have not heard—fall under condemnation.[16] While evangelical inclusivists also affirm that Jesus Christ is the ontological basis of salvation, they insist that He need not be the epistemological basis.

To clarify some of the soteriological questions, three propositions will be considered:[17] (1) Jesus Christ is the only way of salvation. (2) Christ's work on the cross is imputed to any and all sinners who will be saved. (3) To receive salvation one must place direct faith in Jesus Christ as his or her Savior in this life, or face eternal damnation in the next.

The extent to which these are considered absolute, universal, and unqualified determines where one falls within the spectrum from liberal (universalism), to lenient (inclusivism), to limited (exclusivism[18]).

JESUS CHRIST IS THE ONLY WAY OF SALVATION

Though classic universalism denies this first proposition, evangelicals (both inclusivists and exclusivists) affirm it as absolute, universal, and unqualified. The proposition may be supported by four affirmations:

1. Jesus claimed that He is the only way of salvation.[19]
2. Jesus' followers claimed the same.[20]
3. Jesus claimed other ways of salvation are false.[21]
4. Jesus' followers claimed the same.[22]

The conclusion could be stated in this way: Positively, Jesus Christ is the only way of salvation; negatively, other ways of salvation are false.

CHRIST'S WORK ON THE CROSS IS IMPUTED TO ANY AND
   ALL SINNERS WHO WILL BE SAVED

This statement follows from the first, and is again absolute, universal, and unqualified. Taken together, these first two propositions comprise the ontological basis of salvation. Universalists deny the second proposition, along with the first; evangelical inclusivists and exclusivists affirm both.[23]

TO RECEIVE SALVATION ONE MUST PLACE DIRECT
   FAITH IN JESUS CHRIST AS HIS OR HER SAVIOR IN
   THIS LIFE, OR FACE ETERNAL DAMNATION IN THE
   NEXT

Here the disagreement begins between evangelical inclusivists and exclusivists. This third proposition reflects the epistemological basis for salvation. How much content must one know to be saved, and by whom (Whom?) must it be known? If the object of faith (God) knows, is it necessary that the believing subject holds this knowledge? Does ignorance abort grace? Evangelical exclusivists maintain that only Jesus is the Way, and that the redeemed must demonstrate explicit faith in Jesus Christ.[24] Evangelical inclusivists, however, maintain that only Jesus is the Way, and that the salvific knowledge resides in God, but not necessarily in the redeemed. In other words, while God knows Jesus is the only Way to salvation, the redeemed untold do not. In fact other religions may function as "schoolmasters" to lead people, albeit indirectly, to Christ.[25] Some inclusivists would say that those in non-Christian religions who are saved without direct knowledge of Christ are saved *in spite of* their religion (considered an *attempt* at salvation[26]); others would say they are saved *through* it (considered a *way* of salvation[27]).

The Wideness in God's Mercy

At least three solutions are put forth to argue against the third proposition: the eschatological solution, the election solution, and the exception solution. All three maintain (in some degree) that this proposition is particular, not universal, and is relative, not absolute. Each has been embraced by some inclusivists.

The eschatological solution takes two forms. Some hold a "later light" view: though exclusivism is true, the untold will indeed have opportunity for salvation postmortem, based on 1 Peter 3:18–22.[28] The untold are not saved in this life, but will have a chance to believe in Jesus Christ in the future.[29] Though different in kind, a second form of eschatological solution that attempts to relieve the perceived problem of eternal injustice is annihilationism.[30] This view redefines the traditional understanding of damnation—it is destruction, not eternal conscious torment in hell. Pinnock combines both forms of the eschatological solution and maintains that after the untold are confronted by Jesus Christ, those who reject Him will be destroyed in hell.[31]

The election solution is an inclusivist position. The moment of redemption for the untold is not future (the eschatological solution) but is present due to "other possible present states." Those who hold this view maintain that since God knows all possible worlds, He knows whether any particular untold person would have believed had he or she been born in the United States, rather than in, say, Sri Lanka. God elects the individual to salvation according to His knowledge of a potential present world rather than according to decisions made in this actual world. Thus the third proposition is not universal or absolute; its referent is not this actual world, but its application is informed by God's "middle knowledge" of other potential worlds.[32]

The exception solution offers a form of inclusivism which reasons that redemption of the untold takes place in this life (not in the future or in other possible present worlds), even though the individual makes no explicit choice for Christ. The argument is analogical and runs like this: God made a divine exception— similar to "those who have not heard" are "those who had not heard" (the redeemed of the Old Testament): Enoch, Job, Melchizedek, Jethro, and others. Since God redeemed those who had not heard (who were ignorant of Jesus through no fault of their own), would not God be consistent to extend His mercy also to the untold (who fall into the same circumstantial category)? Thus an analogy from past redemption (for those living before Christ's First Advent) supports a redemption model for the salvation of the untold (those living after Christ's First Advent). The chronologically premessianic believers become the test case for the untold, who are informationally premessianic, though living after Christ's Incarnation.

Another analogy Sanders and Pinnock pursue is the case of "those who cannot hear"—infants, small children, and the severely retarded. Many Christians believe that infants who die are saved through the intervening grace of God.[33]

The point is that most evangelicals embrace the principle of gracious exceptions—due to special circumstances which tug at God's mercy—to the requirement that all who will be redeemed will be in heaven only by believing specific content.[34] If so, God has set a precedent: there exists a category of human beings who might be saved apart from conscious assent to the gospel. Should some untold people be placed there as well? Both Sanders[35] and Pinnock[36] argue strongly that evangelicals who are lenient toward these "innocents" should extend their reasoning further and embrace the untold.

Clark Pinnock and John Sanders: A Critique

In some ways the suggestions made by Sanders and Pinnock are winsome and therefore are gaining wide attention among evangelicals. The following are seminal objections, reflections, and suggestions for those who take this approach.

First, the exception solution has problems with the use of the analogies. For the argument from those who had not heard to make its point, these must be without special salvific revelation in this life. Pinnock identifies as "pagan believers" Enoch, Job, Abimelech, Melchizedek, Jethro, and others.[37] The assumption is that since they were saved apart from believing in Christ, this same provision must apply today (since God's character is unchanged) to the unevangelized who are theologically pre-Christian. In fact Pinnock and Sanders see some of these individuals as God's agents for expanding knowledge of and appreciation for other religions.

But there is a missing element in Pinnock's argument—the assumption that none of these received salvific revelation. Special revelation may take several modalities: dreams, visions, theophanies, mighty acts (Ex. 14:13–31), prophets, all of which were used in the Old Testament (Abraham "saw my day," etc.).[38] Enoch (Gen. 5:22), Job (Job 39–42), Noah (a preacher of righteousness, 2 Peter 2:5), Melchizedek (king of righteousness), and Jethro (father-in-law of Moses, to whom Yahweh was revealed), were indeed recipients of special revelation, thus invalidating the strongest point of the analogy.

Other problems are confronted in applying the analogy of those who cannot hear to the untold. Infants are guilty of sin (Ps. 51:5), but not of sins (Isa. 7:15). Furthermore they do not have the capacity to respond to general revelation or conscience. Both of these points may be variables that weigh heavily with God's mercy, and neither of these is true for the untold. (This objection would count little with Sanders and Pinnock; for them the sin that condemns is not original sin or actual sins, but only the sin of rejecting Christ.[39] Sin and sins, it is suggested, either are dealt with in this life or were dealt with on the Cross).

Further, arguments by analogy are tenuous, and their probability depends on the number of correspondences between the situations being compared.[40] The analogies from "those who *had* not heard," and perhaps from "those who *cannot* hear," have some points of correspondence with the case of "those who *have* not heard," but not enough for the confidence with which many evangelicals would baptize the untold.

Second, much is made of Cornelius as a paradigm for conversion from a believing redeemed non-Christian to a believing redeemed Christian. Sanders observes, "Cornelius was already a saved believer *before* Peter arrived, but he was not a Christian believer."[41] However, does the analogy hold?[42] New Testament "God-fearers" believed in the truth of propitiatory sacrifices, and as a God-fearer, Cornelius had already received and responded to special revelation (Acts 10:3–6). However, to say Cornelius would have been saved if he had died before Peter arrived is not the same as saying he is paradigmatic of those who are saved without special salvific revelation. Also it was not till Peter preached in Cornelius's house that Cornelius heard "the good news of peace through Jesus Christ" (Acts 10:36, NIV), received "forgiveness of sins" (v. 43), and was "saved" (11:14).[43]

Third, the exegetical arguments of Sanders and Pinnock reflect hermeneutical sleight-of-hand. When examining a putative exclusivistic passage (e.g., John 14:6; Acts 4:12), both Pinnock and Sanders try to show that wider parameters of interpretation are possible. For example Jesus' spoke of the small gate and narrow road (Matt. 7:13–14) because "at the time when he spoke this warning the number of disciples was few."[44] The "narrow way" statements are thus not applicable today.[45] Sanders argues that Peter broadened the definition of those who "fear God" (Acts 10:2) to mean "those who trust and obey God to the extent of the revelation they have."[46]

Pinnock seems to assume that once a possible reinterpretation toward leniency is conceived, it should be accepted as reality. Why? Because, he says, the character of a loving God transforms the possible into the probable. If there is any grammatical flexibility, or any possible positive nuance within the semantic range of the terms used, Pinnock accepts it as normative. Those who disagree are guilty of "hardening of the arteries,"[47] and are "niggardly," "miserly," and "offensive."[48] However, a possible interpretation is not the same as a likely interpretation.

Fourth, the controlling principles of this approach have broader applications than simply to the unevangelized. As this writer stated elsewhere,

> Thus far Pinnock, Donald Bloesch[49] and other evangelicals have tendered this offer only to the Untold, but one wonders if this stopping point will hold. Once "fairness" is used as a criterion (and exceptions inevitably tend to proliferate), other inequities besides ignorance vie for attention: some may have heard the gospel from a parent who abused them, or from a pastor who later committed adultery. Others may be told about Christ from someone whose intellectual abilities did not commend Christianity as a faith for thoughtful people. Still others are unfortunate enough to have wealth—a tremendous hindrance to salvation (Matt. 19:24). All of these, through no fault of their own, would be negatively disposed toward the gospel. Absolute inductive fairness is elusive.[50]

Indeed, Pinnock and Sanders go beyond this in their views. Some of Pinnock's suggestions may make evangelicals uncomfortable and exclusivists blanch. He maintains that all mankind will have an eschatological opportunity to accept or reject Christ's love.[51] Also he says Socrates will face Jesus,[52] and all the evangelized who rejected Christ will have a postmortem opportunity for salvation. Further, in the eschaton anyone who stands before God and asks Him for mercy will receive it; up to the point of annihilation (!) the books are never closed.[53] Even further, God may redeem an individual not only because of his faith, but by the "directionality" of his heart toward God.[54] Also an atheist may be redeemed—if the ethical component is in place.[55] With these views one is not surprised to read this statement by Pinnock:

> When we approach the man of a faith other than our own, it will be in a spirit of expectancy to find how God has been speaking to him and what new understandings of the grace and love of God we may ourselves discover in this encounter. Our first task in approaching another people, another culture, another religion, is to take off our shoes, for the place we are approaching is holy. Else we find ourselves treading on men's dreams. More seriously still, we may forget that God was here before our arrival.[56]

In this view religions are on a spectrum[57] of friendly competitors[58] who are all in transition, and thus Christians have opportunities to aid them in seeking truth through dialogue.[59]

Sanders assures readers that there is no slippery slope here; the "wider-hope" is not universalism, as C sharp is not B flat.[60] But the views expressed here demonstrate that the slope has already been well negotiated.

Fifth, Pinnock implements "Logos" Christology from the second-century apologists. "Though Jesus Christ is Lord, we confess at the same time that the Logos is not confined to one segment of human history or one piece of world geography. . . . God the Logos has more going on by way of redemption than what happened in first-century Palestine.[61] Again, "The Logos is at work in the whole world like a schoolmaster bringing people to Christ. . . . Those who respond belong to the larger people of God."[62] Pinnock's point focuses not on the incarnation of the Logos (contrary to the focus in John 1:14), but on the nonincarnate—and universal—Logos.[63]

Sixth, Pinnock and Sanders emphasize that their views will cause no decrease in missionary fervor, particularly because avoidance of God's wrath is not a proper motivation for mission.[64] Much of what they say is helpful here. Still, while avoidance of God's wrath may not be the highest of missionary motives, Boone does identify it as the single most important motivator in evangelism.[65] Though "wider-hope" views may not directly result in a shrinking missionary population, Hunter argues that they do and have.[66] The "trickle down" from academicians to missions is indeed cause for serious concern.

Seventh, in application, these exceptions become the rule. They become paradigmatic—rather than exceptions—of how God has dealt and presently deals with the bulk of mankind. This is curi-

ous: while explicit faith in Christ should be the norm, in effect
(because of all those who have lived over the millennia) the
functionally normative means by which most people in the
eschaton will have been redeemed will be through some method
other than that described in Romans 10:14–15.

Eighth, believers of course should *adapt* the gospel message
to current needs, but they should not *adopt* teachings that contradict earlier understandings unless exegetical or theological warrant arises. One must not allow apologetic motives to govern
exegesis. Though Pinnock believes that "wideness" will refresh
Christian apologetics, the more inclusive approach will become
a part of evangelical theodicy (as indeed both Sanders and
Pinnock suggest). This in turn will blunt the offense of the Cross
and thus compromise evangelism and missions.

Pinnock and Sanders are gracious and compassionate men, to
whom three warnings may be addressed. First, they must be
cautious about labeling speculations (even those they deem probable) as certainties. Second, they must be cautious about the
extent to which their inclusivism becomes a component within
their apologetics. Third, they should guard against the assumption that God must have some special arrangements for the
unevangelized, because otherwise, as they argue, God would
then be less worthy of worship, and is less just and loving than
humans.[67]

Conclusion

In a world in which the concept of absolute truth is denied
(absolutely), the offense of the Cross may become increasingly
offensive, and the exclusiveness of Jesus Christ (as both the
ontological and epistemological basis for salvation) may become
a watershed issue among evangelicals. One can certainly applaud Sanders's goal: "We must not adopt an agnostic stance
before we have made a thorough investigation."[68] But once that
investigation is made, and one still disagrees, what then? As
Newbegin observed, "the problem is that we want unity on our
terms, and it is our rival programs for unity which tear us apart.[69]

Contrary to Pinnock[70] and Sanders,[71] those who are agnostic
or even exclusivist on this issue are not guilty of dysfunctional
soteriology, but—in the spirit of Pascal's wager—would rather
err on the side of safety than gamble on speculative leniency. In
a sense Christians must be partially agnostic, for Scripture does

not clearly reveal God's arrangements for the untold. Apparently God did not feel it necessary to inform those to whom (by definition) those plans would never have immediate relevance.[72] When an individual adopts a view on which Scripture is not explicit, he is making assumptions. He is no longer in the realm of exegetical certainty but is dealing (at best) in probability and inference. Putative, implicit speculations that have such broad-ranging implications should be approached with great caution.

Nicole gives a timely warning. "It is dangerous to be more generous than God has revealed himself to be."[73] It is better to err on the side of exclusivism—while hoping that that view is wrong. In other words, while remaining open to the logical possibility that God has made special arrangements for the untold, this "negative agnostic" approach suggests that the wisest course is to assume that the untold remain under condemnation and that Christians should therefore get on with obeying the Great Commission.

CHAPTER 10

Major Flaws in Liberation Theology

J. Ronald Blue

L iberation theology is one of the most significant movements springing from contemporary Latin America. What began among a few Latin theologians has grown into a recognized movement with influence all over the world. From the earliest expressions of the liberation theme by missionary Richard Schaull in 1955, the liberation motif appeared with increasing frequency in a number of progressive Roman Catholic councils and ecumenical conferences in the 1960s.[1] It gained widespread recognition at the second Latin American Episcopal Council (CELAM II) in Medellín, Colombia, in 1968.

Liberation theology is a "new way of 'doing theology' that radically challenges traditional concepts and practices."[2] Liberationists propose to free persons from all that enslaves them—socially, economically, and politically through peaceful protest or, if necessary, through revolutionary violence. While the social conditions that prompted the birth of liberation theology can be verified, the liberationist solutions need to be challenged. Several major flaws invalidate the proposed liberation cures.

Conditions in Latin America

The social frame of reference for liberation theology lies in the reality of poverty. Liberationism is rooted in the struggle to free people oppressed by unjust economic structures. As Fuentes has declared, "South of your border, my North American friends, lies a continent in revolutionary ferment—a continent that possesses immense wealth and nevertheless lives in misery and a desolation you have never known and barely imagined."[3] The poverty, illiteracy, and hunger in Latin America are undisputed facts.

POVERTY

Of Latin America's 400 million people, 60 percent are reported to have incomes of less than $50 a year, and another 30

126

percent earn between $50 and $190 a year. This means 90 percent of the people have incomes below the subsistence level.[4]

An evident tension exists between these poor masses struggling for survival and the privileged elite who control the power structure comprised of large landowners, industrialists, professionals, bureaucrats, and the military and religious leaders. It is the power elite who primarily benefit from any economic advance in Latin America. The top 10 percent eat 41 percent of the meat and get 44 percent of the clothes, half the electric appliances, 74 percent of the furniture, and 85 percent of the motor vehicles.[5]

These statistics, however, do not adequately portray the overwhelming burden that poverty inflicts on the individuals caught in its grasp. Mooneyham turns from abstract statistical analysis to specific reality in the case of Juan Díaz, a coffee worker in El Salvador.

> He and three of his five daughters spend long, hard days in the coffee fields of Montenango. On a good day, Juan picks enough coffee to earn $1.44; his daughters make a total of $3.35. With $1.24 of these wages, Juan and his wife, Paula, are able to feed their family for one day. In bad times, Juan and his daughters make as little as $.56 a day—less than half the money they need just to eat.
>
> At the end of the six-week coffee season, Juan does odd jobs around the hacienda—provided there is work to be done. He can earn about $.90 there for an eight-hour day. Paula de Díaz supplements her husband's earnings by working in the market. When people have enough money to purchase the tomatoes, cabbages and other home-grown vegetables she sells, Paula can make about $.40 a day.
>
> The hacienda provides a simple dwelling for the Díaz family, but no modern facilities. Candles are used for light, water has to be hauled from a well, and furnishings consist of little more than a table and some chairs. Aside from a dress and shoes for each of the girls during the coffee season, the family has not been able to buy much else in the last five years. Whatever money doesn't go for food is spent for visits to the health clinic ($.40 each time), the high interest on bills at the company store, expenses for the children in school, and for the burial of Juan's father, who died last year.
>
> "You know, I look forward to a better life for my children," Juan says. "I dream that if it is possible—if I can possibly afford it—my children will not follow in my footsteps, that they will break out of this terrible way of life. But the money problems we face every day blot out those dreams. I feel bad, nervous, I don't sleep nights worrying about how I'll get something for them to eat. I think and think but don't find any answers. I work hard; my wife and daughters do, too. We all do. But still we suffer. Why?"[6]

The nagging question, why, demands an answer. This is not a case of poverty from indolence. In spite of all the hard work, this family remains trapped in a seemingly hopeless state of poverty. The case of Juan Díaz is the case of millions all over Latin America.

ILLITERACY

Related to poverty is illiteracy. The problem of illiteracy contributes to the problems of underdevelopment. It accompanies and has a bearing on undernourishment, disease, and all kinds of economic and cultural problems.

In Guatemala almost two-thirds of the people are unable to read and write.[7] In most of Latin America, the number of illiterates is rising more rapidly than schools can be built and staffed with teachers. Millions of children move toward adulthood without any instruction at all. Others enroll in the primary grades and drop out without ever learning to read or write. In rural Latin America and in the mushrooming slum areas of Latin America's cities, it is a rare child who is privileged to complete the sixth grade. In many countries it is the sixth-grade graduate who then becomes the teacher in the faltering educational system.

Poverty and population factors contribute to the problem. The countries with the least to spend on education and literacy usually have the highest birth rates. Funds are in short supply. In a rapidly growing population the ratio of trained teachers to school-age children often decreases. As a result, many governments once committed to universal education have quietly abandoned this objective.

The lack of minimal educational opportunities only adds to the inequalities between the wealthy and poorer sections of society. In many cases Latin America's so-called elite are in power simply because only the elite are educated. A nation that is largely illiterate can hardly be strong. Literacy is essential for those who would improve their quality of life, achieve social mobility and dignity, and participate in community affairs. Economic poverty is clearly related to educational poverty, and Latin America suffers from both maladies. Poverty and illiteracy yield a third and perhaps even more distressing problem: inadequate nutrition.

HUNGER

Poverty and illiteracy produce hungry people, and hunger is widespread and persistent in Latin America. It affects a vast majority of the population and continues to plague increasing numbers. McGovern reports, "Most of the people in Latin America go hungry. An estimated two-thirds of the population are undernourished."[8]

With so many of the people of Latin America suffering malnutrition, it is difficult to make any progress. A vicious cycle puts the continent into a tailspin. Undernourished people are not usually healthy people; weak, ailing people are not usually productive people; and unproductive people are not usually prosperous people. The result is more poor people suffering greater malnutrition. And the cycle continues to abysmal proportions. Hunger produces poverty, poverty produces hunger, and in many cases poverty and hunger conspire in the tragic finality of death.

In Latin America, malnutrition is said to be the primary or contributing cause in more than half of all deaths of children.[9] In 1988 the infant mortality rate of Latin America was about six times that of North America. While only 10 babies out of a 1,000 died before they reached one year of age in North America, 57 out of a 1,000 infants died in Latin America.[10]

In spite of these disturbing statistics of infant mortality, the population of Latin America continues to explode, often adding to the problems of poverty and malnutrition. The number of mouths to feed increases while the resources necessary to feed them do not increase. While the population of North America, at its present rate of growth, would take 99 years to double, Latin America's population would double in only 32 years. The 429 million people in Latin America in 1988 have been projected to swell to more than 711 million by the year 2020.[11] Latin America is adding four times as many people to its population each year as North America. Mexico alone is adding more people than are the United States and Canada together.[12]

This rapid population growth only aggravates the situation in Latin America. The quality of life continues to decline for the majority of people who are caught in the throes of poverty, illiteracy, and hunger.

Liberation Theology

Liberation theologians of Latin America address the pressing problems that plague their continent. The prevailing poverty, widespread illiteracy, and increasing malnutrition are realities that must be challenged. Little wonder Gutiérrez exclaims, "To characterize Latin America as a dominated and oppressed continent naturally leads one to speak of liberation and above all to participate in the process."[13]

There is no question about Latin America's severe economic problems. The situation in which the continent finds itself is fact. No one can deny it or dispute it. The point of inquiry revolves around the cause and cure for Latin America's economic crisis. Liberation theologians are in general agreement both on the underlying reasons for the prevailing economic inequities in Latin America and on what they propose as the most viable solution to those problems. Both in their analysis and in their answers, liberation theologians are deeply indebted to Marxism.

Salvadoran theologian Núñez writes,

> No one can fail to notice that Marxist thought exerts a powerful influence on liberation theology. And the exponents of liberation theology do not try to hide that influence. On the contrary they seem to pride themselves on the use they make of Marxism both for social analysis and for the action they propose to transform the structures of Latin American society.[14]

The stark reality of need in Latin America provides the setting for the Marxist solutions advocated by liberation theology. The rich are few but powerful, while the poor are plentiful and in most cases pitiably exploited. As DeKoster so poignantly expresses it, "The wealthy live in unimaginable splendor, and the poor in unimaginable squalor."[15] It does not take exceptional intelligence or special emotional sensitivity to recognize something is wrong.

Proposed Solutions

From the undeniable crisis that Latin America is experiencing socially, economically, politically, and religiously, one must turn to the proposed solutions. It is only right to commend liberation theologians for their deep concern for the people of their continent and for their strong commitment to provide a cure for the ills of their society, but it is equally right to question their diagnosis of the ailments and their proposed cure. To administer the wrong treatment might make the patient only worse. If the diagnosis is wrong, the prescription could be erroneous. And if the prescription is faulty, the cure could be deadly.

There are four grave problems in the health of Latin America that liberation theology proposes to cure. In some cases the liberationist prescription needs to be withdrawn and an entirely new one written. In other cases an alteration or addition is needed. In all cases, however, something seems to be lacking. Major flaws exist in each of the prescriptions liberationists have written.

INJUSTICE

What is to be done about never-ending injustices that deny the most basic rights of people and negate the dignity of human beings?

Every person deserves the respect and honor due him or her. Vatican II expresses it well: "Coming down to practical and particularly urgent consequences, this Council lays stress on reverence for man." The Vatican framers expand on this position:

> Whatever is opposed to life itself, such as any type of murder, genocide, euthanasia, or willful self-destruction, whatever violates the integrity of the human person, such as mutilation, torments inflicted on body or mind, attempts to coerce the will itself; whatever insults human dignity, such as subhuman living conditions, arbitrary imprisonment, deportation, slavery, prostitution, the selling of women and children; as well as disgraceful working conditions, where men are treated as mere tools for profit, rather than as free and responsible persons; all these things and others of their like are infamies indeed.[16]

The infamies so eloquently denounced above are the very injustices that continue to plague Latin America. Certainly it is only fair to say that people caught in the throes of such bondage deserve better.

Liberation theology came into being primarily to address these ills. As Sanders put it, "Liberation theology is an ethical theology that grew out of social awareness and the desire to act."[17] It is a clear attempt to relate theological perspectives to ethical responsibility for the complex problems in Latin America.

Gutiérrez concurs that the "task of contemporary theology is to elucidate the current state of these problems, drawing with sharper lines the terms in which they are expressed." He then places mankind at the center of the solution for these problems.[18] Liberation theologians advance a revived humanism in the cure for the continued problems of injustice. They conclude that since mankind caused the problems of injustice individuals must provide the solutions.

They seem to ignore the thought of any kind of divine intervention in the curative process. The divinity developed in liberation theology is the "divinity" to be found in everyone in the human race. The stress is clearly if not almost exclusively on a horizontal plane. Through social revolution driven by love, albeit at times violent love, man is to attack injustice and establish a new society and become a new man. Liberation theology begins with man and ends with man. The strong core of humanism is undeniable.

Herein lies a grave danger in the proposed solution to injustice. Liberation theology has overlooked the creative force of the transcendent Deity. Without God and His transforming power it is doubtful that any lasting change can be realized in society. The alienation between human beings reflects their alienation from God. Humanistic attempts at reform fall short of the mark. People need more than a change of clothes; they need a change of heart.

Most liberationists conclude that God is in every person. It is curious to note that in Gutiérrez's three-step argument to support this conclusion, he uses biblical references to underline two steps—that God was in Christ and is in the Christian—but he has no reference for the third and final step—that God is in *all* individuals.[19] The reason is simple. There is no such biblical reference.

The liberationists' concern for the injustices in society is admirable, but to contend that society can be transformed solely through naturalistic forces is at best misguided if not naive. Social sin is, after all, simply a conglomerate of personal sin. Society does not commit acts of torture, murder, and rape. People do. Therefore society can only be changed when people are changed.

Liberationists would do well to infuse a little more theology of redemption into their theology of liberation. In the focus on humanity, the theologian need not lock out God. In placing humanity at the center of the stage, there is no need to turn out the lights. The spotlights from the upper gallery may be the only way anyone will be able to see his way around the obstacles and put order to the action on stage. Better yet, the light from above needs to become a light within. This will be done only by divine intervention, not by humanistic efforts.

In the attempt to seek new answers for the injustices of Latin America, liberationists would do well to turn back to some of the old themes found in the Bible. The good news of the Lord Jesus Christ, who came to suffer the ultimate injustice of death on the cross to pay the penalty for man's sin and to thereby offer

new life, eternal life, is still the best news of all. Through supernaturally redeemed individuals perhaps society can be relieved
from so much injustice.

INEQUITY

For liberationists there is no injustice so devastating and debili-
tating as the injustice of poverty. The gross inequity between the
rich and the poor is of major concern. The focal point in most
liberation theology writings is the cause of the poor. Julio de
Santa Ana declares, "Whenever theology takes a prophetic stance,
it has to take cognizance of sociological reflection. Similarly,
the biblical proclamation leads us to a basic option for the poor."[20]
Everyone agrees that poverty is a severe problem. Vatican II
sounded a clear call: "Some nations with a majority of citizens
who are counted as Christians have an abundance of this world's
goods, while others are deprived of the necessities of life and are
tormented with hunger, disease, and every kind of misery. This
situation must not be allowed to continue."[21]

Not all agree, however, on the cause of poverty. Fewer still
agree on the cure.

Liberationists have chosen to follow the theories espoused by
Karl Marx. Poverty is the result of a class society, they say, and
people are poor because others are rich. Or to put it more bluntly,
the liberation theologians to the south contend that Latin America
is poor because the United States is rich. Capitalism is the cul-
prit. Gutiérrez says, "There can be authentic development for
Latin America only if there is liberation from the domination
exercised by the great capitalist countries, and especially by the
most powerful, the United States of America."[22]

The Marxist solution follows the Marxist diagnosis. If the
poor are poor because the rich are rich (the dependency theory),
and the poor are getting poorer while the rich are getting richer
(the gap theory), it is clear, it is argued, that the poor are good
and the rich are evil (the dualism theory). The solution is to
revolt against the evil rich, take what they have, and give it to
the poor. This is a glorified Robin Hood approach to economics.

It is far too simplistic to blame capitalism for poverty, and
specifically to blame the United States for the poverty in Latin
America. Marxist theories lead people to some irrational conclusions. There are multiplied factors responsible for the tragic poverty that exists in Latin America. Latin America was built on a

weak foundation of conquest and feudalism. By contrast, the United States was built on a foundation of colonizers and free enterprise. The structures that have emerged and the inequities between them are far more likely the result of the contrasting foundations than they are of subsequent exploitation.

This is not to excuse the exploitation that has occurred. It is the greed and graft, the exploitation that must be attacked, not the so-called "evil system of capitalism." Greed, graft, and exploitation are as evident in socialistic countries as they are in capitalistic countries. The greatest flaw in Marxist theory is that it stops with the system and never reaches the heart of the matter—individual ethics.

Marx rejected the authoritative source that can provide the needed ethical standards to make any system work—the Bible. He declared that he would take a "scientific" approach to the inequities evident in society. By "scientific" Marx meant "naturalistic." Charles Darwin, Sigmund Freud, and John Dewey all used the term in the same way. "Scientific" does not mean the hypothesis will be verified by empirical facts. On the contrary the theories are proposed without any tests or evidence and are declared "scientific" only because they are "naturalistic." They are stripped of any supernatural influence.

Liberationists would do well to interpret Marx in light of the Bible rather than to interpret the Bible through the teachings of Marx. One of the few places where the high ideals of Marx have been achieved was in the early church. Class and racial barriers were broken down (Rom. 10:12) and believers shared all things (Acts 2:44). But this was not achieved through a revolution in which the empire was destroyed, the rich landholders of Rome were exterminated, and a dictatorship of the proletariat was established instead. The only violence recorded was that of authorities against the growing band of Christians. Marx had an admirable goal, but the process he proposed is neither scientific nor scriptural, and therefore it will fail.

Instead of condemning biblical exegesis as an "exegesis of the dominant class" and calling for a "reinterpretation of the Bible from the viewpoint of the poor,"[23] liberationists need to realize the Bible speaks with equal force to rich and poor. Instead of isolating its attack to economic systems, as does Marx, the Bible gets down to the source of the problems—personal ethics and human character. For example the Bible neither condones nor condemns slavery (though by inference it opposes slavery). Rather than attack the system of slavery, the Bible attacks the sins in slavery—the sins of brutality, disrespect, and mistreatment on the part of the owner and the sins of hatred, dishonor, and indolence on the part of the slave. Better yet, the Bible instructs the owner to treat the slave with care and concern as though he were a son, and it encourages the slave to work with dignity and diligence as to the Lord (see the Book of Philemon).

The solution for Latin America's poverty is not to be found in capitalism or socialism. The solution is to be found in a growing number of productive citizens who treat each other with dignity and respect. Instead of championing capitalism or, as does liberation theology, a Marxist-inspired socialism, one should champion increased production and equitable distribution.

> It is clear that absolute economic freedom fails to establish sufficient justice to make it morally viable. It is also clear that consistent socialization or even regulation of property unduly maximizes political power, replaces self-regulating tendencies in the market with bureaucratic decisions, and tends to destroy the initiative which helped to create modern technical efficiency.[24]

The solution is simply "liberty and justice for all." There must be freedom to produce, and there must be justice to constrain inordinate greed and economic power.

In their sincere attempt to help the poor, liberationists are making the situation in Latin America worse. Liberationists have given legitimacy to guerrilla movements that have caused many Latin American countries to be further destabilized (part of the Marxist process) and their economies further eroded.

Liberationists' adherence to Marxist theories as a solution to the economic inequities that plague Latin America has led them to a position that is imbalanced and therefore ineffective. They should not so quickly have abandoned biblical authority. While the Bible condemns ill-gotten gain and the exploitation of the poor, it highly commends those who are generous and it promises material blessing to the righteous. God is Creator of both rich and poor and He desires for all a lifestyle that is "neither mired in poverty nor choked in wealth."[25] The Bible provides a balance that Marxism cannot achieve.

INSECURITY

An essential element in liberation theology is hope. While it is a theology born out of a critical reflection on the present, it is directed almost exclusively toward the future. It is proposed as the best answer to the identity crisis that prevails in Latin America. It supposedly gives purpose and meaning to life through political aspirations for a new society in which people can develop to their fullest potential. They will at last be free from uncertainty and insecurity. Gutiérrez stresses the hope factor: "Hope thus emerges as the key to human existence oriented towards the future, because it transforms the present. This ontology of what 'is not yet' is dynamic, in contrast to the static ontology of being, which is incapable of planning history."[26] This dynamic of hope "assumes a concrete utopic function," says Gutiérrez, "mobilizing human action in history."[27]

There is a strong element of utopianism in liberation theology. The focus on man and his great potential (humanism) through the Marxist lens of socialist theory (Marxism) has led liberation theologians to project a society governed with justice and perfect harmony (utopianism). Liberationists challenge their readers to remove the shackles of uncertainty and insecurity and to forge ahead to build a new society, to establish the kingdom of God on earth.

By adhering so strongly to an earthly, man-wrought, political utopia to be achieved through "historical praxis," liberationists neglect or even deny the eternal, God-wrought heavenly kingdom to be established through divine intervention. While liberationists may feel that talk of heaven or some future messianic kingdom is illusive and "unscientific," their proposals for a utopia in which all men will share their possessions freely and where justice will prevail seems even more illusive and unrealistic. What Thomas More has written in parody,[28] liberationists have proposed as fact. The "no place" ("utopia" stems from Greek words for "no place") island created in the imagination of More has become the "new place" goal of liberation theology. Idealism can provide direction, but it can also project catastrophic, unattainable goals.

In the strong pursuit of historic utopianism, liberationists have turned their backs on eternal reality. The insecurity and the search for identity among the masses in Latin America may be stirred into political action by the promise of utopia, but their hopes will be shattered when their utopia turns out to be a repressive dictatorship or an unrestricted anarchy. Dreams can often turn into nightmares.

Liberation theology has again emerged with an imbalance. The strong dose of human hope in a political utopia needs to be tempered and thus enhanced by the divine hope of an everlasting kingdom, the biblical hope that extends beyond time and the limitations of "historical praxis" and human frailty.

INIQUITY

Only in the realm of religious experience and theological constructs do cultural, economic, and political proposals find ultimate meaning. Liberation theology is, above all, theology. Liberationists are not attempting to propose a new *ideology* for liberation; they present a *theology* of liberation. With sincere pastoral concern, most liberation theologians try to lead the church to see the relevance of religion in a society that is all too often filled with injustice, oppression, and corruption.

Actually the problems of injustice, inequity, and insecurity are byproducts of a deeper social problem called sin. Iniquity abounds, and where iniquity abounds other destructive elements run rampant. The problem is clear: "Theologically, this situation of injustice and oppression is characterized as a 'sinful situation' because 'where this social peace does not exist, there we will find social, political, economic, and cultural inequalities.'"[29] At the heart of the inequalities and injustices of society is the theological question of ethics.

While they recognize the problem of personal as well as social sin, almost all liberationists focus on social sin. Miranda decries the sin incarnated in social structures "which by no means is reducible to the sum of individual sins."[30] Liberationists develop what Scott concludes is the "thoroughly biblical notion that sin is not only individual and private but also institutional and public."[31]

In the strong attack on social sin, there has been a concomitant tendency to excuse personal sin. In the attempt to draw all men into a common cause against societal injustice and to create an ecumenical climate to unite diverse religious groups, liberation theologians advocate a universalistic approach in their solutions. All men are called to join in the battle. Even atheists are included in the universal family, a "family of God" that is said to help curb social sin and to bring about perfect harmony.[32] Liberationists claim that iniquity must be purged from society through the joint effort of mankind.

The proposal sounds admirable, but in the pursuit of social equality through holistic universalism, individual iniquity seems to go unnoticed. Universalism is an attractive whitewash treatment, but the rust of sin keeps seeping through. Liberation based on universalism and ecumenicalism is cosmetic and temporal. It does not provide a lasting freedom from iniquity. Society will be changed as men are changed and the change needed is internal, not external. By adhering so strongly to universalism, liberation theology neglects the uniqueness of the church and the redemptive liberty granted to each individual who is a part of the true church. The revolution so earnestly sought in society and the renewal desired in the church might best be accomplished as greater numbers of people in the society and church experience the revolution of new birth and the renewal of a new life.

Instead of condemning systems, liberationists need to denounce sin—hatred, greed, graft, alienation, exploitation, prejudice, domination, fraud, dishonesty, violence, murder, rape, and theft. These evil acts are wrong no matter who commits them. The place where an inclusive universalism fits is in the condemnation of evil and in the commendation of righteousness. To declare that all men are a part of the family of God, even those who practice iniquity, is confusing and contradictory. Worse yet, to advocate violence to defeat violence is irrational. Organized violence to attack "institutionalized violence" only creates more violence. Sin is sin no matter who commits it, and at the very core of the cultural, economic, and political problems of Latin America, and indeed anywhere in the world, is the theological problem called "sin."

Sin is universal. Sin is destructive and disruptive to human progress and the health of societies. And sin must be denounced. This world is in desperate need of liberation from sin and the heartache and chaos it brings.

The universalism of liberationism only muddies the waters and in many cases allows people who claim to be Christians to engage in reprehensible atrocities. And it welcomes those who deny God's existence to participate if not lead in the so-called "liberating process." All too often this liberation leads to enslavement.

Conclusion

Liberation theology is a sincere attempt to answer real needs. Its critique of the Latin American crisis is both penetrating and convicting. Nonetheless liberation theology and its "critical reflection" bears some critical reflection. By restricting their analyses and cures so stringently to historical time and earthly reality, liberationists have neglected the eternal dimension and divine intervention.

To humanism must be added transcendent Deity. Marxism needs to be subjected to the light of biblical authority. Earthly utopianism needs the added dimension of eternal reality. Holistic universalism will never bring the unity and renewal that redemptive liberty affords. The theology of liberation needs a stronger touch of a theology of redemption. As the dialectic process continues among liberationists who are rightfully admired for their ingenuity and even more so for their concern, perhaps liberation theology will be drawn toward a more balanced position and thereby more effectively minister to the pressing needs of Latin America.

In the meantime it behooves everyone to do all they can to eliminate oppression and provide liberation. Gutiérrez' closing comment in his monumental *A Theology of Liberation* is a classic:

> All the political theologies, the theologies of hope, of revolution, and of liberation, are not worth one act of genuine solidarity with exploited social classes. They are not worth one act of faith, love, and hope, committed—in one way or another—in active participation to liberate man from everything that dehumanizes him and prevents him from living according to the will of the Father.[32]

Whatever the analysis one makes and the solutions one proposes, every person must heed Gutiérrez' challenge to act on behalf of those in need. This is the will of God the Father. True liberation, however, can only come through the touch of the Father. It behooves every believer to follow the Master's example and "preach good news to the poor" and "proclaim freedom for the prisoners" and "the oppressed" (Luke 4:18–19). God's good news will always do more than mankind's good works. Redemptive theology is the answer to the flaws of liberation theology.

CHAPTER 11

An Appraisal of the Signs and Wonders Movement

Ken L. Sarles

One of the most remarkable developments in American evangelicalism over the last decade is the appearance of a new phenomenon known as the "Signs and Wonders movement." The movement is a blending of evangelical commitments and charismatic practices. Those associated with this recent trend affirm the continuation of all the miraculous gifts mentioned in the New Testament and yet refuse to be labeled Pentecostals or charismatics.[1] In this regard the following statement is enlightening:

> Our backgrounds, both Dispensational and Reformed, taught us to believe that the overt gifts of the Holy Spirit ceased with the apostles. To pass our theological exams we all adopted the party line. After varying lengths of time in pastoral ministry, however, each of us came to the same basic conclusions: (1) the cessation of particular gifts was not taught in Scripture; (2) the church was desperately weak and anemic because of the lack of these gifts; and (3) what we were seeing in our own experience suggested that these gifts were available for the church today.[2]

How could such divergent movements as Pentecostalism and dispensational or Reformed evangelicalism converge to produce a new theological hybrid? What are the distinctives of this newly formed matrix and how should those distinctives be evaluated? An attempt will be made to address these questions by considering both the emergence and emphases of the Signs and Wonders movement.

Emergence of the Signs and Wonders Movement

The rise of the movement can be traced through the intersecting ministries of two key individuals: C. Peter Wagner, professor of missions at Fuller Theological Seminary, and John Wimber, pastor of the Vineyard Christian Fellowship in Anaheim, California.[3]

THE MINISTRY OF C. PETER WAGNER

On the mission field. Wagner served as a missionary in Bolivia for 16 years, during which time he opposed what he considered to be Pentecostal excesses.[4] He remarks, "I remember well when the Pentecostal faith healers set up their tent in the city where I lived as a missionary in Bolivia. I was incensed. I told the members of my church not to go. I wrote a nationally circulated article against it."[5] But he adds that he now affirms what he once denied. The change in his thinking occurred when he moved to Fuller Seminary.

At Fuller Theological Seminary. In 1971 Wagner was appointed to the Donald McGavran chair of Church Growth at the Fuller Seminary School of World Mission.[6] His change in *position* led to a change in *perspective*. Originally Wagner had been strongly influenced by dispensationalism on the one hand and Benjamin B. Warfield on the other, and so he held to a cessationist view of the charismatic gifts.[7] In his own words, "My background is that of a Scofield Bible dispensational evangelical. I was taught that the gifts of the Spirit were not in operation in our age; they went out with the apostolic church."[8] However, his study of church growth principles led him to a renewed interest in charismatic practices. His research "forced him to recognize Pentecostalism as a driving force in much of church growth in the Third World."[9] Wagner's approach is largely pragmatic and optimistic. "He has made a career out of finding what is good in growing churches, and affirming it—without asking many critical questions. This enables him to hold up as models of church life . . . just about any . . . church that is growing."[10]

The *problem* with Wagner's change in perspective is that it is based on an inadequate view of church growth. A true measure of church growth must include not only *outward, quantitative* growth but also *inward, qualitative* growth. Detailing the size of a church's physical plant, Sunday school program, and membership roll does not give insight into the commitment, knowledge, and maturity of the congregation.

THE MINISTRY OF JOHN WIMBER

Frustration with the church. According to his own testimony, John Wimber was a fourth-generation unbelieving jazz musician when he was converted to Christianity in 1962.[11] From 1964 to 1970 he and his wife Carol led hundreds of people to Christ and taught numerous Bible studies. Then in 1970 Wimber joined the staff of the Yorba Linda Friends Church. Though he had a successful ministry, all was not well. He summarized his situation this way: "I began to lose the kind of joy and peace that I thought would accompany such success. I was dissatisfied with my life and did not understand why. It was a disquieting and confusing time."[12] Part of the confusion had to do with his understanding of the miraculous gifts and their role in the church's ministry. According to Wimber,

> I had always avoided Pentecostal and Charismatic Christians. . . . Also, my judgment of their ministries was colored by a presupposition that charismatic gifts like tongues, prophecy, and healing were not for today. (As a dispensationalist, I believed the charismatic gifts ceased at the end of the first century.)[13]

However, after encountering what he considered to be miraculous divine healings, he began to question his previous conviction. His experience led him in a new direction. "Frustrated as a pastor of a fast-growing evangelical Friends church, Wimber left to join Wagner in doing church-growth consultations for the Fuller Evangelistic Association."[14] The turning point for Wimber came in 1977 when his wife Carol was dramatically healed of what she called a "personality meltdown." While asleep she dreamed that she was filled with the Holy Spirit and then woke up speaking in tongues![15] This produced a change in Wimber's attitude from skepticism to openness concerning divine healing.[16]

Formation of a new church. Wimber's new perspective led to the formation of a new kind of church—a "noncharismatic" church that focused on miraculous healings and other supernatural gifts. The origin of the church is best described by Stafford:

> Wimber's wife, who had become charismatic, started a prayer group that grew to 50 members. In 1977, at what he believed was very direct guidance from God, Wimber began to pastor it. He soon resigned his position as a church-growth consultant.
>
> The church met in a high school gymnasium. Wimber began to preach from the Gospel of Luke, and was struck by the many healings and exorcisms Jesus did. Wimber offered repeated altar calls for healing, but the church prayed for months without seeing a single healing occur. It was a humiliating, gut-wrenching time when many people left the church in disgust. Yet Wimber would not give up. He believed that God would not let him. He was determined to see God heal people, and eventually— after ten months—he did. One young woman was healed in her home of

a fever, and Wimber's exultation knew no bounds. "We got one!" he yelled at the top of his lungs on the way to his car.[17]

The church became known as the Vineyard Christian Fellowship, located in an industrial area of Anaheim, California. According to one observer, the peak of Disneyland's Matterhorn is clearly visible from the Vineyard's parking lot.[18] The inference seems to be that the church may serve as a religious counterpart to the famous entertainment center. On Sundays the large carpeted warehouse where the church assembles is filled with a "casual, white, middle-class, youthful crowd. . . . They come excited, expecting to see healings, to experience the supernatural at work."[19] This seems to parallel the attitude of certain Jews in the first century who demanded that Jesus show them a sign from heaven (Matt. 12:38; Luke 11:16). But Jesus rebuked their sign-seeking and said that no sign would be given to them except the sign of Jonah, a clear reference to His death and resurrection (Matt. 12:39–40; Luke 11:29–30).

The church went through a watershed experience in 1981 which launched its present ministry of power evangelism. A young man preaching at a Sunday service said, "Come, Holy Spirit." The results were rather bizarre.

> One fellow, Tim, started bouncing. His arms flung out as he fell over, taking a mike stand down with him. He was tangled up in the cord, with the mike next to his mouth. He began speaking in tongues, and the sound carried throughout the high school gymnasium in which we met. . . . The majority of the young people were shaking and falling over. At one point it looked like a battlefield scene, bodies everywhere, people weeping, wailing, speaking in tongues.[20]

It should be observed that though the Vineyard Christian Fellowship is most noted for its emphasis on divine healing, other charismatic practices such as speaking in tongues and being slain in the Spirit are also incorporated in the church's ministry.

Influence of the Vineyard church. The *record* of growth has been nothing short of phenomenal. In less than 10 years the Vineyard group has grown from a home Bible study of 17 to a church of over 6,000.[21] In addition scores of similar churches have been spawned around the country, producing what many would call a mini-denomination.[22]

The *reason* for the growth is more difficult to ascertain. One of the more probable reasons is Wimber's own style of ministry. He is far removed from the popular image of an overly zealous, undereducated rural Pentecostal preacher. His approach has been characterized as follows:

> The rotund Wimber speaks in an offhand, unrehearsed manner—a lovable teddy bear. He is also a thoughtful, original Bible expositor. He communicates to educated evangelicals. His style—cool, humorous, and fatherly—is exactly pitched to baby boomers. It is a style redolent of Ronald Reagan: an awfully nice neighbor leaning over the back fence, presenting what used to be considered extreme without sounding mean or pushy.[23]

Wimber's apparent honesty, sincerity, and genuineness are very attractive to upwardly mobile middle-class audiences.

Initiation of a new course at Fuller Seminary. The rapid expansion of the Vineyard ministry caught the attention of church-growth expert Peter Wagner. In the fall of 1982 a new course was offered at Fuller's School of World Mission, cotaught by Peter Wagner and John Wimber, who had been appointed adjunct professor. The course was MC510 "The Miraculous and Church Growth." It was the most popular and also the most disruptive course on Fuller's campus. According to Fuller's president David Hubbard, then president of Fuller Seminary,

> It was launched with considerable fanfare: for perhaps the only time in American church history an academic course preempted an entire issue of a national religious magazine—*Christian Life* (October, 1982). The fanfare at large was matched by ruffles and flourishes at home: the course broke all enrollment records at Fuller.[24]

At the close of each lecture, laboratory sessions were held in which demons were exorcised, words of knowledge were received, and divine healings were performed. In this way students were able to discover what miraculous gifts they had been given. Even the coteacher, Peter Wagner, was able to demonstrate that he had the gift of "leg lengthening."[25] Wagner's enthusiasm for the miraculous seems to know no bounds. After interviewing several people who claim to have been raised from the dead, he recently concluded: "I, too, now believe that dead people are literally being raised in the world today. . . . I would not be surprised if it were happening several times a year."[26]

Concerns were raised about the implications of MC510 by several of the theological faculty at Fuller Seminary, resulting in a moratorium on the course in the spring of 1986.[27] Hubbard then appointed a faculty task force to study the biblical, theological, and psychological impact of the course on the curriculum.[28] The ensuing published report addressed two questions: (1) Is there scriptural warrant for signs and wonders as a central focus of the church's ministry? (2) Is a course on signs and wonders appropriate for a theological curriculum? The response to the first question was a qualified no. Signs and wonders were said to be exceptional rather than normative in the life of the church. The answer to the second query was also no.[29]

Impact of the Signs and Wonders movement. Regardless of what happens at Fuller Seminary, the Signs and Wonders movement has become so pervasive that it is now being referred to as the "third wave" of the Holy Spirit's power in the 20th century. According to Wagner, the first wave represents the Pentecostal movement at the turn of the century, the second wave was the charismatic movement, beginning about midcentury, and the third wave, appearing about 1980, constitutes "a gradual opening of straightline evangelical churches to the supernatural ministry of the Holy Spirit without the participants becoming either pentecostals or charismatics."[30] The significance of this development is that the distinctions between charismatic and noncharismatic evangelicals are becoming increasingly blurred. A new theological creature has now appeared on the scene known as a "third wave, noncharismatic evangelical"! For the first time in American religious history a noncharismatic segment of conservative evangelicalism has adopted a charismatic view of signs and wonders without accepting the charismatic label. This astounding turn of events has created both a confusion of categories and a sense of consternation among noncharismatic evangelicals who are not part of the Signs and Wonders movement.

Many churches are now wrestling with this problem and a clarification of the issues is desperately needed. A clearer focus on the question can be achieved through an examination of the emphases of third-wave Christians.[31]

Emphases of the Signs and Wonders Movement

The great difficulty in painting a portrait of a new movement is to portray accurately a characterization of it without creating a caricature of it. An attempt will be made here to reflect the essential features of the movement as the basis for an evaluation of its assets and liabilities. The central emphases of the Signs and Wonders movement include a perspective on world views, the presence of God's kingdom in this age, and power evangelism as a working concept for reaching the Third World.

PERSPECTIVE ON WORLD VIEWS

A "world view" is such an enormous, all-encompassing proposition that it is next to impossible to define it precisely. A careful treatment of the concept is beyond the scope of the present article. However, for the purpose of discussion a working definition may be provided:

> Cultures pattern perceptions of reality into conceptualizations of what reality can or should be, what is to be regarded as actual, probable, possible, and impossible. . . . The worldview is the central systematization of conceptions of reality to which the members of the culture assent (largely unconsciously) and from which stems their value system. The worldview lies at the very heart of the culture, touching, interfacing with, and strongly influencing every aspect of culture.[32]

This is a helpful definition if one keeps in mind that it is not intended to be a comprehensive statement.

CHARACTERISTICS OF A WESTERN WORLD VIEW

Wimber has used the notion of world view to reveal why so many Western Christians are reluctant to accept supernatural phenomena as normative.[33] His leading thesis as to why some of his fellow evangelicals are skeptical about the miraculous is that they have been overly influenced by four negative characteristics of a Western world view.

The first negative characteristic, according to Wimber, is *secularism.* "To think secularly, is to think within a frame of reference bounded by the limits of our life on earth: it is to keep one's calculations rooted in this worldly criteria."[34] The corollary to this is that secularists have closed off the known universe from the possibility of divine intervention. For them truth is pursued through a combination of rational thought and empirical means.[35]

The second characteristic is *rationalism,* which "seeks a rational explanation for all experience, making reason the chief guide in all matters of life."[36] Westerners tend to reject what they cannot logically explain, including of course the miraculous.

The third characteristic of a Western world view is *materialism,* which "assumes that nothing exists except matter and its movement and modifications. For a materialist, only what can be seen, tested, and proved is real."[37] By definition a materialist denies the existence of the supernatural.

The fourth characteristic is *mechanism*. Mechanists "construe the universe as a magnificent nexus of physical causes and effects, a world where all things are and all events occur only because of physical antecedents that can be located, identified, and . . . manipulated."[38] Mechanism explains the way in which a materialistic world operates. Mechanistic materialism has no room for divine intervention.

The contention is that these unbiblical characteristics have infiltrated the thinking of Western Christians who reject the Signs and Wonders movement. Furthermore according to third-wave people, the Western world view has produced a "gap" in Christian thought between the supernatural and the natural. This gap is known as the "excluded middle."

Concept of the excluded middle. This concept was developed by Paul Hiebert, professor of anthropology and South Asian studies at the Fuller School of World Mission, as a way of explaining the difference between Eastern and Western world views. The Eastern world view recognizes three levels of reality. The first level is equivalent to the natural world perceived in the West. The second level, however, is quite different. It is inhabited by

> spirits, ghosts, ancestors, demons, and earthly gods and goddesses who live in trees, rivers, hills and villages. These live not in some other world or time, but are inhabitants with humans and animals of this world and time. In medieval Europe these included trolls, pixies, gnomes, brownies and fairies who were believed to be real. This level also includes supernatural forces such as manna, planetary influences, evil eyes, and the powers of magic, sorcery and witchcraft.[39]

The third level deals with the transcendent realities of heaven and hell, and the so-called cosmic forces of karma and kismet.

Hiebert equates the second level of reality in the Eastern world view with the "excluded middle" in the Western world view. Reflecting on his own experience as a missionary in India, he notes:

> I had excluded the middle level of supernatural but this-worldly beings and forces from my own worldview. As a scientist I had been trained to deal with the empirical world in naturalistic terms. As a theologian, I was taught to answer ultimate questions in theistic terms. For me the middle zone did not really exist. Unlike Indian villagers, I had given little thought

to spirits of this world, to local ancestors and ghosts, or to the souls of animals.[40]

The excluded middle constitutes a blind spot in the Western world view, according to Hiebert. Christians raised in the West have failed to see an entire realm of reality that has long been recognized in the East. Western Christians ministering in the Third World are caught in the clash of two world views. The excluded middle of their own world view prevents them from answering the questions Third-World people are asking. For instance,

> What does one say when new tribal converts want to know how the Christian God tells them where and when to hunt, whether they should marry his daughter to that young man, or where they can find the lost money? Given no answer, they return to the diviner who gave them definite answers, for these are the problems that loom large in their everyday life.[41]

In Hiebert's opinion Western Christians can provide the definite answers Easterners are looking for through the practice of signs and wonders. Tribal people can receive specific divine guidance through dreams, visions, and words of knowledge. Animistic pagans can be won to the gospel through miraculous signs, demonstrating that the Christian God is supreme over all other gods. Those in the Signs and Wonders movement believe they have bridged the gap between East and West by proclaiming a gospel authenticated in miraculous power.[42]

Consequences regarding world views. In assessing the Signs and Wonders perspective on world view, several positive and negative comments can be noted. First, on the positive side it is certainly true that Christians in the West have been greatly influenced by a Western world view.[43] Second, many evangelicals recognize that Western society is marked by a rationalistic, materialistic, secularist viewpoint.[44]

On the negative side of the ledger, the conclusion, drawn from the two preceding premises, that Western evangelicals have been overly influenced by a rationalistic, empiricist world view, does not necessarily follow.[45] Wimber has phrased the question this way: "Could it be that many Western evangelicals have subconsciously developed a theology that excludes the possibility of supernaturally inspired dreams and visions, harmonizing 'Christian doctrine' with Western rationalism?"[46] However, the question could just as plausibly be phrased another way: Since

Christianity has had such an enormous impact on the history of Western civilization, could it not be that Western rationalism is an appropriate philosophical expression of "Christian doctrine"?

Obviously the key to the formulation of the question is the meaning of the term "rationalism."[47] It can be used positively or pejoratively, depending on one's perspective. For instance rationalism in its positive sense can be seen in Walter Chantry's conviction that

> the gospel must approach the human heart through the intellect. The great revivalists like Jonathan Edwards and George Whitefield were insistent on this. They were always asking whether experiences, however emotional or powerful, were in direct response to understood truth. If not, they were discounted as fanaticism.[48]

The beneficial use of rationalism in evangelistic preaching to guard against emotional extravagance is ignored by Wimber. According to Chantry,

> it is not surprising that Wimber belittles rational truth. He prefers to recount illustrations of sinners whose hearts were made receptive to Christ by the miraculous, before they knew anything of him. He prefers to tell of conversions where minimal scriptural teaching was needed.[49]

Another drawback to the Signs and Wonders critique of the Western world view is the failure to discuss existentialism as part of that world view. ("Existentialism" is used here in its popular sense, referring to the primacy of experience in seeking for truth [rather than in its technical, philosophical sense, involving metaphysical implications of the statement "existence precedes essence"]). Though Wimber does not *analyze* a Western experience-oriented perspective in his writings, he *evidences* that perspective in some of his statements. At one point he concludes, "So God uses our experiences to show us more fully what he teaches in Scripture, many times toppling or altering elements of *our* theology and worldview."[50] This statement is true only insofar as theology is not based on Scripture. If theology is authentically biblical, God-ordained experience will enrich it, not alter it, because God cannot contradict Himself.[51] Rather than beginning with a valid interpretation of the Bible and then allowing the Scriptures to interpret his experience, Wimber seems to start with his own experience, which he then allows to inform his understanding of the biblical text.[52] The implication is that Wimber himself has an "existentialist blind spot" in his understanding of how one's world view governs one's approach to Scripture. This would explain why he categorizes those who allow the text to sit in judgment on their experience as being overly rationalistic.

More serious than this apparent blind spot, however, is Wimber's misuse of biblical passages. For instance he applies Matthew 13:11–16 to those who oppose his position. Jesus explained to His disciples that He was speaking to the people in parables, "because while seeing they do not see, and while hearing they do not hear, nor do they understand" (v. 13). Jesus then related this to Isaiah's prophecy (Isa. 6:9–10).

Wimber applies Jesus' comments and Isaiah's prophecy to fellow evangelicals who do not accept the validity of present-day signs and wonders. He correctly points out that the central problem with those who do not see or hear is a hardened heart. But then in summarizing he states, "A hard heart may incline us toward a worldview that excludes the supernatural or it may prevent us from altering a faulty worldview to include the supernatural."[53] By "supernatural" he means the current manifestation of miraculous gifts.[54] Therefore an evangelical who believes in a supernatural realm of reality and the supernatural intervention of God in history, but does not acknowledge the divine origin of contemporary signs and wonders would be classified by Wimber as having a hardened heart.

A closer look at the passage in Matthew yields an interpretation more accurate than Wimber's view. The issue Jesus was addressing was the rejection of His messiahship by the leaders of the nation Israel just as the nation had rejected Isaiah's prophetic ministry centuries earlier.[55] Now the mysteries of the kingdom would be revealed to the disciples but concealed in parables from the scribes and Pharisees.[56] This touches on the truth of reprobation, whereby God withholds knowledge of Himself from those who continually resist Him.[57] In short, there is a world of difference between the rejection of the Messiah by first-century Jewish leaders and the rejection of present-day signs and wonders by certain 20th-century evangelicals!

Another difficulty in the area of world view pertains to the concept of the excluded middle. The fact that the Eastern world view contains a second level of reality excluded in the Western world view does not necessarily make the existence of that particular realm of reality legitimate! Evangelical theology of the Western variety need not be compromised because of a *perceived* blind spot. If a Third World animist asks a question from the "excluded middle," the question does not automatically imply that an answer can be given from the so-called middle level of reality. That is to say, desiring a revelatory word of knowledge, for example, does not necessarily mean that such a revelation of divine guidance will be forthcoming. The only way to determine whether such a middle level of reality exists is to study not the Eastern or Western world views, but the *biblical* world view. The Signs and Wonders perspective on world view is simplistic in its formulation and deficient in its biblical support.

PRESENCE OF THE KINGDOM

In the Signs and Wonders movement the existence of the miraculous gifts is directly linked to the teaching of the kingdom of God on earth. The movement has capitalized on a certain view of God's kingdom that provides the theological undergirding for the practice of signs and wonders.

Kingdom theology explained. According to Wimber, "the Greek word *basileia* means 'kingship' or 'royal rule.' It is normally translated 'kingdom.' It implies exercise of kingly rule or reign rather than simply a geographic realm over which a king rules."[58] Wimber's understanding of the kingdom has been greatly influenced by the views of George Ladd.[59] Ladd, a nondispensational premillennialist, holds that the future kingdom of God is now present in some respects.[60]

> The Kingdom of God belongs to The Age to Come. Yet The Age to Come has overlapped with This Age. We may taste its powers and thereby be delivered from This Age and no longer live in conformity to it. This new transforming power is the power of The Age to Come; it is indeed the power of the Kingdom of God. The Kingdom of God is future, but it is not only future. Like the powers of The Age to Come, the Kingdom of God has invaded this evil Age that men may know something of its blessings even while the evil Age goes on.[61]

The kingdom of God is both "already" and "not yet." Wimber concurs with this position.

> The future age, the kingdom of God, invaded the present age, the kingdom of Satan. To use an expression of George Ladd's, we live in "the presence of the future." We are between the times, as it were, between the inauguration and the consummation of the kingdom of God.[62]

Since the kingdom is present today, the power and authority of the kingdom are available to the subjects of the kingdom:

"We must understand power and authority in the kingdom. . . . Power is the ability, the strength, the might to complete a given task. Authority is the right to use the power of God."[63] After complaining of a weak Christianity in which Christians are not exercising the authority they have as subjects of the kingdom, Wimber concludes, "We must learn how to hear and believe Jesus' commands if we expect to be the vehicles of signs and miracles for the kingdom."[64]

In exercising his authority the believer is to follow the two-fold pattern of Christ's own ministry, involving *proclamation* followed by *demonstration.* After proclaiming His message Christ performed miraculous signs to demonstrate the authenticity of His message.[65]

> There is no difference between the *words* and *works* of Jesus. The *works* have exactly the same message as the *words.* The message and words concentrated on the announcement of the Kingdom of God. The miracles and works show us what the Kingdom is like. . . . The *words* and the *works* of Jesus both center on the Kingdom of God. They are a unity. They both *show* and *tell* what the Kingdom is.[66]

The assumption is made that the believer as a subject of the kingdom in the present age may today perform the same kind of miraculous works Jesus performed to authenticate the kingdom message. Wimber is quite descriptive in explaining the exercise of kingdom authority in performing works of healing as Jesus did.

> Words of command come with a burst of faith. I feel the confidence and power of God rise in my heart and release it through my speech. Typically I will lay hands near the afflicted area and say, "I break the power of this condition in the name of Jesus," or "Stop it!" . . . I speak directly to evil spirits, commanding them to leave. . . . My hands usually tingle and are warm, and I feel something like electricity come out of them when I speak a word of command. I have come to associate feelings like tingling and heat with an anointing of the Holy Spirit on me for healing.[67]

Kingdom theology evaluated. Of interest to dispensationalists is the fact that the new kingdom emphasis of Wimber and others was forged out of a premillennial, dispensational heritage. However, that heritage has been altered in several significant ways.

The first area concerns dispensational distinctives in Christ's earthly ministry. Differences are overlooked between the pre-resurrection and postresurrection commissionings of Christ to His disciples. In His preresurrection commission, "Jesus sent His disciples out with authority to heal people's sicknesses, to cleanse lepers, to cast out demons, and even to raise the dead (Matt. 10:1, 5–10; Mark 6:7–13; Luke 9:1–6)."[68] Third-wave Christians attribute a universal character to this commission, making it applicable to every disciple in every church in every age. But this commission was unique and time-bound. Jesus instructed His disciples, "But rather go to the lost sheep of the house of Israel" (Matt. 10:6). The disciples were offering the messianic kingdom in the person of the Messiah to the nation Israel. The preresurrection commissionings "were not general, timeless mandates, but specific and limited mandates for specific occasions."[69] In contrast to this, Christ's postresurrection mandate is to preach repentance and forgiveness to all the nations (Luke 24:47). Apart from one highly disputed passage, Mark 16:15–18, which is not contained in most ancient Greek manuscripts, no connection is made between the postresurrection Great Commission and the practice of miraculous gifts. To put it succinctly:

> Jesus' instructions to his disciples to prepare his way to the "lost sheep of the house of Israel" are not the same as his instructions to his universal church. . . . the church at large was not commissioned to heal the sick and raise the dead, and . . . when Jesus sent his disciples on a special mission to heal the sick and raise the dead (Matt. 10; Luke 10), he did not commission the church to do the same.[70]

A second area, closely related to the first, involves the dispensational characteristics of the apostles' ministry. Historically, dispensationalists have argued that the signs and wonders performed by the apostles were temporary in nature.[71] The purpose of the miraculous gifts was to authenticate the authority of the apostles and to validate their message. By the end of the first century A.D., with the death of the apostles and the completion of the New Testament canon, the purpose of the sign gifts associated with apostleship had been fulfilled. Therefore they ceased to occur because they were no longer necessary. Of course this understanding of the temporary nature of signs and wonders is not limited to dispensationalists. Nondispensationalists have articulated the same view.[72]

The cessation of miraculous gifts as propounded by dispensationalists is a theological deduction made from certain New Testament passages. For instance Acts 14:3; Romans 15:18–19; and 2 Corinthians 12:12 indicate that the signs and wonders performed by Paul were a confirmation of his claim to apostleship.[73] In Ephesians 2:20 the apostles and prophets are said to be the foundation of the church. Once the foundation is completed and the superstructure is begun, the foundational gifts are no longer necessary.[74] Even more significant is Hebrews 2:3–4: "After it was at the first spoken through the Lord, it was confirmed to us by those who heard, God also bearing witness with them, both by signs and wonders and by various miracles and by gifts of the Holy Spirit according to His own will." The Greek grammar of these verses in Hebrews suggests that the signs, wonders, and miracles had ceased by the time the epistle was penned. As one commentator has explained it,

> The verb "was confirmed" (*ebebaiothe*) is past (aorist) tense. Apparently this confirmation was not going on at the time of writing. The present tense of the participle, "bearing witness," relates to the main verb, "was confirmed." God was not bearing witness at the time Hebrews was written.[75]

Hodges gives an excellent summary of the theological principle derived from these passages.

> Accordingly, inasmuch as Protestant theology generally has clearly recognized the cessation of the apostolic gift in the first century, at the same time that it rightly denies any form of apostolic succession, all such Protestant theology becomes basically committed to the *principle* of temporary gift. For clearly the apostleship was itself temporary, and, if the principle be established, it is perfectly legitimate to inquire whether there may not be other first-century gifts which were likewise temporary.[76]

Since the gift of apostleship was temporary, this seriously undermines the Signs and Wonders concept of kingdom authority as the basis for performing miraculous feats today. In addition the evidence Wimber offers (feelings of tingling and heat) to substantiate his authority to command demons and diseases to depart is highly subjective and is more than a little suspect.

As pointed out earlier, Signs and Wonders leaders, including John Wimber, Peter Wagner, and George Mallone, claim to have been dispensationalist in their thinking. What is interesting to note is that they have rightly associated the cessationist view of the miraculous gifts with their dispensationalist heritage. They have since rejected that view and for the most part have abandoned dispensationalism. It seems fair to conclude from this that at the very least one could not remain a *consistent* dispensationalist and adopt the kingdom theology of the Signs and Wonders movement.

POWER EVANGELISM

The ingredient in third-wave theology that explains how the kingdom operates in the present age is known as "power evangelism." This concept is at the heart of the movement. Power evangelism as a working hypothesis can best be understood by noting its practice, its purpose, and its problems.

Practice of power evangelism. The operation of power evangelism is explained by what is called "power encounters." A power encounter represents a clash between the kingdom of God and the kingdom of Satan.[77] According to Wimber, *"Any system or force that must be overcome for the gospel to be believed is cause for a power encounter."*[78] From his missionary experience in the Third World, Wagner has defined a power encounter as "a visible, practical demonstration that Jesus Christ is more powerful than the false gods or spirits worshipped [*sic*] or feared by a people group."[79]

The classic example of a power encounter is found in the Old Testament, in Elijah's confrontation with the 450 prophets of Baal on Mount Carmel (1 Kings 18).[80] Wimber says this contest provides the working model for power encounters in the present day. "Primitive peoples often need to see the superior power of the gospel demonstrated for them to believe."[81] In this connection Wagner has given what he believes is a contemporary Third World parallel to Elijah's experience:

> A dramatic power, reminiscent of Elijah's on Mt. Carmel, involved a witch doctor in Mandala, India. He took home a flyer with a picture of Jesus and put it on a shelf with pictures of many other gods. He was beginning to believe that Jesus was the true God, but he needed a test. So he placed a tiny ball of dried cow dung fuel in front of each picture, believing that the most powerful one would ignite the fuel. Almost immediately the dung in front of Jesus' picture burst into flames. He is now a fervent evangelist for Jesus Christ.[82]

It is believed that power encounters of this sort are needed if the church is to grow in non-Western cultures.

The source of power encounters is the Holy Spirit.

> It is the Holy Spirit, the "go-between God," who holds the key to power encounters. Our openness and availability to its direction and enabling, anointing, and power is the catalyst for fulfilling the great commission.
>
> Clearly the early Christians had an openness to the power of the Spirit, which resulted in signs and wonders and church growth. If we want to be like the early church, we too need to be open to the Holy Spirit's power.[83]

No believer dares suggest that Christians should not be open to the Holy Spirit, but whether He is continuing to operate in precisely the same way as He did in the first century is questionable.

Purpose of power evangelism. This new kind of evangelism may be defined as

> a spontaneous, Spirit-inspired, empowered presentation of the gospel. Power evangelism is evangelism that is preceded and undergirded by supernatural demonstrations of God's presence. . . . In power evangelism, resistance to the gospel is overcome by the demonstration of God's power in supernatural events.[84]

Power evangelism supposedly includes an element missing in other forms of evangelism—supernatural evidence that authenticates the gospel message.

There is a great need for this new brand of evangelism, according to Signs and Wonders people. In their view Western Christianity has become secularized because the world is actually "evangelizing" the church more effectively than the church is evangelizing the world.[85] This is the reason American churches are not experiencing dramatic growth like that which is occurring overseas.[86]

Evangelism as commonly practiced in the West is described by Wimber as programmatic evangelism.

> Programmatic evangelism attempts to reach the minds . . . of people without the charismatic gifts. Programmatic evangelism is usually characterized by message-centered communicators who present the gospel primarily through rational arguments. . . . Usually it is one-way communication, a prepared message given by the speaker to passive listeners. There is also an emphasis on organization and technique, a search for the one most effective presentation of the gospel, and the tacit assumption that if people understand the propositions of the gospel they will decide to become Christians.[87]

Because of what is considered to be an overweening rationalism, an intellectualist approach is taken to the gospel in programmatic evangelism with a corresponding emphasis on answering theological objections.[88]

In his analysis of programmatic evangelism, Wimber has listed two weaknesses he feels are corrected in power evangelism. The first weakness involves the *program* in evangelism. His point is that "programmatic evangelism is often incomplete, lacking demonstration of the kingdom of God in signs and wonders."[89] The second weakness is in the *person* doing the evangelism. While doctrinal correctness and character development are important, much more is added when the evangelist can perform miraculous works of power.[90] As Stafford has observed, "Traditionally, the church has emphasized the power of God in the proclamation of the gospel and in the moral improvement of Christian lives. Wimber says this is deficient."[91]

Problems with power evangelism. In evaluating the Vineyard movement it appears that the "deficiencies" with which Wimber is concerned are matched by deficiencies in his own thinking. The first problem area concerns the concept of power encounter. A second look at Elijah's Mount Carmel experience casts doubt on the biblical justification for power encounters. First, Elijah was an Old Testament prophet, not a New Testament saint. A whole range of covenantal and spiritual differences exists between these two categories of redeemed people.[92] Therefore Elijah's confrontation with the prophets of Baal is not *necessarily* a model for evangelizing Third-World pagan cultures today. Extreme caution should be exercised in establishing Old Testament principles for New Testament practices. Second and far more significantly, Elijah's power encounter did not produce its intended result. It is true that after witnessing the miracle on Mount Carmel the Israelites cried out, "The Lord, He is God; the Lord, He is God" (1 Kings 18:39). But the Israelities of the Northern Kingdom did *not* repent of their sin and turn to God and so were eventually led into captivity by the Assyrians. And Baalism was certainly not rooted out of Israel by Elijah's Mount Carmel victory.

The example of Elijah reveals the underlying fallacy in a power encounter, namely, the more dramatic the evidence, the more persuasive the argument. This thesis is disproved in Jesus' own public ministry. His greatest miracle was calling Lazarus out of the tomb after he had been dead for four days. But instead of acknowledging Him as Messiah, the Pharisees who witnessed the miracle began plotting together to kill Him (John 11:38–53). The apostles experienced the same opposition in spite of their signs and wonders. When Peter and John healed the lame beggar at the temple, they were arrested and brought before the Sanhedrin. The testimony of the council says it all: "What shall we do with these men? For the fact that a noteworthy miracle has taken place through them is apparent to all who live in

Jerusalem, and we cannot deny it. But in order that it may not spread any further among the people, let us warn them to speak no more to any man in this name" (Acts 4:16–17).

These biblical examples demonstrate that the *real* miracle in conversion is not the *persuasion* of the mind by sensationalized supernatural evidence, but the *reorientation* of the mind by the biblical evidence that already exists! This reorientation of perspective is a supernatural work accomplished only by the Holy Spirit in regeneration. What is needed is not new *objects* to see (signs and wonders) but new *eyes* with which to see (regeneration) the object that is already there (the testimony of Scripture).

Wagner's description of Jesus setting a ball of cow dung on fire hardly comports with the sovereign majesty of the Spirit's work in opening the hardened heart to the truth of the gospel. In this regard it should also be recalled that Wimber is somewhat careless in his description of the Spirit's ministry. In an earlier quotation on the Spirit as the source of power encounters, Wimber uses the impersonal pronoun "it" when referring to the Holy Spirit. Furthermore according to Wimber the speaker who was influential in directing the Vineyard Church in its present course also used the impersonal pronoun when speaking of the Holy Spirit.[93] Though it cannot be proved, it can at least be asked, Does a heavy emphasis on the outward, visible manifestations of the Spirit lead to a corresponding deemphasis on His personhood? Subtly, it seems, one's attitude can drift so that the Spirit is viewed more as a *force that works* rather than a *divine Being who wills.* He is appreciated more for His *power* than His *personality.* However, the Holy Spirit is not a "genie in a bottle," but the omnipotent God who works how, when, and where He pleases.[94]

The second problem area, along with power encounters, is the distinction between power evangelism and programmatic evangelism. On the positive side it must be noted that Wimber has accurately assessed programmatic evangelism as it is practiced by many American evangelicals since Charles Finney.[95] It is true that the presentation of the gospel must be more than an exercise in apologetics. The gospel appeals to the whole person, not just the intellect. It is also true that in certain circles there has been a preoccupation with method and technique. But this does not necessarily mean that power evangelism is the preferred alternative.

What is most disconcerting about power evangelism is the

suggestion that godliness of life is not enough. This suggestion limits the supernatural power of God to physical miracles. But considering the human condition, the greatest demonstration of God's supernatural power is the inner transformation of human character in spite of outward circumstances. Packer has given eloquent expression to this truth.

> There are many of us for whom the role model is Joni Eareckson rather than John Wimber. We see the powers of the kingdom operating, but mainly in regeneration, sanctification, the Spirit as a comforter, the transformation of the inner life, rather than in physical miracles which just by happening prevent much of that other kingdom activity whereby people learn to live with their difficulties and glorify God.[96]

Consequently the real power in power evangelism is not the power to perform miracles and remove suffering, but the power to live a Spirit-directed holy life in the midst of suffering.

Conclusion

The penetration of the Signs and Wonders movement into mainstream American evangelicalism is certainly one of the most provocative developments of the day. It remains to be seen what direction evangelicalism takes as a result. As Stafford has concluded,

> However, one thing is sure: Signs and Wonders is part of a bigger Pentecostal movement that is changing the church worldwide. Noncharismatic evangelicals are trying to come to terms with this movement, and in a less dramatic way, the Pentecostal movement is trying to come to terms with the wider church.[97]

It is incumbent on American evangelicals to evaluate the Signs and Wonders movement carefully in light of larger issues such as the nature of the gospel, the continuation of the miraculous gifts, and the exercise of kingdom authority.

Clearly whatever "fruit" is produced by the movement is of the Pentecostal variety and must be judged accordingly.

> Signs and Wonders offers what the Pentecostal movement has offered generally, a challenge to experience, and not just talk about, God's unmanageable presence. Its temptations are also those that have dogged Pentecostals—schism and spiritual elitism and supernatural showmanship eclipsing the gospel.[98]

CHAPTER 12

The Cessation of the Sign Gifts

Thomas R. Edgar

R eferring to the charismatic movement, Hollenweger states that "in the not too distant future there will be more Christians belonging to this type of Christianity than to the Anglican community. They will number almost as many as all other Protestants together."[1] He feels that the numerical and perhaps the spiritual center of Christianity will shift to "Indigenous Non-white" or "Third World Pentecostal" churches.[2] The validity of such a prevalent force is an issue that cannot be ignored.

The Essential Question: From God or Not from God?

As with any other doctrinal issue it is important to know the truth or the error of the "charismatic" position. This is not a purely doctrinal matter, since in the charismatic movement in all its various forms, such as Pentecostalism, neo-Pentecostalism, "power evangelism," and the Signs and Wonders movement,[3] emphasis is placed on phenomena and subjective experiences. These experiences, which transcend doctrinal considerations and doctrinal boundaries, are the *raison d'etre* of the movement. They are not merely the daily *outworking* of one's doctrine as distinct from his doctrinal position, but are usually crisis events that allegedly go beyond normal, traditional Christian experience. These so-called "spiritual" experiences are either from God or not from God. There can be no neutral or partially true position. Either they are biblically true or they are false experiences. If they are biblically false then the issue is much more serious than merely another view of the Christian life, since the charismatic movement involves a spiritual experience that attempts to be in direct contact with supernatural forces. Whether the charismatics are correct can only be determined from the Scriptures and other relevant facts. By the very nature of the issue, the "gifts," such as tongues, healings, and signs and wonders, so prevalent in today's charismatic movement, are either from God or not from God. There can be no middle ground.

160

Evidence Contrary to the Validity of the Phenomena

Several factors give evidence that the phenomena of the charismatic movement are not the gifts and activities of the Holy Spirit in the New Testament. On the other hand charismatic proponents have given no evidence, other than their assumption, that these are the same phenomena. That their numbers are growing, that the followers are enthusiastic, and that there are alleged miracles are not evidence that the phenomena are from the Holy Spirit, since all these occur in other religions. To argue that the New Testament gifts could occur today or that no verse rules out such a possibility is not enough; it must also be shown that the modern charismatic "gifts" are the same as in the New Testament. The proponents of the charismatic movement have been unsuccessful in proving either the first (the possibility of the gifts today) or the second (that these are the same phenomena). Are all phenomena automatically from the Holy Spirit simply because someone makes such an assertion, unless a verse can be found that directly states they are not? It is not enough merely to assert that charismatic phenomena are New Testament phenomena. There must be evidence that they are the same.

THE EVIDENCE OF HISTORY

If the miraculous gifts of the New Testament age had continued in the church, one would expect an unbroken line of occurrences from apostolic times to the present. If they are of God, why should such miracles be absent for centuries?

The entire controversy exists because the miraculous gifts of the New Testament age *did* cease and did not occur for almost 1,900 years of church history and certainly have not continued in an unbroken line. Questions about their presence today as well as differing opinions, even among charismatics, regarding the nature of tongues, prophecy, and certain other gifts are due to the fact that they ceased. Chrysostom, a fourth-century theologian, testified that they had ceased so long before his time that no one was certain of their characteristics.[4]

History contradicts the charismatics. Though some have attempted to prove that tongues and other miraculous gifts have occurred in the postapostolic history of the church, the very paucity and sporadic nature of alleged occurrences is evidence against this claim.[5] Referring to alleged instances of tonguesspeaking, Hinson, a church historian, sums up the situation this way: "The first sixteen centuries of its history were lean ones indeed. . . . if the first five centuries were lean the next were starvation years for the practice in Western Christendom and doubtful ones in Eastern Christendom."[6]

After a few alleged instances in the second century there is a gap of almost one thousand years before a few more occur. Obviously it would not have been difficult to produce evidence for these gifts during the apostolic age. Why then is there such a dearth of evidence if the gifts continued throughout church history? The alleged instances are even more rare if restricted to genuine believers, and if hearsay evidence is omitted. If instances of the gift of healing rather than supposed answers to prayer are considered, the alleged instances all but vanish. That these miraculous workings ceased in the past can hardly be refuted,[7] and this is recognized by many charismatics. Dayton feels that many charismatics actually prefer to grant that certain gifts ceased, since they regard today's phenomena as a latter-day pouring out of the Spirit.[8]

Explanations are unrealistic. It is one thing for a doctrine such as justification by faith to be temporarily lost due to man's frailty. It is another thing entirely for miraculous signs and wonders to be missing. Those at Pentecost were not expecting to speak as they did. In Acts no tongues speaker was previously aware of the existence of the gift; yet they spoke. They could hardly have had faith in their ability to perform miracles or to speak in tongues, since they were unaware of such gifts. They did not obtain or lose the ability because of their belief or lack of belief in the charismata. If God gave these gifts during the history of the church, they would have occurred regardless of man's frailty. To argue that the gifts faded away in the postapostolic church because of a failure to believe in miracles evades the facts of history and has no biblical support.

First Corinthians 12–14 implies that the early church was only too inclined toward such gifts rather than against them. In almost every religion men have been inclined toward the miraculous rather than toward rejecting obvious miracles. And yet some argue that miracles ceased or nearly so in the early church— an era when belief in the supernatural was rampant and when the signs and wonders actually occurred—because of disbelief in miracles![9] Yet it is claimed that in the most rationalistic of ages, when no miracles were occurring, 19th- and 20th-century Christians believed to the extent that the gifts reoccurred, and reoccurred on the scale of today's claims. Since modern Christians are so receptive to signs and wonders and modern man is so willing to believe the charismatic claims, on what basis can one assume that the early Christians would refuse to do so? Those willing to believe religious miracles are always plentiful. To claim that this "miraculous infusion" of the Spirit gives joy, purpose, power for service, and revitalization of the church, and at the same time claim that such a tremendous working was ignored, rejected, and allowed to drop out of the early church which experienced it, is illogical. *The only reasonable explanation for the lack of these gifts in church history is that God did not give them. If He had given them, they would have occurred.*

Since these gifts and signs did cease, the burden of proof is entirely on the charismatics to prove their validity. Too long Christians have assumed that the noncharismatic must produce incontestable biblical evidence that the miraculous sign gifts did cease. However, noncharismatics have no burden to prove this, since it has already been proved by history. It is an irrefutable fact admitted by many Pentecostals. Therefore the charismatics must prove biblically that the sign gifts will start up again during the Church Age and that today's phenomena are this reoccurrence. In other words they must prove that their experiences are the reoccurrence of gifts that have not occurred for almost 1,900 years.

"Latter day" explanations are inadequate. Many Pentecostals hold that the sign gifts did cease and that they have reoccurred in these "latter days." This must be demonstrated from Scripture, however. There is no biblical evidence that there will be a reoccurrence of the sign gifts in the church or that believers will work miracles near the end of the Church Age. However, there is ample evidence that near the end of the age there will be false prophets who perform miracles, prophesy, and cast out demons in Jesus' name (cf. Matt. 7:22–23; 24:11, 24; 2 Thess. 2:9–12). During the Church Age there will be false leaders who fashion themselves as ministers of righteousness (2 Cor. 11:13–15). During the Tribulation period, there is no indication that believers, other than the two witnesses of Revelation 11:3–12, will perform miracles. Those performed by the two witnesses are exceptional, and their actions are comparable to those of Old Testament prophets rather than to those of the apostles. The two witnesses

are not part of the church, and if they were, they could hardly be considered typical of the church.

The "latter rain" arguments are incorrectly based on verses that actually are referring to seasonal rainfall in Israel. Hosea 6:3 and Joel 2:23, for example, refer not to some unusual outpouring of the Holy Spirit in the last days of the Church Age. They refer instead to spring rains, in contrast to early rains in the fall.

The arguments based on the expression "in the last days" in Acts 2:16–21 are also invalid. If the "last days" referred to in Acts 2:17 includes the day of Pentecost, the beginning of the Church Age, and "if this is that" (v. 16) includes Pentecost, then it cannot mean at the same time the "last days"*of* this Church Age. On the other hand if the "last days" do not include Pentecost, then Pentecost was not a fulfillment of Joel's prophecy, and Acts 2:16–21 refers specifically to Israel and is still future. Either way this passage gives no evidence for a reoccurrence of miraculous gifts during the "last (latter) days" of the church. The present charismatic movement is characterized by phenomena that began in the church about 100 years ago, which apart from any historical connection or evidence are claimed to be the same as the miracles performed in the apostolic age. It is simply naive to accept this claim without some direct historical link or solid biblical evidence that these present phenomena are the same as those in the days of the apostles. The most reliable evidence would be a direct historical link with the apostolic gifts due to their continuity in the church. However, as already argued, history testifies to the contrary. The gifts ceased and there is no reason to expect their presence or reoccurrence today.

LACK OF SIMILARITY WITH THE NEW TESTAMENT

For any phenomena to make credible claim to be the same as the gifts and miracles of the apostolic age there must be great similarity between the two. Any phenomena can be intentionally duplicated or copied. Therefore similarity alone cannot prove the modern phenomena are genuine. Conversely a lack of similarity is definitely evidence against the claim that they are the same as the New Testament gifts and miracles.

An examination of the New Testament reveals that the modern charismatic phenomena are not sufficiently similar to those of the apostolic age. Where are the tongues of fire and the rushing of a mighty wind as on the day of Pentecost? Do missionaries blind their opponents as Paul did? Do church leaders discern hypocrisy and pronounce the immediate death of members as in Acts 5:1–11? Do evangelists amaze an entire city with miracles as did Philip (8:5–8)? Are they then taken to another place of ministry by the Holy Spirit (vv. 39–40)? Are entire multitudes healed by merely being in the shadow of the healer (5:15)? Do prophets give specific prophecies that come to pass soon after (11:27–28)?

The miracles and signs of the apostolic age were clearly and overtly miraculous. Even the opponents of the gospel could not refute the miracles of the apostolic age. But today's "signs and wonders" cannot be verified even by those who are neutral or friendly to the movement. A detailed comparison with specific individual gifts shows an amazing lack of similarity between the New Testament gifts and the modern "charismatic" gifts.[10]

The gift of healing. The New Testament gift of healing is a specific gift to an individual enabling him to heal. It is not to be confused with healing performed by God in answer to prayer. New Testament healings include those with verifiable afflictions and handicaps such as the man who was crippled from birth (Acts 3:1–10). The healings were instantaneous, complete, and obvious to all. The man crippled from birth had never walked, but he was instantly able to walk and jump. The healings in the apostolic age never failed regardless of the faith of the recipient. They did not depend on direct physical contact (5:15). There were no preliminaries, healing meetings, or incantations. The healer merely stated to the individual, even when the individual was unaware of the intention to heal (3:1–10), something equivalent to the words, "In Jesus' name, stand up and walk." The healings were usually in public, performed on unbelievers, and often *en masse.*

The modern charismatic movement made little impact on the basis of speaking in tongues alone. It was not until "healing" was added that the movement began to grow in significant numbers. Today's healers admittedly often fail. This is blamed on the lack of faith of the sick rather than on the healer. The alleged healings are seldom instantaneous or complete. They usually are not healings of objectively verifiable illnesses; they often pertain to internal disorders such as "emotional healing."[11] Rather than being irrefutable, they are unverified or even denied by those neutral. They involve healing meetings, preliminaries, incantations, and usually repeated visits. They are not performed in the streets, *en masse,* or at a distance. In a crowd they are usually performed on only a select few. They are never performed on those who are not aware of the "healer" or his intention to "heal."

There is little correspondence between modern-day charismatic "healings" and the healings recorded in the New Testament. The differences are so vast that many of today's healers are careful to point out that they do not have the gift of healing, but are merely those to whom God often responds with healing. No one heals today in such a way that it is clearly the New Testament gift of healing.

Exorcism of demons. The miraculous ability to exorcise demons directly also needs to be differentiated from answers to prayer (James 5:14). The exorcisms in Acts concerned those clearly recognized as "possessed," including a girl with a mantic gift (Acts 16:16–18). They were clearly differentiated from those who were merely ill (5:16). They were not nebulous cases of emotional problems such as "personality meltdown," frustration, tension, the "demon of worry," the "demon of drugs or alcoholism," as is often the case in alleged exorcisms today. Such can hardly be considered demonism in the New Testament sense.

The New Testament instances of exorcism never failed, were without preliminaries, were instantaneous, were usually performed in public, often *en masse,* usually on unbelievers, and in the case of the mantic girl (Acts 16:16–18) apart from any cooperation of the demonized. Today's "exorcisms" often fail, often require repeated sessions, are usually unverified as demonism, are never *en masse,* seldom if ever occur in public, and are only on the cooperative "faithful." Many cases are similar to common psychiatric or religious counseling sessions that are claimed to be "demon exorcism."[12] This is not to suggest that genuine cases of demon possession may not exist. The point is that merely *claiming* to exorcise demons gives no evidence that one is actually doing so.

Raising the dead. Dorcas had been dead for some time when Peter apart from fanfare instantaneously raised her (Acts 9:40). The incident regarding Eutychus (20:7–12) concerns a boy who fell three stories and was dead. Paul with no fanfare pronounced him alive. In the apostolic age with all the miracles, exorcisms, healings *en masse,* and so on, there are only these two low-profile incidents of raising the dead. This action was apparently rare even for the apostles. There is no reason to expect this today. No modern-day "raising of the dead" has been verified. Wimber refers to a man who fell, hit his head, was apparently unconscious for three minutes, and "came to" with a bump on his head. After Wimber and others prayed the bump eventually went away.[13] This is incredible, not as a miracle, but that anyone would consider this as a possible raising of the dead. Would anyone have been convinced by such a "miracle" that Jesus was the Son of God or that the apostles represented God?

The gift of tongues. The nature, purpose, and other characteristics of the gift of tongues, including a complete exegetical discussion and refutation of the concept of private or devotional tongues is included elsewhere.[14] The tongues of the apostolic age were genuine miracles, since they were the ability to speak previously unlearned foreign languages, rather than the "charismatic tongues" of today, which can easily be duplicated. The only passage describing the nature of tongues speaking is Acts 2:4–11, where they are definitely languages. Peter stated that the tongues-speaking in Cornelius' house (10:46) was the same as on the day of Pentecost (11:17). And there is no reason to assume the instance in Acts 19:6 was different. Since 1 Corinthians 14 repeatedly states that the tongues-speaking in Corinth was *in an assembly* of believers, why then was it mysterious and why was there lack of understanding? It was because the believers did not understand the foreign languages of the tongues-speakers. The mystery was not because the tongues in 1 Corinthians differed in nature from the tongues in Acts.

New Testament tongues were verifiable foreign languages. The term γλῶσσα means "language" and is never used for ecstatic speech. By contrast, today's "tongues" have never been verified as actual languages. All objective studies by impartial linguists indicate that they do not have the characteristics common to languages.

The New Testament gift of tongues is specifically said to be a sign for unbelievers (1 Cor. 14:22). This is how it functioned at Pentecost. All instances were public, not private. The people who spoke in tongues in Acts (2:4; 10:46; 19:6) were not previously aware that the ability or gift existed, and in Acts 10:46 and 19:6 the people were not previously aware of the gospel of Jesus Christ. They could not have been seeking or in any way exercising belief in such a gift, and yet they received it. There is no indication that the New Testament speakers spoke in a trance; they were in control of the phenomenon. Perhaps the most outstanding contrast is usage. The gift of tongues in the New Testament functioned, as did all the other gifts, for ministry to others (1 Cor. 12:1–30; 1 Peter 4:10), rather than primarily for the benefit of the speaker as in the modern charismatic movement.

There is no similarity between today's tongues and the New Testament gift. Today's charismatic proponents are wrong regarding the nature, purpose, use, and every other aspect of tongues. There is no reason to assume merely on the basis of their claim that they are correct in identifying their tongues-speaking—which can easily be duplicated and is common to man—as the New Testament gift of tongues.

Conclusion. The "charismatic gifts" of today are not similar to the New Testament phenomena either in general perspective or in the details. There is no evidence to conclude that they are the same; there is every reason to conclude that they are not. The historical fact that the New Testament gifts ceased long ago and the fact that there is no historical link whatever between the charismatic phenomena and the New Testament gifts require the same conclusion. The only remaining possibility for giving credence to the modern charismatic claims would be to produce direct statements of Scripture that the apostolic phenomena will always be present in the church, or that they will specifically be in the modern church despite their cessation through most of church history. Even if this were produced, there must also be evidence that the charismatic phenomena are somehow the same phenomena referred to in the passages. However, there is no specific biblical evidence such as this. There is no biblical statement that requires a denial of historical fact or that requires an equation of such dissimilar entities merely on the assertion of the proponents. All objective evidence is contrary to the charismatic claims. It is not sufficient to assert that by faith their claims must be taken contrary to the evidence. This is existential naiveté, not faith. Faith is trust in biblical evidence rather than in experience.

BIBLICAL EVIDENCE FOR CESSATION

No Bible verse specifically states that tongues, signs, and wonders will continue throughout the Church Age. Nor is there a verse that specifically states they will cease at the end of the apostolic age. However, this does not mean that one cannot take a position on this issue. Many doctrines, such as the Trinity, are not directly stated but are derived from the study and correlation of passages of Scripture. There are several indications in the Scriptures that the gifts of tongues, healing, and miracles (signs and wonders) will not continue. The charismatic movement in all its forms rests not on exegetical evidence that the gifts will continue, but on the assumption contrary to history that since they occurred in the apostolic age they should also occur today. The foundation for this assumption is nonexistent.

The New Testament church was not characterized by power and miracles as the charismatics assume. It was characterized by the problems addressed in the epistles (including, e.g., the problems that beset the Corinthian church) and the problems of the churches described in Revelation 2 and 3. Miracles were performed with very few exceptions only by the apostles (Acts 2:43; 5:12). Those who "turned the world upside down" were the apostles, not the churches as a whole. The charismatics assume that the church today should be like their imaginary church. They assume that the entire church today should be able to do all the apostles did in the New Testament.

If the church as a whole had performed miracles, it is only an assumption, apart from evidence, that this should be true today. This assumption is not interpretation. The assumption that the miraculous events recorded in the Book of Acts should occur today is "a distinct hermeneutic, a distinctively Pentecostal manner of appropriating the Scriptures."[15] This development of theology on the basis of narrative rather than on direct teaching of Scripture is always a precarious methodology.

General biblical evidence. Moses performed a series of miracles. However, they did not continue throughout the Old Testament nor were other believers expected to do the same. The Old Testament prophets occasionally performed miracles, but Israel in general was not expected to do so, nor did the miracles continue throughout Israel's history. The fact that some individuals on special occasions in biblical history performed miracles did not result in others doing the same or in a continuity of those miracles. So there is no reason to assume that since the apostles and a few members of the early church performed miracles, they are to be expected today.

Specific biblical evidence. In addition to evidence from history there is also specific biblical evidence that certain gifts were temporary. The term "apostle," commonly used in ancient times in the sense of "representative," in a few passages describes representatives of a local church. This is not the New Testament gift of apostleship. Nor can this term, contrary to its normal meaning and contrary to the New Testament descriptions, be equated with the modern missionary merely on the basis of etymology. The only individuals in the New Testament who clearly possessed the miraculous gift of apostle of the Lord Jesus Christ and could perform miracles as required of an apostle (2 Cor. 12:12) were the Twelve and Paul. Perhaps Barnabas and James can be included. Almost every branch of the church, including most Pentecostals, has held that apostles in this sense have not continued in the church. The charismatic reliance on the narrative of Acts is often avoided when defining "apostles" or "prophets," as too restrictive.[16] These gifts can be precisely delineated,[17] however. Imprecise use of Scripture is a common failing among charismatics.[18] No matter how one tries to broaden the term "apostle," there is little doubt that apostles such as the Twelve and Paul did not continue. If they did not, then all things are *not* as they were in the New Testament church, all miraculous gifts did not continue as in the beginning church, and at least one gift in the New Testament did not continue.

In addition the New Testament sets standards for an apostle that preclude the continuance of this gift. Not only must an apostle be able to perform miracles (2 Cor. 12:12), not only was the early church very careful about granting anyone, even Paul, the title of "apostle" (Gal. 2:1–10), but also an apostle must have seen the resurrected Lord (1 Cor. 9:1–2; Acts 1:22–26). Paul explicitly stated that he was the *last* one to see the resurrected Lord (1 Cor. 15:8), and he specifically connected this fact with his apostleship.[19] This requirement for apostleship refers to genuine appearances of the resurrected Christ and not to "visions." There have been no resurrection appearances since the apostolic age. Paul clearly stated that the last appearance was to him. (Revelation 1:12–18 refers to a vision, and is not an appearance of the resurrected Lord in bodily form on earth.) Therefore apostles in the sense of the Twelve and Paul cannot occur today.

When Paul wrote that all gifts were given to the church (1 Cor. 1:7) and benefited the church, he did not mean that all believers were apostles or *performed* miracles, but that the apostolic, miraculous ministry was experienced by and benefited the

Corinthian church. Paul wrote in Ephesians 2:20 that the apostles and prophets are the foundation for the universal church.[20] This at least implies that they were only for the beginning, and this accords with the other specifics mentioned above. Since "apostle" in the full sense of the gift was only a temporary gift and did not continue in the church, the biblical precedent is established that some gifts given in the apostolic age did not continue and were only temporary. It is contrary to Scripture to assume that all gifts and all happenings of the apostolic church are to continue and to be expected in today's church.

Since the ones who performed the miracles were only in the beginning church, it is logical that the miracles themselves were only for the apostolic age. Since the ability to perform such miracles was evidence of apostleship (2 Cor. 12:12), then with rare exceptions others could not have performed such signs and wonders, and they would not continue when the apostles ceased. In addition to this implication the temporary nature of miracles is directly supported by Scripture. Mark wrote that the apostles went forth in accord with the Lord's instructions and preached (aorist tense) everywhere and the Lord confirmed their word with signs. This is all placed in the past at the time of Mark's writing (Mark 16:20; the time of the present participle is relative to the past tense of the main verb). The same is true in Hebrews 2:3–4, which says miracles were performed by eyewitnesses of the Lord (apostles), and were performed by God to confirm the word of the eyewitnesses. All this was past at the time Hebrews was written (the main verb is past tense and the participle is relative in time to the main verb "was confirmed"). In both cases the signs, wonders, and miracles are referred to as being in the past at the time of writing; they were not referred to as occurring at that time. In both passages miracles were performed by the apostles (eyewitnesses) and are described as intended by God as evidence to authenticate the apostles' preaching.

James 5:14 does not instruct the sick to look for a healer or for someone with the ability to heal. Rather it instructs the sick to call for the elders and they are to pray for him. This is basically in accord with the procedure in noncharismatic churches, but is in direct contrast to what would be expected if the gift of healing were available for believers. Either the gift was not to be used to heal believers, or the only other option is that it had ceased.

Conclusion. There is ample biblical evidence that the miraculous gifts ceased with the apostolic age. To assume that such gifts are permanent is contrary to the Scriptures in general and to the biblical precedent that some gifts such as full apostles of the Lord definitely ceased. History is against the charismatic claims. The dissimilarity between the New Testament gifts and the alleged gifts of the charismatics also contradicts their claims. The assumption that because these gifts existed in the apostolic age they should also exist today is a gratuitous assumption contrary to objective evidence. It is also an assumption contrary to scriptural principles and specific biblical evidence. There is no teaching in Scripture that the church should look for such miraculous gifts, nor are they referred to in the passages discussing the fruit of the Spirit (Gal. 5:22–23), spiritual warfare (Eph. 6:10–18), the life of faith (Eph. 5:18; Col. 3:12–17), and requirements for church leaders (1 Tim. 3:1–13; Titus 1:5–9) as necessary for the believer to lead a spiritual life.

Characteristics That Refute Charismatic Claims

Various present-day forms of the charismatic movement are offshoots of Pentecostalism. All have the same basic ideology and all have arisen because of the modern Pentecostal movement. The primary focus for the individual, no matter how their theologians may describe it, is experiential. Many people in the charismatic movement emphasize the miraculous nature of this experience seemingly for personal benefit more than service to others.

THEOLOGICAL ASSOCIATIONS

In Pentecostalism the doctrine of Christian perfectionism assumed a specific form in the inaccurate concept of a postconversion crisis experience,[21] a "second blessing." This teaching with its concept of an effusion of power from the Holy Spirit resulted in the expectancy of and search to obtain overt "power" as described in Acts.

The movement crosses all theological boundaries. Speaking in tongues is present in non-Christian religions such as Buddhism and Hinduism, and in cults such as Mormonism. Healing, miracles, and exorcisms are also common in non-Christian religions. In conventional Christian circles the charismatic movement includes Protestants and Roman Catholics, liberals and conservatives, and individuals in many denominations. Those who believe in the inspiration of the Bible, justification by faith, and many other doctrines—as well as those who do not—are also involved.

QUESTIONABLE THEOLOGY

The concept of the "second blessing" or "baptism or fullness of the Spirit" presupposes that while Jesus' death on the cross paid for sin, it is insufficient to empower for service, to enable one to be spiritual, or to give effectiveness in prayer. This differs drastically from the teaching of the New Testament.[22] The view that only those who speak in tongues have real communication with God is contrary to the biblical teaching that all believers have full access to God. Romans 8:26 states that all believers are helped in prayer by the Spirit with *inaudible, nonuttered,* internal groanings.

The tongues movement presupposes that communication with the spiritual realm is more direct when it is apart from the mind.[23] Such a concept, though found in various religions, is contrary to biblical Christianity. This emphasis on a level of communication that bypasses the mind and is not direct communication from the believer to God is a dangerous teaching. This interest in "supernatural" events, not primarily as convincing signs but as the daily experience of believers that supposedly places them in contact with the supernatural, is dangerous. This middle-level, spirit realm, called the "excluded middle," is an area of charismatic emphasis.[24]

The emphasis on experience, particularly in this level above the rational, often results in emphasizing "experience" over Scripture. In a recent nationally televised program on the subject of televangelism several charismatically oriented evangelists appealed to the "call" as the license for a sinning preacher to continue his ministry. They made no appeal to the Scriptures.

SIMILARITIES TO NON-CHRISTIAN RELIGIONS

The modern-day charismatic movement is disturbingly similar to practices common in paganism, while at the same time it lacks correspondence to biblical miracles. Trancelike states and communications on a level apart from the mind are common in paganism. An emphasis on physical healing and exorcism for the benefit of adherents is common. The experience of a power or force "overcoming" the participants is similar to pagan practice. The bizarre and often wild practices of early Pentecostalism seem similar to pagan religion. The idea of contact and interest in the spirit world, the "excluded middle" between God and man, is also common to pagan religions.

THE EFFECTS OF THE MOVEMENT

All groups and doctrinal persuasions of Christendom have experienced theological and moral problems with both their leaders and laymen. As other Christians have experienced, so a number of charismatic leaders have led lives that are morally or ethically contrary to Scripture. If not more common, this is at least as common as among noncharismatics. Therefore it may be safely concluded that all the alleged miracles and so-called tongues-speaking have not produced any genuine spiritual advance over noncharismatics. It has produced enthusiasm for the miraculous, but this is not to be equated with spirituality.

All these supposedly miraculous events have produced no advance in biblical knowledge or spiritual living. The basic doctrines common to the movement are not original with charismatics. Their main claim to biblical knowledge is the assumption that the current church should be like the early church. Since the movement has not produced more spiritual believers or any advance in biblical or theological knowledge, what has it accomplished? Is it not amazing that a movement that claims to have restored power for service, ability to communicate with God more than others have, ability for self-edification, power to heal and perform other miracles, and ability to prophesy and receive direct revelation, has produced no significant advance in spirituality or in biblical or theological knowledge? Is it not inconsistent that a movement that claims to be in direct contact with the Holy Spirit, to have all gifts such as prophecy, apostleship, and the word of knowledge, to communicate directly with God by tongues-speaking and other means, can at the same time include Roman Catholics, conservative and liberal Protestants, amillennialists, premillennialists, Calvinists, Arminians, those who deny the verbal inspiration of the Bible, and those who reject Christ's vicarious atonement on the cross?

Apparently the Holy Spirit is not concerned with communicating any information to correct all these differences, many of which are crucial and some of which are incorrect. All this direct communication with the Spirit has apparently done nothing to correct even basic errors. It has not even produced unity among charismatics regarding the nature and purpose of many of the gifts. This movement has solved no theological issue, produced no advance in biblical knowledge, and has not produced more spiritual Christians. Would such an effusion of the genuine Spirit of God produce so little? Other than enthusiasm there seems to be no spiritual advantage to this movement and the noncharismatics are not missing out on any genuine spiritual benefit. On the negative side the movement has split churches, and through its televangelists the movement has had one of the most significant negative impacts on the testimony of the church in recent history. These characteristics are evidence that the charismatic phenomena are not the New Testament phenomena, that the genuine gifts are not present.

Conclusion

In every attempt to prove that the New Testament gifts exist today, the charismatic movement fails. The objective evidence of history and lack of correspondence with the New Testament indicate that the genuine miraculous gifts ceased and have not reoccurred. Biblical evidence indicates that these gifts ceased with the apostolic age. The theological associations and results of today's so-called miraculous gifts are contrary to gifts given by God. The movement has not produced Christians who are more spiritually mature, as would be expected of a genuine occurrence of the New Testament gifts. Apparently a Christian experiences no spiritual loss by *not* becoming involved in the charismatic movement.

On the other hand there is a dangerous similarity to non-Christian practices, there is a dangerous interest in supernatural phenomena that give no evidence of being from God, and there is a disturbing interest in the spiritual world somewhere between God and man. Since evidence points to the cessation of the miraculous gifts in the apostolic age, no one can be confident that the charismatic phenomena are from God. Since believers are warned to avoid contact with the intermediate spiritual world and since they should do only what they are confident God approves, no one should experiment in the realm of the supernatural phenomena.

CHAPTER 13

When Will the Gift of Prophecy Cease?

F. David Farnell

I n discussing the cessation of New Testament prophecy, two essential areas should be examined. First, prophecy's miraculous nature must be stressed. Because prophecy is a miraculous gift mediated by the Holy Spirit, any attempt at describing or defining the gift without proper consideration of this element may result in a marked misunderstanding of the nature and operation of prophecy. Current novel attempts at defining prophecy impugn the miraculous nature of New Testament prophecy. True New Testament prophets declared Spirit-inspired messages that were fully authoritative and completely accurate—not "merely human words" that could be "mistaken" or accepted and rejected by the congregation on a "take it or leave it" basis.[1]

Second, strategic arguments demonstrate that the gift of prophecy, like the other miraculous gifts of apostleship and tongues, has ceased. The gift of prophecy played a vital role in the foundational aspects of the church. With the church firmly established through the ministry of the first-century apostles and New Testament prophets, prophecy passed from the scene.

The Miraculous Nature of New Testament Prophecy

In both the Old and New Testaments, prophecy's essential nature is that of a miraculous gift involving the direct reception of revelatory information from God to the prophet. This miraculous nature of prophecy can be demonstrated in several ways. The following facts illustrate the supernatural character of the prophetic gift.

THE PROPHET AS SPOKESPERSON FOR THE LORD

The chief function of the prophet (προφήτης) or of prophecy (προφητεία) was not necessarily found in the element of prediction of future events.[2] Though prediction was an important factor in the prophetic role, the predictive aspect is considered a later development in the significance of the word group.[3]

A primary function of the prophet in both extrabiblical and biblical usage was to proclaim or announce the will of God to the people.[4] As such, the prophet was the "immediately inspired spokesman" for God.[5] Since every prophet declared something that was not his own, the synonym that comes closest to the primary function of the prophet is the Greek word κῆρυξ (verb, κηρύσσω), for the κῆρυξ also declared what he had received from another.[6] Thus the προφήτης occupies a mediatorial role, for he was both the mouthpiece of and spokesman for God.[7] In that role a prophet had the potential to claim much authority in a believing community, particularly since he announced the will of God to His people.[8]

This primary function of the biblical prophet as spokesman or mouthpiece for the Lord also underscores the essentially miraculous nature of both Old and New Testament prophecy.[9] That is, the basic nature of the genuine biblical prophet was someone who, through the inspired prophetic state, was in direct contact with God in the performance of his gift in a way that others were not.[10] Prophecy's miraculous nature centers strategically in the supernatural reception of revelation from God to the prophet.[11] Importantly, such a gift had to be completely miraculous in character, for if that gift did not involve a Spirit-mediated, miraculous element, the community could not guard itself against doctrinal confusion and error.

PROPHECY AND REVELATION

Prophecy is a sovereignly bestowed charisma through which revelations from God occur (1 Cor. 2:10; 12:10; 13:9; 14:6, 29). The same gift of prophecy was active whether the revelation involved canonical matters or the impartation of immediate guidance to the church (e.g., the writing of the Book of Revelation [Rev. 1:10] or the command of the Holy Spirit through church prophets to send out Barnabas and Saul [Acts 13:1–4]). Also the same gift was involved whether that revelation came from apostles who possessed the gift of prophecy or from nonapostolic New Testament prophets (Eph. 2:20; 3:5; 1 Cor. 14:29–31). For this reason prophecy involved speech based on direct reception of revelatory information from God through the prophet(s) which, in turn, guided the people of God in matters of faith and practice.[12]

Furthermore the revelation did not have to entail exclusively predictive elements to be miraculous. Such a statement does not minimize the predictive characteristic exhibited in prophecy, for prophecy is frequently predictive,[13] but it reduces prophecy to its primary characteristic of Spirit-inspired speech based on direct revelatory communication from God involving information which often could not be known on an ordinary, human basis.[14] Even prediction involves the communication of divine truth which could not be known by ordinary means, that is, supernatural communication between God and the prophet.[15]

Inclusion of Gentiles in the church (Eph. 3:5–10) illustrates this point. This concept, revealed through the apostles and New Testament prophets to the church, is primarily doctrinal and does not necessarily encompass prediction. The revelatory nature of Paul's message did not involve solely predictive elements but also reception of the true nature of the gospel of Jesus Christ and justification by faith (Acts 9:3–6, 20; Gal. 1:12, 16–17). In Acts 13:1–3, God revealed His will through the prophets regarding sending Barnabas and Saul on their first Gentile mission. In Matthew 26:67–68 (cf. Mark 14:65 and Luke 22:64), the Jews sarcastically asked Jesus to prophesy who hit Him, thus indicating supernatural discernment but not necessarily requiring prediction. In John 4:19 the woman at the well perceived Jesus to be a prophet, not on the basis of prediction, but because of His miraculous knowledge of her marital history. Luke 7:39 indicates that the Pharisees considered a prophet to have supernatural discernment of the true character of people. In 1 Corinthians 14:29–31 prophets are linked with the miraculous ability to determine true prophets from false prophets rather than merely setting forth predictive prophecies (cf. 12:10).[16] Hence the miraculous nature of prophecy has its basis in the reception of revelation. Such revelation frequently involved the reception of information that exceeded normal human cognitive functions.[17] As spokespersons for God, biblical prophets in both Testaments distinguished themselves as prophets primarily by the possession of a supernatural ability to receive revelations directly from God. Therefore prophecy, reduced to its basic function, is Spirit-inspired utterance based on the direct, miraculous reception of divine revelation.[18]

Another important point about the miraculous nature of prophecy must be addressed, namely, wrongly equating prophecy with mere comfort, admonishment, or encouragement. This reflects a fundamental misunderstanding of 1 Corinthians 14:3 in which Paul wrote that "one who prophesies speaks to men for edification and exhortation and consolation." However, Paul was not defining prophesy but, in context, "merely uses the fact that prophecy is understandable and therefore results in edification, exhortation, and encouragement."[19] Since prophecy, in contrast to tongues, contributed directly to the understanding of the congregation, it had an edifying effect on the whole group, including the speaker (1 Cor. 14:4).[20] Godet notes,

> The conclusion is often drawn from this verse, that since to prophesy is to edify, exhort, comfort, whoever edifies, exhorts, comforts, merits according to Paul the title prophet. This reasoning is as just as it would be to say: He who runs moves his legs; therefore, whoever moves his legs, runs; or, to take a more nearly related example: He who speaks to God in a tongue, speaks to God; and therefore whoever speaks to God, is a glossalalete. No, certainly; one may edify, comfort, encourage, without deserving the title of prophet or prophetess.[21]

These latter concepts are better viewed as the results of prophecy and not as references to the content of prophecy.[22] Hence the result of prophecy was edification, exhortation, and comfort.[23]

For example the Book of Revelation is labeled "revelation" (ἀποκάλυψις) and also as "prophecy" (προφητείας) that John the prophet received in the prophetic state (ἐγενόμην ἐν πνεύματι, (Rev. 1:10) directly from Jesus Christ or angelic ministers (1:1). Brown notes, "Although the words *parakaleō* and *paraklēsis* do not occur, the letters to the seven churches (chs. 2 and 3) and indeed the whole work constitutes a series of messages of consolation and exhortation. The work carries the authority of the exalted Christ, speaking through the Spirit (Rev. 22:18 f.)."[24] The vast portion of the Book of Revelation exhibits the miraculous element of predictive prophecy in which John was transported to the future (chaps. 4–22).[25] Even in the messages to the seven churches, which are considered "historical" in nature (i.e., chaps. 2–3 written to seven historical churches—"the things which are" [cf. 1:19]), miraculous elements predominate. For instance supernatural knowledge of the spiritual conditions of these churches emphasizes the miraculous nature of these messages (e.g., Rev. 2:2–6, 9–10, 19–28; 3:2, 4–5, 7–12, 15–18), which brought comfort to some churches (e.g., Smyrna, 2:8–11, and Philadelphia, 3:7–13) and admonishment to others (2:10; 3:14–19).[26] Prediction also forms an important part in these messages to the churches. Smyrna was warned of impending persecution ("you will have tribulation ten days"); in Thyatira the false prophetess Jezebel would be cast on a bed of affliction and go into great tribulation for her wicked deeds; Philadelphia was promised deliverance "from the hour of testing which is about to come upon the whole world" (3:10) and those of the "synagogue of Satan" would be made to bow down at their feet (3:9).

Similarly Paul miraculously prophesied (predicted) in Acts 27:22–26 that not one life would be lost in the shipwreck on his journey to Rome. Not only did this constitute a marvelous vindication of Paul as God's prophet to the unbelievers who guarded him, but it also comforted and encouraged those who, along with Paul (e.g., Luke who wrote "we" in 27:27, 29), faced the ordeal.

In light of this, whether the information involved elements of prediction or *resulted* in edification, comfort, or encouragement does not militate against its essence as being the miraculous impartation of revelation to the prophet by the Holy Spirit which, in turn, is proclaimed to members of the Christian community. Therefore it is unlikely that a proclamation made apart from immediate revelation may strictly be termed "prophecy."[27]

THE ECSTATIC STATE OF THE PROPHET

The ecstatic[28] or prophetic state of the prophet also demonstrates the unique revelatory role of the prophet as a spokesperson for the Lord. In the Old Testament certain stereotyped phrases reveal the prophetic state.[29] For example "the Holy Spirit entered into" the prophet and that prophet received revelation (e.g., Ezek. 2:2; 8:3; 11:5–12, 24; 12:1), or "the hand of the Lord" was on the prophets when prophetic communication was received (e.g., 3:14, 22; 8:1; 33:22; 37:1). Sometimes the phrase "the Spirit of God came upon" is used to describe the revelatory state (Num. 24:2; 1 Sam. 10:10; 11:6; 19:20; 2 Chron. 15:1; Isa. 61:1), or the phrase "the word of the Lord came to" is used (1 Kings 19:9; 1 Sam. 15:10; 2 Sam. 24:11; Jonah 1:1; Hag. 1:1; 2:1, 20; Zech. 7:1; 8:1). Another phrase is "filled with power, with the Spirit of the Lord" (Mic. 3:8).[30]

New Testament prophets exhibited a similar prophetic state. In the state of ecstasy (ἔκστασις) Peter received revelation regarding the inclusion of uncircumcised Gentiles like Cornelius into the fellowship of the church (Acts 10:10; cf. ἐκστάσει in

11:15). Paul related that in the ecstatic state (ἐκστάσει) he was warned to depart from Jerusalem because of the hostility of the Jews and was commissioned to be an apostle to the Gentiles (22:17; cf. 9:26–30). John was "in the Spirit" on the Lord's day (Rev. 1:10, ἐγενόμην ἐν πνεύματι) and because of this prophetic state he was enabled to receive the contents of the Book of Revelation (cf. 4:2, ἐγενόμην ἐν πνεύματὶ and 17:3 and 21:10, καὶ ἀπηνέγκέν με ἐν πνεύματι). "Through the Spirit" (ἐσήμαινεν διὰ τοῦ πνεύματος) Peter predicted the coming famine during the reign of Claudius (Acts 11:28). In the prophetic state Paul received "visions" (ὀπτασίας) and "revelations" (ἀποκαλύψεις) from the Lord (2 Cor. 12:1). Genuine New Testament prophets who were in the prophetic state (ἐν πνεύματι θεοῦ) were guarded from erroneous revelatory statements because of the intimate ministry of the Spirit of prophecy (1 Cor. 12:3).[31] The Holy Spirit exercised sovereign control over the true prophet's prophetic activity. These verses also serve to stress the special relationship the Holy Spirit maintains to the prophetic state, which demonstrates the miraculous and rational nature that such experiences entailed for both Old and New Testament prophets.[32]

In summary, prophecy was a Spirit-mediated miraculous gift. Several factors demonstrate this. First, the primary characteristic involved was Spirit-motivated speech centering in direct reception of revelation from God. Without such revelation, prophecy does not function. Second, supernatural discernment, insight, and knowledge were frequently involved in conveying information that could not have been obtained by ordinary human means. Third, prophecy often involved prediction. Prediction was a vital element in biblical prophecy in contrast to secular examples of προφητεία. Fourth, edification is better understood as the effect of prophecy on the listener rather than as its content. Fifth, the Spirit-mediated prophetic state of the prophet reinforced the supernatural element involved. This miraculous element of prophecy is frequently neglected in determining the meaning, nature, and function of the gift.

A Comparison of Prophecy to Related Gifts

A comparison of gifts related to the gift of prophecy is also needed since erroneous equations of the prophetic gift are made because of failure to give due recognition to the miraculous nature of prophecy.

THE PROPHET AND THE TEACHER

Prophets and teachers are frequently mentioned as the most significant proclaimers of the Word in the church (Acts 13:1; 1 Cor. 12:28; Eph. 4:11; Rom. 12:6). Like teachers, prophets mediated knowledge, so that one could learn from them (1 Cor. 14:31; Rev. 2:20; cf. *Didache* 11.10–12). Prophets instructed the church regarding the meaning of Scripture, and through revelations they gave information about the future.[33]

However, prophecy is not the same as teaching. Because it was based on direct divine revelations, the ministry of the prophet was more spontaneous than that of the teacher. Teachers, on the other hand, preserved and interpreted already existing Christian tradition, including relevant Old Testament passages, the sayings of Jesus, and traditional beliefs of earlier Christian teaching.[34] Furthermore while the teacher considers the past and gives direction for the present on the basis of what took place or what was said previously, the prophet looked toward the future and guided the path of the believing community forward.[35]

In the New Testament the presence or absence of revelation distinguishes prophecy from teaching.[36] Prophecy always depended on a revelation from God, but by contrast no human speech act which is called a διδαχή or διδασκαλία ("teaching") done by a διδάσκαλος ("teacher") or described by the verb διδάσκω ("to teach") is ever said to be based on ἀποκάλυψις ("revelation").[37] Furthermore no ἀποκάλυψις in the New Testament is ever said to result in a "teaching" of one man to another. Instead teaching is put in contrast to divine "revelation."[38] Teaching is simply an exposition or application of Scripture (Acts 15:35; 18:11, 25; Rom. 2:20–21; Col. 3:16; Heb. 5:12) or a repetition and explanation of apostolic instruction (Rom. 16:17; 1 Cor. 14:17; 2 Thess. 2:15; 2 Tim. 2:2; 3:10).[39]

THE PROPHET AND THE PREACHER

Some commentators assert that prophecy is essentially another name for preaching. An example of this is Redpath, who asserts that prophecy "is the gift of the man who in the name of the Lord and in the power of the Spirit is able to speak with authority from the Book to the day in which he lives."[40] MacArthur distinguishes between revelatory prophecy, which has ceased, and prophecy today, which he defines as "the ability to proclaim truth powerfully."[41] Perhaps this association has been built up because of the "forthtelling" aspect in the prophetic activity of the prophet as the spokesman for God.

However, to equate preaching with the spiritual gift of prophecy is fallacious.[42] Such an equation is also quite artificial. While preaching is essentially a merging of the gifts of teaching and exhortation, prophecy has the primary elements of prediction and revelation.[43] As Friedrich notes, "All prophecy rests on revelation, (1 Cor. 14:30). The prophet does not declare what he has taken from tradition or what he has thought up himself. He declares what has been revealed to him."[44] Friedrich's further comment is relevant: "Whereas teachers expound Scripture, cherish the tradition about Jesus and explain the fundamentals of the catechism, the prophets, not bound by Scripture or tradition, speak to the congregation on the basis of revelations."[45] Therefore, since the preacher is not in contact with God as was the prophet, the preacher is not the modern equivalent of a prophet. While both preacher and prophet proclaim, the reception of direct revelation from God is the crucial essence of the prophetic gift that qualitatively separates it from other forms of proclamation and preaching. Furthermore, while preaching includes teaching, the ministry of the prophet was more spontaneous, being based on direct divine revelation.

THE PROPHET AND THE EVANGELIST

Like the prophet, an evangelist (εὐαγγελιστῆς) utilizes proclamation. Similarly, prophecy is not addressed solely to Christians but may also have an evangelistic value for unbelievers (cf. 1 Cor. 14:24–25). This evangelistic value of New Testament prophecy is also seen in its Old Testament counterpart (e.g., Jonah 3:5). Yet important differences in the two gifts mark out their distinctiveness. Evangelism is addressed primarily to unbelievers who have not yet heard or accepted the message concerning Jesus Christ, while prophecy has its primary focus on believers in the congregation (1 Cor. 14:3, 29–37). The content of both gifts must also be distinguished. The evangelist proclaimed the content of the gospel, while prophecy is based on the miraculous impartation of immediate revelation which could not be known through ordinary human means (the "secrets of his heart are disclosed," 1 Cor. 14:25).[46]

THE PROPHET AND KNOWLEDGE

First Corinthians 13:8–12 deals with prophecy and γνῶσις ("knowledge"). They are similar in that both are charismata of the Spirit, both are concerned with knowledge of mysteries, and both are fragmentary rather than definite or perfect (13:9).[47] In contrast, however, γνῶσις is not superior to prophecy, but prophecy is the supreme gift of grace. Furthermore they differ in the way the knowledge of mysteries is attained and in the use to which this knowledge is put. Γνῶσις is a rational gift of the Holy Spirit which deals with the ability to grasp the logical nature and relations of truths revealed,[48] whereas prophecy rests on direct revelation. Furthermore, while γνῶσις is individualistic, prophecy is by its very meaning and nature concerned with proclaiming to others.

Arguments for the Cessation of Prophecy

The temporary nature of miraculous gifts as espoused by many cessationists is based on theological deductions made from certain New Testament passages. Though many verses are sometimes used (e.g., Rom. 15:18–19; 2 Cor. 12:12; Rev. 22:18),[49] two prominent passages will be discussed: Ephesians 2:20 (ἐπὶ τῷ θεμελίῳ τῶν ἀποστόλων καὶ προφητῶν—the foundational nature of New Testament prophecy) and 1 Corinthians 13:10 (ὅταν δὲ ἔλθῃ τὸ τέλειον—the temporal nature of New Testament prophecy).[50] The theological argumentation for the cessation of prophecy also is enforced by a comparison of the biblical data regarding prophecy with current practices of so-called "prophecy" exhibited among noncessationist groups. Also in the same way Old Testament prophecy ceased and the canon of the Old Testament was closed, New Testament prophecy reasonably may be considered to have ceased following that same analogy.

EPHESIANS 2:20

An important verse arguing for the cessation of such gifts as New Testament prophecy is Ephesians 2:20. In verses 19–21 Paul, employing the temple structure as a metaphor to describe the church, distinguished between apostles and prophets on the one hand and individual Christians on the other by relating them to one another as a foundation is related to the walls resting on it (cf. 1 Peter 2:4–8). Paul portrayed the apostles and New Testament prophets as comprising the foundation of the church (appositional genitive) with Jesus Christ as the chief Cornerstone. The entire church is said to be built on the foundation of those apostles and prophets and on no one else.

Ephesians 2:20 clearly refers to the universal church, not to some local church or mission field.[51] Paul's predominant usage of ἐκκλησία elsewhere in Ephesians demonstrates this. In 3:5 he wrote that the apostles and prophets were closely related to the foundational revelation that Gentiles as well as Jews would be united in the one universal body of Christ (cf. v. 10). He also used this universal sense in 3:21. In 5:23–27 the illustration of the husband and wife shows Christ's relationship to the universal church. This universal church is described as "His body" (v. 30) and also as a mystery (v. 32), referring back to 3:5.[52] Paul's words therefore cannot be properly applied to local or national churches throughout this age, inasmuch as Paul's representation of the church throughout this passage and elsewhere describes the church in the most universal and pervasive of terms (e.g., "God's people" and "God's household" in 2:19). Therefore Paul was referring to the foundation of the universal church in Ephesians 2:20. This foundation, by implication and by its very nature, can be laid only once since foundations are necessarily laid only once at the beginning of any structure.[53]

Ephesians 3:5–10 helps interpret 2:20, for it deals with the revelatory impact the apostles and New Testament prophets had in the church.[54] From 3:5 it becomes clear that apostles and New Testament prophets were of primary importance as vehicles of revelation, thereby providing the foundation for the church: the mystery (μυστήριον) of Jewish and Gentile inclusion in the universal body of Christ, the church (3:9–10).[55] This mystery was disclosed to the whole church, not to just a local congregation (1:8–10, 17, 18) through the apostles and prophets, of whom Paul was one (2:20). Paul said this revelation about Gentiles being included in the church had not been made known previously (3:5) but "has now" (ὡς νῦν) been revealed to the apostles and prophets and is contained in canonical revelation (e.g., Ephesians). This mystery was fully revealed to the body of Christ by the end of the apostolic era through proclamation (as evidenced in the Book of Acts and epistles like Ephesians). This first generation laid the foundation through the reception of such revelation. This can be seen by the ὡς νῦν, which contrasts the former age, in which people did not know of Gentile inclusion, with the present time of the writing of Ephesians, and also by the use of the culminative aorist indicative ἀπεκαλύφθη, signifying the attainment of effort or process. Once that revelation had been made, it no longer needed to be given by the Spirit again since it was proclaimed by the apostles, particularly Paul. Once a mystery is revealed, it is no longer a mystery and does not need to be revealed again.

Furthermore apostleship in Ephesians 2:20 must correspond to a narrow definition, being restricted to first-century apostles, especially since this verse is related to the apostles of 3:5–10 and the mystery of Gentile inclusion in the church is no longer being revealed. The direct relationship of 3:5–10 with 2:20 makes it most likely that the apostles mentioned in 2:20 were those commissioned directly by Christ, who received such important revelations (Acts 10; 2 Cor. 12:1–2; Gal. 1:11–12) and were the primary instruments in the spread of the gospel in the first century (to the Jews, Acts 2; to the Samaritans, Acts 8; to the Gentiles, Acts 10; and as far as Rome in the case of Paul, Acts 13–28). The term θεμέλιος ("foundation") is a key term, for the foundation was obviously established during the first century when apostles, as eyewitnesses of Christ's ministry and commissioned by Him, were still alive (cf. 1 Cor. 9:1–2; 15:8; 2 Cor. 12:12).[56]

Moreover, the prophetic gift was closely associated with the gift of apostleship.[57] Prophets are found alongside apostles in the New Testament as playing a special role in laying the foundation (Eph. 2:20) and in receiving revelation (1 Cor. 12:28; Eph. 2:20; 3:5; 4:11; Rev. 18:20). This close association of the two gifts is verified by the *Didache,* Ignatius, and the *Muratorian Fragment.*[58] To second-century writers, apostleship was a thing of the past. If the first century marked the end of the apostolic gift, it is probable that it marked the end of the prophetic gift also.[59]

Since Paul was referring to the universal church in Ephesians 2:20 and the apostles and prophets laid the church's foundation by receiving and transmitting revelation (3:5), the strong implication is that once the church was established, the gift would be discontinued. By its very nature, a foundation cannot be continuously relaid. This verse clearly implies that Paul viewed revelation as occurring during a specific, nonrepeatable era, with the church of subsequent ages commanded to discover its foundation in those apostles and prophets, or more specifically, in their doctrine as it is recorded in the Scriptures. Since the passage labels prophecy in itself as a foundational gift, the inevitable conclusion is that New Testament prophecy ceased along with the gift of apostleship.

The major objection to this reasoning is that it is a theological deduction from the text and not something the passage explicitly states. Mallone argues, "The intention of this verse is not to say that these gifts have ceased but only that a gift exercised must be in harmony with the instruction of the founding apostles and prophets."[60] In reply, it has already been demonstrated that Ephesians 2:20 signifies that the foundation consists of the apostles and prophets (appositional genitive) and does not refer to their teaching activities (subjective genitive). Since they are the foundation, the building illustration clearly seems to indicate the idea of the cessation of such gifts. While it is true that all teaching and instruction must be in harmony with that of the apostles and prophets, the central thrust of the illustration is the foundational role of such individuals in the church's formation and, as such, would indicate the temporary character of such offices by the very nature of the illustration. As already noted, once the foundation has been laid by the apostles and prophets of the first century it does not need repeated formation by others.[61]

Some may respond by saying that perhaps the definitions of apostle and prophet are too restricted, and that other apostles and prophets may be a part of the superstructure besides those referred to by Paul here in Ephesians.[62] True, apostleship can have both a general and a limited meaning. In a general sense the word ἀπόστολος ("apostle") means "one who is sent" (from ἀποστέλλω, "to send"), or "a messenger." The Latin term is equivalent to the word "missionary." Hence in a general sense every Christian is a missionary or an apostle, because he has been sent into this world to render a testimony for Christ. Epaphroditus illustrates this idea, for the word "apostle" is used of him (Phil. 2:25).[63]

However, in the specialized sense of the gift of apostleship, the word ἀπόστολος refers to the office of apostleship (Acts 1:20–26). Paul apparently had this specialized sense in mind in Ephesians 2:20.[64] The apostles, like Paul and the Twelve, were a distinct group far different from those designated by any general usage of the term. The first-century apostles and New Testament prophets received special revelations and participated in the foundation (θεμέλιος) of the church (Eph. 3:5). Once that foundation had been laid by those in the first century who possessed the gifts of apostleship and prophecy, no further need to relay the foundation by subsequent generations is implied. Therefore no ground exists for seeing need for any further apostles and prophets since they have fulfilled their primary purpose and the church builds on that foundation as Ephesians 2:20 naturally implies.[65] The burden of proof for seeing a general class of apostles and prophets continuing in the superstructure must rest on those asserting that such a class exists today. Furthermore such contentions go far beyond the purpose of Paul's illustration in the context and rest on tenuous definitions.

FIRST CORINTHIANS 13:8–13

Much of the controversy surrounding spiritual gifts, particularly the miraculous gifts like prophecy, tongues, and knowledge, has concentrated on 1 Corinthians 13:8–13 as providing a *crux interpretum* regarding the continuance or cessation of the gift. Both sides have centered on this passage to argue either for or against the cessation of the prophetic gift.

All groups would agree that 1 Corinthians 13:10 indicates that gifts such as prophecy, tongues, and knowledge are temporary. That such gifts will cease is not at issue so much as when those gifts will cease and what particular time is being indicated by the phrase ὅταν δὲ ἔλθῃ τὸ τέλειον in 13:10. Whenever τὸ τέλειον arrives, then these gifts will no longer be necessary. While the analyses of the passage have produced a variety of interpretations, the major views essentially reduce to two possible ways of rendering τὸ τέλειον.[66]

The first view understands τὸ τέλειον in an absolute sense of "perfect" and has reference to Christ's Parousia.[67] Here the significance of τὸ τέλειον is identified as "the perfection" that will exist after Christ returns for His church, as seen in 13:12. At that time, all spiritual gifts, not just prophecy and knowledge, will cease. The only virtue that has permanent significance is love (v. 13).

Several arguments are advanced in favor of this view. First, this view is the only one that adequately satisfies the explanatory confirmation of 13:12 where the ideal, final state is in view. Second, the meaning of "perfect" best describes the period after Christ's return. Third, the verb ἔλθῃ can refer only to the precise moment of Christ's second coming.[68] Fourth, Pauline statements of eschatological hope center in Christ's return (1 Cor. 1:7–9; 15:20–34; 1 Thess. 4:13–18). Fifth, Paul and other New Testament writers used the related term, τέλος, of the same period (Rom. 8:18–30; 1 Cor. 1:8; 15:24; Matt. 24:6, 13–14). Sixth, maturity and the end are related in Paul's writings (Col. 1:5, 22, 27–28).[69]

The second view is that τὸ τέλειον refers to what is "mature" or "complete" rather than "the perfect state."[70] Understood in this sense, τὸτέλειον draws on the figure of the church as Christ's body collectively growing up during the age since the day of Pentecost.[71] The gifts of 1 Corinthians 13:8–9 gradually ceased with the close of canonical revelation and the increasing maturity of the body of Christ (cf. Eph. 4:11–16, esp. v. 13, εἰς ἄνδρα τέλειον, "the mature man").

Admittedly any decision on these two options is not easy. However, the second view ("maturity") is the more viable. Arguments for the second view also constitute a rebuttal of the first view. First, Pauline usage of τέλειος never conveys the idea of absolute perfection, and such a philosophical meaning is also questionable in the rest of the New Testament.[72] Only this view allows τέλειος a relative sense. Second, Paul's constant use of the νήπιος . . . τέλειος antithesis supports this interpretation. Τέλειος elsewhere always possesses a relative meaning of "mature" when used in proximity to νήπιος (13:11, ὅτε ἤμην νήπιος, "when I was a child"; cf. 1 Cor. 2:6; 3:1; 14:20; Eph. 4:13–14). Furthermore the occurrence of τέλειος is what suggests the νήπιος illustration of 1 Corinthians 13:11 (cf. Heb. 5:13–14). Whenever the adjective is used in connection with νήπιος, it always carries the connotation of gradual increase, not of an abrupt change. Third, this view gives an adequate sense to the illustrations in 1 Corinthians 13:11 and 12. In verse 11 a relative maturity is signified, while verse 12 indicates an absolute maturity. Provision also exists here for the ultimate state after the Parousia, according to the demands of verse 12, in that maturity is of two kinds: one that is constantly changing and increasing (v. 11), and the other that is final and absolute (v. 12). The latter type is viewed in verse 12 as a future goal.

Fourth, Ephesians 4:13–14 more explicitly presents the picture of the maturing of Christ's body collectively. A number of striking resemblances between 1 Corinthians 13 and Ephesians 4 tie these passages together in reference to gradual maturity.[73]

The parallels between these two passages are strengthened also by the historical connection of the writing of 1 Corinthians while Paul was ministering at Ephesus (1 Cor. 16:8).[74] Since Ephesians 4:13–14 pictures a gradual development of Christ's body from the beginning to the end, Paul's picture in 1 Corinthians 13 would also convey the same concept. Fifth, this view provides for Paul's uncertainty as to the time of the Parousia and status of a written canon.[75] Sixth, as already suggested in note 69, the contrast with ἐκ μέρους in 13:9 requires a quantitative idea ("complete") rather than a qualitative idea ("perfect").[76]

In light of this, Paul's development from childhood to adult-hood in verse 11 illustrates the progressive growth of the church through the critical period of its history. Ultimate maturity is another matter, as is illustrated in verse 12, when growth reaches its culmination at Christ's return. Thus this view is comprehensive enough to embrace the relative maturity implied by the illustration in verse 11 as well as the absolute maturity depicted in verse 12. It pictures believers collectively growing up together in one body, beginning with the birth of the church on the day of Pentecost. The body of Christ attains different states of maturity during this period until complete maturity is reached at the Second Coming of Christ. The contrast in verse 13a is that gifts of the earlier part of the paragraph were possibly to extend only through a portion of the church's existence, whereas faith, hope, and love would characterize the entire earthly ministry. Beyond this, only one of the three virtues will survive the Parousia, and that is love itself. For this reason, it is declared to be the greatest gift.[77] As Thomas concludes,

> "When the mature comes" gathers together into one concept both the period of church history after the need for the gifts of direct revelation has ceased to exist (relative maturity illustrated in v. 11) and the period after the return of Christ for the church (absolute maturity illustrated in v. 12). By comparing these gifts to the maturity of the body of Christ Paul shows their temporary character (in contrast with love). A certain level of maturity has been reached once the N.T. canon has been completed and is in hand, and so the result is almost the same as that of [the completion of the New Testament canon view]. Yet Paul expected an imminent return of Christ and could not know, humanly speaking, that there ever would be a complete N.T. canon of 27 books before Christ returned. Hence, he was guided by the Spirit to use the more general language of maturity to allow for this.[78]

Thus the gift of prophecy, along with tongues and knowledge, was a temporary gift which is no longer operative today.[79]

THE ARGUMENT FROM THE REVELATORY AND
MIRACULOUS NATURE OF PROPHECY

Much regarding this argument has already been hinted at in this chapter. Current attempts at prophecy parallel one of the flaws displayed in the second-century heresy known as Montanism: the phenomenon of false prophesying. False prophesying was a strategic reason why the church soundly rejected Montanism's claims of being a genuine "prophetic" movement. Accordingly the New Testament (Acts 2:17–21) and the postapostolic early church[80] saw a fundamental continuity, not discontinuity, between Old and New Testament prophets and prophecy.[81] Therefore false prophesying still remains one of the key signals for detecting false prophets.

As this study has shown, according to both the Old and New Testaments the miraculous nature of genuine biblical prophets and prophecy is that true prophets are one-hundred percent correct in all that they prophesy.[82] Either a prophet was always and completely accurate or he was to be rejected as a false prophet.

Stress also must be given to another often-neglected axiom of Scripture. Even if the prophecy of a so-called "prophet" comes true, no guarantee exists that such an individual is a true prophet, for even false prophets are capable of occasional true prophecies and "signs" or "wonders" (Deut. 13:2). While true prophets always prophesied accurately, false prophets sometimes prophesied accurately. The inaccuracy of the false prophets' prophesying constituted them as false prophets. Hence constant vigilance is required (1 Cor. 14:29–31). Prophets must be closely scrutinized. Any prophet who even once prophesied falsely was to be rejected summarily by God's people. "The prophet who shall speak a word presumptuously in My name which I have not commanded him to speak . . . that prophet shall die" (Deut. 18:20).[83] Proponents of the current practice of "prophecy" attempt to assert that Old Testament commands no longer apply to present-day "prophets."[84] However, no evidence exists that the apostles, who were Jews steeped in the Old Testament, ever thought that such Old Testament requirements were substantially modified or abrogated in judging prophets. Paul's warning in 1 Corinthians 14:29–31 to judge prophecies is a direct develop-

ment from such Old Testament warnings and also corresponds
to Jesus' warnings against false prophets who will try to deceive
God's elect by false signs (Matt. 7:15–16; 24:11, 24; Mark 13:22;
1 John 4:1; cf. Hos. 4:6). Constant vigilance and careful examination by God's people are required in dealing with prophets who
prophesy falsely or who exhibit false "signs" and "wonders."[86]
Geisler identifies a crucial issue regarding fallible prophets.

> Many today claim to be receiving visions, dreams, and revelations from
> God. The problem is that their "revelations" are not infallible. Some of
> them are flatly wrong. But a fallible revelation from God is a contradiction
> in terms. . . .
>   The problem with making testable prophecies in the name of the Lord
> is that they might prove to be false. This might not seem to be too
> significant until we remember that the test of a prophet is not whether he
> is sometimes right but whether he is ever wrong. Moses declared, "If
> what a prophet proclaims in the name of the Lord does not take place or
> come true, that is a message the Lord has not spoken. That prophet has
> spoken presumptuously" (Deuteronomy 18:22). The penalty for false
> prophecy under the Old Testament law was death (v. 20). If that law
> were still in effect today, there would undoubtedly be far fewer persons
> claiming prophetic powers.[86]

Several other recent works have also cataloged false prophecies by modern-day charismatic proponents who assert that the
gift of prophecy is still active.[87]

Any one claiming the prophetic gift today must be scrutinized
in light of the nature of the gift as revealed in the New Testament.
Those who assert such activity must be subject to the regulations
set forth in Scripture. By claiming the prophetic gift, they are
asserting that they have direct contact with Jesus Christ, which is
nonnormative and unique among the rest of the members of the
body of Christ.[88] Prophecy involves a miraculous impartation of
revelatory information not known on a mere human basis. This is
further substantiated by the fact that the New Testament prophetic
gift involved much more than teaching, preaching, evangelism, or
the possession of certain kinds of knowledge. While these latter
activities may be accomplished on a purely human level, the New
Testament prophetic gift was a miraculous and supernatural
revelatory gift that differed antithetically from what may be
accomplished by naturalistic means.

Because of the miraculous nature of prophecy, current novel
attempts at defining prophecy have also impugned the basic substance of prophecy.[89] That is, nothing miraculous exists in a gift

that is conceptualized to include the possibility of "mistaken" prophecy whereby the prophet is sometimes accurate and sometimes not. Even modern fortunetellers can claim varying degrees of partial or intermittent accuracy. However, genuine biblical prophets and prophecy are qualitatively different from any such novel practices. Recent attempts at redefining prophecy are directly contrary to its essential nature as a miraculous gift. Grudem, whose book constitutes the mainstay of defense for the Vineyard movement's approach to "prophecy," directly admits that Vineyard prophets can be and are mistaken at times. "Prophecy in ordinary New Testament churches was not equal to Scripture in authority, but was simply a very human—sometimes partially mistaken—report of something the Holy Spirit brought to someone's mind."[90]

Any prophetic pronouncements must stand the test of accuracy and uniqueness found in such places as Deuteronomy 13:1–5; 18:20–22; 1 Corinthians 14:28–32; and 1 John 4:1–3. The moment that a prophetic pronouncement demonstrates itself as being inaccurate or wrong, then such prophecy must be labeled as a false prophecy given by a false prophet. It would seem reasonable to contend that no person today who would presently claim the prophetic gift could ever make claims to such an absolutely perfect record of supernatural and miraculous accuracy which is required of true biblical prophets. Indeed, a close examination would reveal an overwhelming trend to a great level of inaccuracy. If persons claiming prophetic status are evaluated on the basis of a correct understanding of the biblical data and requirements for prophets, the light Scripture sheds on such activity demonstrates that the genuine gift of prophecy has ceased.[91]

THE ARGUMENT FROM THE ANALOGY OF THE END OF OLD TESTAMENT PROPHECY

Judaism as a whole in the time of Jesus held that prophecy had ceased since the time of Malachi. Though there were claims to prophetic activity (as in, e.g., the Essene community of Qumran), such claims need to be distinguished from genuine prophecy in terms of canonical recognition and general Jewish acceptance. Early Christians also knew the opinion of Judaism on this issue. If they viewed Old Testament prophecy as having ended, then it is reasonable that they also entertained the same possibility for New Testament prophecy.

Grudem attempts to escape this conclusion by his definitional bifurcation of the gift. He distinguishes between canonical revelation of the apostles and an alleged form of edifying prophecy in 1 Corinthians 12–14. He contends that because such prophets "mistakenly" misunderstood the nature of the prophetic gift as speaking the "actual words of God," which was reserved for apostolic prophets, they were eventually rejected by the church.[92] However, Grudem's dichotomizing here is highly tenuous. Such distinctions in prophetic authority have been shown to be unsound. Contrary to Grudem, church history reveals that a rise of false prophecy led to the outright rejection of those claiming the prophetic gift, as especially evidenced in the church's decisive repudiation of Montanism. The first-century church and postapostolic church applied Old Testament standards to judge New Testament prophets and prophecy. Hence in light of the analogy of the end of Old Testament prophecy, the church increasingly emphasized the close of the New Testament canon as that canon was recognized.

Conclusion

The evidence demands the view that the New Testament prophetic gift ceased its operation very early in the history of the church. Furthermore, although no one single argument alone demonstrates this, the aggregate weight of the total evidence decisively points to this conclusion. When claims to prophetic activity today (and indeed throughout church history) are compared to the biblical record, woeful inaccuracy and inadequacy of such practices are evidenced. If the data from Scripture regarding the nature and practice of the biblical gift of prophecy and the testimony of church history are used as the standard to judge claims of the present possession of the gift of prophecy, the Vineyard movement's practice of prophecy and the prophetic practices of "charismatic" groups as a whole show the need for the body of Christ to reject soundly such claims. It is of paramount importance to make a diligent, careful scrutiny of the scriptural evidence regarding such activities. Only by such a close examination can the body of Christ guard against serious doctrinal error and misunderstanding which can and does result from such concepts of "mistaken" prophecy. The sincerity of those claiming the prophetic gift today is not called into question by this series. However, the support for such claims is what is called into serious doubt and is completely rejected. When such an examination is conducted, contemporary claims are rendered entirely suspect.

Christ's warning to His church must be heeded: "Beware of the false prophets . . . You will know them by their fruits" (Matt. 7:15–16a; cf. 24:11, 24; Mark 13:22; Acts 20:28–31). While the cessationist camp arguably may have "survived" the tongues issue of previous years, this Vineyard and charismatic concept of a form of "mistaken" or fallible prophets and prophecy that is sweeping across traditional lines has the potential of doing untold harm to God's people (Jude 3).

CHAPTER 14

The New Age Movement

Norman L. Geisler

Background: A Shift in World Views

On Mars Hill the Apostle Paul faced the Epicureans and the Stoics (Acts 17:18). The Epicureans were the atheists of the day and the Stoics were the pantheists. Today Christianity again stands between the materialist and the mystic. Present-day "Epicureans" are secular humanists, and contemporary "Stoics" are proponents of what has come to be known as the New Age movement.

Western Society is experiencing an ideological shift from an atheistic to a pantheistic orientation. The basic difference between these two views is that atheists claim there is no God at all, but pantheists say God is all and all is God. Atheistic materialists believe all is matter, but mystics hold that all is mind.

The shift from secular humanism[1] to the New Age pantheism has occurred gradually over the past few decades. It has been a relatively smooth transition because of the commonalities of these two world views. Both atheism and pantheism hold in common a basic naturalistic approach to the world. (1) Both deny an absolute distinction between Creator and creation. Both deny there is any God beyond the universe. (2) Both deny that a God supernaturally intervenes in the universe (by miracles).[2] (3) And in the final analysis both believe that man is God (or Ultimate), though not all atheists admit this.

Western atheism and Eastern pantheism also have a common enemy. They are both diametrically opposed to Judeo-Christian theism. As Alice Bailey clearly declared, New Agers are committed to "The Gradual Dissolution of Orthodox Judaism."[3] Benjamin Creme is just as emphatically anti-Christian. "To my way of thinking," he says, "the Christian Churches have released into the world a view of the Christ which is impossible for modern people to accept: as the one and only Son of God, sacrificed by a loving Father to save us from the results of our sins—a blood sacrifice, straight out of the old Jewish dispensation."[4]

Other New Age sources are equally emphatic in their rejection of biblical theism. Pantheism does not reject a God in nature. "It only refuses to accept any of the gods of the so-called monotheistic religions [such as Judaism and Christianity], gods created by man in his own image and likeness, a blasphemous and sorry caricature of the ever unknowable."[5]

The shift from the Old Age humanism to New Age pantheism is manifest in numerous ways in today's culture. First, there is the growth in pantheistic religions and cults. Along with Christian Science, Unity, Bahai, and Scientology, the growth in "guruism" in the West has been phenomenal. Transcendental meditation, yoga, Hare Krishna, the Church Universal and Triumphant, and the Unification Church are only a few of the more popular cultic manifestations of New Age thought. Along with these are dozens of space cults and the more popular religion of the Force.[6]

Second, New Age thought permeates the media. Many of the most popular movies of the past decade are pantheistic, including "Star Wars," "The Empire Strikes Back," "Return of the Jedi," "Poltergeist," "The Exorcist," "Raiders of the Lost Ark," "Indiana Jones and the Temple of Doom," "ET," "Close Encounters," and "The Dark Crystal" (by Jim Henson, a fairy tale of pantheism). Television too has experienced more than its share of occult, magic, and other Eastern influences, from "I Dream of Jeannie" to "Bewitched." Even children's cartoons feature "He Man," "Masters of the Universe," and numerous magical manifestations of Eastern mysticism. And children's comics are literally filled with occult manifestations of New Age thought.

Third, much of pop pantheism was generated by the Beatles when they embraced the Maharashi. George Harrison expressed this in "My Sweet Lord," a song of praise to Krishna. This same trend continues unabated to date and has even manifested itself in outright satanic lyrics in some hard rock songs.

Fourth, pantheistic influence surfaced in the public schools through the teaching of transcendental meditation (popularly known as TM). Despite the fact that they were found by the courts to be religious in nature, TM and other forms of yoga, meditation, imaginary guides, and exploration of "inner space" and "confluent education"[7] continue in public schools. Likewise the human potential movement and pantheistic forms of positive thinking methods are frequently taught in schools.

Fifth, the broader culture evidences numerous influences of pantheistic thought from EST (now FORUM) business seminars to holistic health fads (usually vegetarian), relaxation techniques, biofeedback, and biorhythms. The popularity of horoscopes and the supranormal are also indications of New Age thought. The increased belief in reincarnation is an amazing evidence of the turn to the East. A Gallup poll in 1982 showed that nearly one-fourth of all Americans believe in reincarnation, with 30 percent of college students believing it.[8] And the most important fiction writer of the New Age is the bestselling author Carlos Castenada, who wrote *The Teachings of Don Juan, Tales of Power, The Ring of Power*, and others.

Basic Principles of the New Age Movement

Unlike most religious movements the various New Age religions have no central headquarters or organization.[9] However, they do have a commonality of core beliefs and goals, and a common consciousness.

DEFINITION OF NEW AGE RELIGIONS

Various terms have been used to describe this rise of pantheistic thought in the West. It has been called the Aquarian Conspiracy, New Consciousness, New Orientalism, Cosmic Humanism, Cosmic Consciousness, Mystical Humanism, Human Potential movement, and Holistic Health movement. But the umbrellalike term that encompasses them all is the New Age movement.

As a working definition, the New Age movement is a broad coalition of various networking[10] organizations that (a) believe in a new world religion (pantheism), (b) are working for a new world order, and (c) expect a New Age Christ. Of course not all who participate in the New Age movement are necessarily conscious of all these aspects.

NEW AGE JARGON AND SYMBOLS

Words common to New Age thought include awakening, centering, consciousness, cosmic energy, force, global village, holistic, human potential, initiation, interdependent, network, planetary vision, rebirth, spaceship earth, synergistic, transcendent, transformational, transpersonal, and unity.

Of course New Age belief has no franchise on these words. Not everyone who uses these words is necessarily buying into New Age pantheism. All meaning is discovered by context and usage.

A number of symbols, some old and some new, have been adopted by the New Age including the rainbow, pyramid, triangle, eye in a triangle, unicorn, pegasus, concentric circles, rays of light, swastika, yin-yang, goathead on a pentagram, and even the numerals 666 worked into art. But here again, not all who use some of these symbols belong to the New Age movement. After all the rainbow was set up by God as a sign of His promise, and no New Ager should rob a Christian of its true significance.

NEW AGE PRAYER

The New Age movement has a prayer known as "The Great Invocation," which has been translated into over 50 languages. It is often found as a book marker in New Age literature. According to George Trevelyan, leader of the New Age movement in England, "it expresses truths common to all major religions, and is now being used across the world by people of many differing faiths and creeds. It is a prayer which focuses the call for help from man to the Higher Worlds."[11] It reads as follows:

> From the point of Light
>   within the Mind of God
> Let light stream forth into
>   the minds of men.
> Let Light descend on Earth.
>
> From the point of Love
>   within the Heart of God
> Let love stream forth into
>   the hearts of men.
> May Christ return to Earth.
>
> From the center where the
>   Will of God is known
> Let purpose guide the little
>   wills of men—
> The purpose which the
>   Masters know and serve.

> From the center which we
>   call the race of men
> Let the Plan of Love and
>   Light work out.
> And may it seal the door
>   where Evil dwells
> Let Light and Love and
>   Power restore the Plan on Earth.

Since most of the words seems "innocent" enough, the prayer needs some explaining. To the author(s) of this prayer, "God" is a pantheistic God, not a theistic one. "Love" is not a volitional act of compassion by a person but is an impersonal cosmic energy that unifies everything. "Christ" refers not to Jesus Christ but to the so-called universal "Christ spirit," which they believe has dwelt in different great religious leaders including Buddha, Jesus, and other gurus. "Masters" refer to occult leaders who give revelations. "The plan" is the occult plan whereby a new world order is to be established by the cooperative participation of the masses in occult powers.

NEW AGE "HOLY BOOKS" AND FUNDAMENTAL TEACHINGS

Like most religious movements the New Age has books with "revelations" of New Age religious thought. Some of the more important ones are these: *Isis Unveiled*, by Helena P. Blavatsky (1877); *Oahspe*, by Newbrough (1882); *The Secret Doctrines*, by Helena P. Blavatsky (1888); *The Aquarian Gospel of Jesus the Christ*,[12] by Levi Dowling (1907); *The Urantia Book*, by Bill Sadler (1955); *Revelation: The Birth of a New Age*, by David Spangler (1976); and *Messages from Maitreya the Christ*, by Benjamin Creme (1980).

The last two writers have written many books that supposedly present revelations, prophecies, and teachings of the New Age.[13] Creme for example claims to receive telepathic messages from "the Christ." David Spangler claims that the revelations now being received by New Agers like himself are every bit as important as what were given to Jesus.

There are several summaries of New Age "fundamentals" by their own writers. Blavatsky, the famous Russian mystic and foremother of the New Age movement, listed three basic beliefs or "secret doctrines": impersonal, eternal God; eternal cycles of nature; and man's identity with God and reincarnation.[14]

The English follower of Blavatsky, Alice Bailey, summarized New Age teaching in four beliefs: the fact of [pantheistic] God, man's relationship to God, the fact of immortality and of eternal persistence, and the continuity of revelation and the divine approaches.[15]

Benjamin Creme, the self-appointed "John the Baptist" of the New Age Christ, lists four fundamental teachings of New Age religion: God's [pantheistic] existence, man's immortality, continuing revelations from messengers, and man's ability to evolve into Godhood.[16]

In an excellent book evaluating the New Age movement, Groothuis lists six basic beliefs: all is one, all is God, humanity is God, change in consciousness, all religions are one, and cosmic evolutionary optimism.[17] At least 14 doctrines are typical of New Age religions. While not all New Age groups hold all these beliefs, most groups embrace most of them. And all groups are characterized by the pantheistic perspective reflected in them. These beliefs are: (1) an impersonal god (force), (2) an eternal universe, (3) an illusory nature of matter, (4) a cyclical nature of life, (5) the necessity of reincarnations, (6) the evolution of man into Godhood, (7) continuing revelations from beings beyond the world, (8) the identity of man with God, (9) the need for meditation (or other consciousness-changing techniques), (10) occult practices (astrology, mediums, etc.), (11) vegetarianism and holistic health, (12) pacifism (or anti-war activities), (13) one world (global) order, and (14) syncretism (unity of all religions).

Some Leaders of the New Age Movement

The New Age movement has many dimensions. Its ancient pantheistic roots go back to Hindu and Greek thought. The modern Western roots reach into the last century.

MODERN SOURCES

The Russian mystic, occultist, and cofounder of theosophy, Helena Petrova Blavatsky, is the grandmother of the New Age movement. She is the author of *Isis Unveiled* (1877) and *The Secret Doctrines* (1888). These books are mystical "Bibles" of New Age thought.

Alice B. Bailey (d. 1949) was an English mystic who received telepathic communications from Tibetan occult master Djwhal Khul (known as D.K.) for 30 years about "The Plan" for a new world order. She is the author of numerous works, including *Letters on Occult Meditation* (1922), *Discipleship in the New Age* (1944), *The Reappearance of Christ* (1948), and *The Externalisation of the* [occult] *Hierarchy* (1957). Bailey contributed much of the vocabulary to the New Age movement.

CONTEMPORARY SPOKESPERSONS

General presentation. Marilyn Ferguson's book *The Aquarian Conspiracy* (1980) is one of the best overall popular presentations of New Age thought.

Religious dimension. David Spangler is one of the foremost writers of New Age religious belief. His main works include *Revelation: The Birth of a New Age* (1976) and *Reflections on the Christ* (1978). Benjamin Creme's works fit into this category as well. He wrote *The Reappearance of the Christ* (1980) and *Messages from Maitreya the Christ* (1980). Also George Trevelyan's books, *A Vision of the Aquarian Age* (1977) and *Operation Redemption* (1981), have been quite influential.

Political dimension. Two names stand out here: Mark Satin, *New Age Politics: Healing Self and Society* (1979), and Robert Muller, *New Genesis: Shaping a Global Spirituality* (1982).

Scientific dimension. In the area of the new physics, *The Tao of Physics*, by Fitjof Capra, is a notable New Age work, as are David Bohm's *Quantum Theory* and *Wholeness and the Implicate Order.* In the area of cosmology, Paul Davies's books, *God and the New Physics* and *Superforce*, are a modern pantheistic explanation of origins.

Psychological dimension. Abraham Maslow's work, *The Farthest Reaches of Human Nature* (1971), and *Religions, Values, and Peak Experiences* (1980), are part of the New Age phenomena. Other psychologists, such as Carl Jung, Carl Rogers, and Rollo May, have New Age themes. Barbara Brown has produced a New Age anthropology in her book *Supermind* (1983).

Health and dietary dimensions. Viktoras Kulvinskas produced *The New Age Directory of Holistic Health Guide* (1981). There is also *Survival into the 21st Century: Planetary Healer's Manual* (1925), and Leslie Kaslof's *Wholistic Dimensions in Healing* (1978).

Historical and cultural dimensions. Two New Age historians and cultural apologists stand out: Theodore Roszak, *Where the Wasteland Ends* (1972), and *Unfinished Animal* (1977), and William Irwin Thompson, *From Nation to Emanation* (1982).

There are endless other New Age groups, including communes, camping programs, music, schools, even New Age businessmen's organizations and centers (like Findhorn Community, Scotland). There are ecology groups, political action organizations, lobbying groups (such as New Directions) and even New Age publishing houses (such as Lucis Publishing Company, formerly Lucifer Publishing Company). A complete list of these groups is included toward the back of Mark Satin's book, *New Age Politics.*

NEW AGE MAGAZINES AND JOURNALS

Among the numerous publications with New Age themes the following should be mentioned: *East-West Journal, Yoga Journal, New Age, New Realities,* and *Whole Life Times.* Of course New Age articles can be found in the magazines of most of the pantheistic religions, including Buddhism, Hinduism, Christian Science, Unity, Scientology, and others. New Age articles even appear in *Science Digest* and other mainline magazines.

New Age Doctrines

A brief analysis of some New Age teachings about God, the world, man, Christ, salvation, and the future will be helpful in understanding the movement.

REVELATION

New Agers believe in social and continual revelations. In fact they believe that

> the Word of God [is] revealed in every age and dispensation. In the days of Moses it was the Pentateuch; in the days of Jesus, the Gospel; in the days of Mohammed, the Messenger of God, the Qur'an; in this day, the Bayan; and in the Dispensation of Him Whom God will make manifest, His own Book—the Book unto which all the Books of former Dispensations must needs be referred, the Book that stands among them all transcendent and supreme.[18]

That is, there is a progression of continual revelations, with the latter superseding the former.

As for the Bible, Alice Bailey adds, "Little as the orthodox Christian may care to admit it, the entire Gospel story in its four forms or presentations, contains little else except symbolic details about the Mysteries."[19]

The Hindu leader, Mahatma Gandhi, declared clearly, "I do not regard everything said in the Bible as the final word of God or exhaustive or even acceptable from the moral stand-point."[20] Of the Gospels he said,

> I may say that I do not accept everything in the Gospels as historical truth. And it must be remembered that he [Jesus] was working amongst his own people, and he said he had not come to destroy but to fulfill. I draw a great distinction between the *Sermon on the Mount* and the *Letters of Paul*. They are a graft on Christ's teaching, his own gloss apart from Christ's own experience.[21]

In short, New Agers pick and choose in the Bible as it fits their own purposes. Indeed, Levi Dowling rewrote the Gospels to make Christ into a pantheistic occult magician who believed in reincarnation.[22]

Contemporary New Age writers speak of "revelation," "inspiration," "overshadowing," and "visions." Creme described his telepathic communications this way:

> It descends on me and comes down as far as the solar plexus and a kind of cone is formed, like that, in light. There is an emotional outflow as well. It is the mental overshadowing which produces the rapport so that I can hear, inwardly, the words. The astral overshadowing allows what is called the True Spirit of Christ, the energy of the Cosmic Christ, to flow out to the audience and through the audience to the world. . . . I am aware of His Presence, I can sense part of His mind in my mind. It is difficult to describe, but it is there.[23]

Likewise, Spangler tells of receiving his revelations as follows:

> I found that my consciousness came into contact with a force or a presence. It could not be accurately described as a being but definitely as a point of relation, an error of sorts. This resulted in six statements of vision, six communications, which were put out in little booklets from Findhorn and which inspired a number of questions. In an attempt to answer the questions I ended up writing the book called, *Revelation: The Birth of a New Age*.[24]

In this book Spangler said,

> When I sat down to write, I envisioned a publication of about twenty to thirty pages. I had no intention of writing a book. However, as I began, it was as if I were overlighted by another aspect of this presence of Limitless Love and Truth. Insights which I had gained over the years through my

> communions with higher levels, new information, and a deeper
> identification with some of the processes, behind that presence all came
> together in a synthesis of inspiration, and I found myself writing non-
> stop for several days.[25]

These "revelations" are continual. For, as Bailey put it, "Never
has Deity left Itself at any time without witness. Never has man
demanded light that the light has not been forthcoming. Never
has there been a time, cycle or world period when there was not
the giving out of teaching and spiritual help which human need
demanded."[26]

Since revelations from the occult Masters are not infallible
and are even contingent on human cooperation, their prophecies
are not infallible. Indeed, they often conflict. In spite of this,
some claim a unique role for their "revelations." Spangler, for
example, claims:

> No other revelation to equal it has been offered to humanity, but all
> revelations of the past have led up to it. Jesus gave the great bridge through
> proclaiming our kinship with God, our sonship with him. Buddha gave the
> great bridge in enabling us to find the balance of our own being so that the
> energies we receive are expressed in harmony with the whole. Through
> knowing wisdom and through knowing love we now should be at a point,
> and we are at a point, where God can reasonably say to us, "All right, I
> have given you the keys. I have given you the tools. Now build with me."[27]

GOD

The New Age view of God is pantheistic. God is all and all is
God. God is an impersonal force or energy. The most popular
presentation of such a God is in George Lucas's "Star Wars"
movie series. Lucas wrote,

> When you are born, you have an energy field around you. You could call
> it an aura. An archaic description would be a halo. . . . When you die,
> your energy field joins all other energy fields in the universe, and while
> you're still living that larger energy field is sympathetic to your own
> energy field.[28]

Or as Creme put it, "God is the sum total of all that exists in the
whole of the manifested and unmanifested universe."[29] God is
"Limitless Love."[30] By love some New Agers mean "a great
cosmic energy" that streams from the center of the universe.[31]

But yet God, according to New Agers, is literally indefin-
able.[32] He is beyond all thought and speech,[33] and is literally
"unspeakable, incomparable, beyond description . . . what is
that? It is impossible to say!"[34]

Thus the pantheistic God is not a definite person but a presence that transcends all individual beings. As Spangler claimed, "Am I God? Am I a Christ? Am I a Being come to you from the dwelling places of the Infinite? I am all these things, yet more."[35] What is more than God? In Spangler's words, it is a "presence" that transcends all concepts of God, an infinite reality.[36] Thus "that central Reality can be called by any name that man may choose according to his mental or emotional bent, racial tradition and heritage, for it cannot be defined or conditioned by names."[37] Indeed God is called both good and evil. He has a "light side" and a "dark side."[38]

Spangler even went so far as to say that the ultimate force in the universe has two sides—the "Christ" side and the "Lucifer" side.[38]

> Christ is the same force as Lucifer but moving in seemingly the opposite direction. Lucifer moves in to create the light within through the pressure of experience. Christ moves out to release that light, that wisdom, that love into creation so what has been forged in the furnace of creation can become a light unto the world and not simply stagnate within the being.[39]

JESUS CHRIST

The New Age view of Jesus Christ involves a separation of the human Jesus from the divine Christ spirit (or office), which New Agers believe dwelt in Him and other great religious teachers. According to Creme, "Christ" said, "I am your Friend and Brother, not a God."[40] Again, "the Christ is not God."[41] When a woman knelt to worship Jesus, He supposedly replied, "Good woman, stay; take heed to what you do; you may not worship man; this is idolatry."[42]

Jesus is divine "in exactly the sense that we are divine."[43] That is, "He is Divine, having perfected Himself and manifested the Divinity potential in each of us."[44] For according to some New Agers, "Christ was the most advanced human ever to walk on this planet."[45] But this same Christ spirit dwelt in "Hercules, Hermes, Rama, Mithra . . . Krishna, Buddha, and the Christ." All these were "perfect men in their time, all sons of men who become Sons of God, for having revealed their innate Divinity."[46] So, as Creme admits, "in the esoteric [occult] tradition the Christ is not the name of an individual but of an office in the Hierarchy" (of occult masters). That is, Christ is a master occult magician who, according to Dowling, solved "the problem of the ages" by showing that "human flesh can be transmitted into flesh divine."[47]

Actually many pantheists believe that Jesus did not die.[48] As Dowling affirms, "Jesus did not sleep within the tomb."[49] He was alive, though unmanifest. In His resurrection He simply transmuted from "carnal flesh and blood to flesh of God."[50] Jesus took on a body of a "higher tone," that is, a spiritual one.[51] Even this is not unique, for the pantheistic Christ said, "What I have done, all men will do; and what I am, all men will be."[52] Occultists relate all this to degrees of initiation. Jesus was a third-degree "initiate" when He entered the world. He became a fourth-degree "initiate" at His crucifixion and a fifth-degree "initiate" at the resurrection. The same process is open to all men.

MAN

According to New Age thinkers man is basically a spiritual being, not a material one. That is, he is "energy." "Man is a thought of God; all thoughts of God are infinite; they are not measured by time; for things that are concerned with time begin and end."[53] Man is a soul force. "It is a subatomic force, the intelligent energy that organizes life. It is . . . everywhere—[it] is that [which] we call 'God.'"[54]

Man is the "Breath made flesh."[55] "The spiritual being, Man, descended from a subtler plane to assume a body, the necessary sheath in which to live amid earth vibrations."[56] But his "body" is not real. "It is a manifest; is the result of force; it is but naught; is an illusion, nothing more."[57]

Man is basically spirit, and he is essentially good. As Shirley MacLaine put it, "mankind and life, is basically good."[58] Thus "we ascend until we reach the pinnacle of that which life is spent to build—the Temple of Perfected Man."[59] For "at the Transfiguration Christ revealed the glory which is innate in all men."[60] Thus Dowling's Jesus said, "What I can do all men can do. Go preach the gospel of the omnipotence of Man."[61]

Since man is infinite and omnipotent, his main task is to discover his own divinity. As one writer stated, "One of the major teachings of Christ [is] the fact of God immanent, immanent in all creation, in mankind and all creation, that there is nothing else but God, that we are all part of a great Being."[62] Marilyn Ferguson illustrates this as she vividly describes the story of a man watching his sister drink milk: "All of a sudden I saw that she was God and the milk was God. I mean, all she was doing was pouring God into God."[63]

A New Age "Christ" (known as Lord Maitreya) supposedly gave this message: "My purpose is to show man that he need fear no more, that all of Light and Truth rests within his heart, that when this simple fact is known man will become God."[64] So "man is an emerging God and thus requires the formation of modes of loving which will allow this God to flourish."[65] Accordingly "the tragedy of the human race was that we had forgotten we were each Divine."[66]

But if man is God, to whom does man pray? Creme gives a forthright answer:

> One doesn't pray to oneself, one prays to the God within. The thing is to learn to invoke that energy which is the energy of God. Prayer and worship as we know it today will gradually die out and men will be trained to invoke the power of Deity. This is one reason why the Great Invocation was given out—to enable us to learn the technique of invocation.[67]

Actually New Agers believe in "prayer" not as intercession but as meditation. They believe in consciousness-altering techniques such as yoga, hypnotism, biofeedback, peak experiences, psychotherapies, and psychotechnologies.[68] The goal of prayer is "attunement" or "at-one-ment" with God. It is the modern version of Plotinus's mystical union with God.[69]

Not only is man infinite, omnipotent, and immaterial, he is also essentially immortal, according to New Age thinkers. "Man cannot die; the spirit is one with God, and while God lives man cannot die."[70] So eventually "man will come to know himself as the Divine Being he is."[71]

SIN AND SALVATION

New Age thought has no place for sin. Man is basically good. "Evil" is not moral guilt but spiritual imbalance. As Spangler put it, "Man holds the ultimate responsibility for the redemption of what we have come to call 'evil energies,' which are simply energies that have been used out of timing or out of place, or not suited to the needs of evolution."[72]

In *The Aquarian Gospel* one reads that "evil is the inharmonious blending of color, tones, or forms of good."[73] "Evil" exists only on the lower level. As the Zen masters claim, for a man of "character," "the notions of right and wrong and the praise and blame of others do not disturb him."[74] New Ager Mark Satin agrees, saying, "In a spiritual state, morality is impossible."[75] So for New Agers, as "for Hindu thought there is no problem of

Evil."[76] As Mary Baker Eddy claimed, evil is an illusion, an error of mortal mind.[77]

Belief in good and bad is a form of dualism rejected by the monistic views of New Agers. New Age ethics "is not based on . . . dualistic concepts of 'good' or 'bad.'"[78] New Age religion "does not share the Western view that there is a moral law, enjoined by God or by nature, which it is man's duty to obey."[79]

This is not to say New Agers are without moral values, but only that the ones they have are *chosen* by man, not *revealed* by God. As Satin put it, "We recognize that we're responsible for choosing everything—our parents, our personalities, everything. We even experience events as if we've created or willed them in some way."[80]

Rather than believing in opposites like good and evil, right and wrong, New Age proponents hold to one all-embracing cosmic force called "love." This "love" is "a totally impersonal but *all inclusive* cohesive, binding force which draws all men and all things together, and holds them together. It is the energy which makes humanity One."[81]

Since there is no sin (such as breaking of moral law), there is no need for a payment for sin. Thus New Agers do not believe Christ died for man's sin. In fact the "Jesus" of *The Aquarian Gospel* opposed the concept of a Passover lamb. Dowling records these words:

> I am disturbed about this service of the paschal feast. I thought the temple was the house of God where love and kindness dwell. Do you not hear the bleating of those lambs, the pleading of those doves that men are killing over there? Do you not smell that awful stench that comes from burning flesh? Can man be kind and just, and still be filled with cruelty? A God that takes delight in sacrifice, in blood and burning flesh, is not my Father-God. I want to find a God of love, and you, my master, you are wise, and surely you can tell me where to find the God of love.[82]

Creme rejects orthodox Christianity because it presents "a picture of the Christ impossible for the majority of thinking people today to accept—as the One and Only Son of God, sacrificed by His Loving Father to save Humanity from the results of its sins; as a Blood Sacrifice straight out of the old and outworn Jewish Dispensation."[83] Bailey adds, "It is impossible to believe that they [New Agers] are interested in the views of the Fundamentalists or in the theories of the theologians upon the Virgin Birth, the Vicarious Atonement."[84]

How then can a person be saved? According to New Age

religions, "salvation" is not redemption from sin; it is reunifica-
tion with God. It is overcoming the inexorable law of karma,
which condemns one to suffer in the next life for things done in
this one. As Shirley MacLaine, movie star and "pop" theologian
of the New Age, stated, "If you are good and faithful in your
struggle in this life, the next one will be easier."[85] So in Spangler's
words, "man is his own Satan just as man is his own salvation."[86] This salvation is achieved by some form of consciousness changing or meditation by which one overcomes duality,
multiplicity, and inharmony and becomes one with the One
(God).[87] This then is the "attunement" or at-one-ment that constitutes New Age "salvation."

According to the New Age "prophet," David Spangler, it is
Lucifer who helps bring unity or wholeness into one's life. "Lucifer works within each of us to bring us to wholeness, as we
move into a new age, which is the age of man's wholeness, each
of us in some way is brought to that point which I term the
Luciferic initiation."[88] Spangler further says,

> Lucifer, like Christ, stands at the door of man's consciousness and knocks.
> If man says, "Go away because I do not like what you represent, I am
> afraid of you," Lucifer will play tricks on that fellow. If man says,
> "Come in, and I will give to you the treat of my love and understanding
> and I will uplift you in the light and presence of the Christ, my outflow,"
> the Lucifer becomes something else again. He becomes the being who
> carries that great treat, the ultimate treat, the light of wisdom.[89]

Lucifer guides all men through a series of experiences geared to
awaken in them a sense or awareness of their inner divinity. This
guidance continues until a "new light" comes into being (within them)
that is capable of manifesting the "One Light" (God). After this light
has come into being, the Christ then works to draw that same light
out of each man so that there will be an outward manifestation of the
newly recognized inner divinity. As Spangler explains,

> Lucifer moves in to create the light within through the pressure of
> experience. Christ moves out to release that light, that wisdom, that
> love into creation so what has been forged in the furnace of creation
> can become light unto the world and not simply stagnate within the
> being."[90]

Thus Lucifer and the Christ are seen as partners in this endeavor.
It is because of Lucifer's benevolent role that Spangler calls him
"an agent of God's love."[91]

The goal of the whole process is "Luciferic Initiation," which refers to a transformation of consciousness. This consciousness is one that recognizes that all past experiences were part of a plan (led by Lucifer) that ultimately led to the recognition and manifestation of one's inner divinity. This is largely what esoteric salvation is. In light of this it is wrong to fear and reject Lucifer. For the person with this type of attitude Lucifer "plays tricks."

Eventually, according to New Age belief, everyone will be saved. "The Exponents and the Representatives of all the world faiths are there waiting—under His [the Christ's] guidance—to reveal to all those who today struggle in the maelstrom of world affairs, and who seek to solve the world crisis, that *they are not alone.* God Transcendent is working through the Christ and the spiritual Hierarchy to bring relief."[92] Or, as Robert Short sees it, the "gospel" of the New Age film series "Star Wars" declares that "eventually everyone—even Darth Vader and the Devil— will thankfully serve Christ and worship him."[93]

There are many ways to salvation, according to New Agers. "There are a number of paths that can help us return to that experience of unity, that can help us feel at home again in the spiritual and religious states of consciousness. In *Unfinished Animal* Theodore Roszak lists over 150 such paths![94] In fact New Agers believe there is unity in all religions. This is why Baha'ism is so popular among New Agers.

> God works in many ways, through many faiths and religious agencies; this is one reason for the elimination of non-essential doctrines. By the emphasizing of the essential doctrines and in their union will the fullness of truth be revealed. This, the new world religion will do and its implementation will proceed apace, after the reappearance of Christ.[95]

FUTURE THINGS

Most New Agers are working for a new world order and unity-in-diversity of all cultures, religions, and countries. Some (e.g., Spangler and Trevelyan) have only a general eschatology, in which Christ "returns" in all humanity. Others have a rather clearly defined doctrine of last things. Bailey gives three basic assumptions of New Age belief about the future.

1. That the reappearance of the Christ is inevitable and assured.
2. That He is today and has been actively working—through the medium of the spiritual Hierarchy of our planet, of which He is the Head—for the welfare of humanity.

3. That certain teachings will be given and certain energies
    will be released by Him in the routine of His work and
    coming.[96]

Creme claims that "the Christ" said He would return in June
1945. This "Christ" laid down four conditions:

[1]   That a measure of peace should be restored in the world;
[2]   That the principle of Sharing should be in process of
controlling economic affairs;
[3]   That the energy of goodwill should be manifesting, and
leading to the implementation of right human relationships;
[4]   That the political and religious organizations throughout
the world should be releasing their followers from authoritarian supervision
over their beliefs and thinking.[97]

Actually the pantheistic "Christ" was not to return but only to
reappear[98] since, according to Creme, "the Christ" reappeared
on July 8, 1977.

He came into the world by aeroplane and so fulfilled the prophecy of
"coming in the clouds." On July 8, 1977, He descended from the
Himalayas into the Indian sub-continent and went to one of the chief
cities there. He had an acclimatization period between July 8th and 18th,
and then on July 19th, entered a certain modern country by aeroplane. He
is now an ordinary man in the world—an extraordinary, ordinary man.[99]

Following this a full-page ad appeared in major newspapers
around the world with the headline, "The Christ Is Now Here."
Creme believes that "one day soon, men and women all over
the world will gather round their radio and television sets to hear
and see the Christ: to see His face, and to hear His words drop-
ping silently into their minds—in their own language."[100] "In
this way they will know that He is truly the Christ, the World
Teacher. . . . Also in this way, the Christ will demonstrate the
future ability of the race as a whole to communicate mentally,
telepathically, over vast distances and at will."[101] Bailey was
frank to admit that "the Christ Who will return will not be like
the Christ Who (apparently) departed."[102]

Furthermore, "The Christ is not God. When I say, 'coming of
Christ,' I don't mean the coming of God, I mean the coming of a
divine man, a man who has manifested His divinity by the same
process that we are going through—the incarnational process,
gradually perfecting Himself."[103]

According to Creme, the present "Christ" is a reincarnation of
the Christ spirit in an occult master who has lived in the
Himalayas for the past 2,000 years.[104] Jesus (of Nazareth), on the

other hand, "now lives in a Syrian body which is some 600 years old, and has His base in Palestine."

> In the last 2,000 years [Jesus has] worked in the closest relation to the Christ, saving His time and energy where possible, and has special work to do with the Christian churches. He is one of the Masters who will very shortly return to outer work in the world, taking over the Throne of St. Peter, in Rome. He will seek to transform the Christian Churches, in so far as they are flexible enough to respond correctly to the new reality which the return of the Christ and the Masters will create.[105]

This New Age occult "Christ" will soon manifest Himself "creating and vitalizing the new world religion."[106] He "will emphasize our inner connectedness as souls, identical with the one soul [God]."[107] This New Age "Christ" will set up a new world order.[108] This will "involve the reconstruction of the world financial and economic order." By his "presence in the world, He seeks to save millions from death and misery through starvation, and to release from bondage those now languishing in the prisons of the world for the 'crime' of independent thought."[109]

> World government will not be imposed on mankind but will be the result of the manifested brotherhood. The sharing and the cooperation of all mankind, the redistribution of the produce of the world, will result in world government. Any attempt to achieve or impose world government without the acceptance of sharing is doomed to failure.[110]

Of course the "Christ's" manifestation is conditional.[111] It depends on human effort to bring about the "kingdom." For "the Christ and the Masters are not going to do anything but show the way. They are not going to build the new age. We have to build it. We have still to make the inner changes. We have still to make the decisions of accepting the Plan."[112] As Spangler says, we are "co-creators" of the New Age. In short, just as secular humanism is a form of postmillennial atheism, the New Age movement is an expression of postmillennial pantheism.

Comparison and Contrasts

One reason professing Christians are being deceived by New Age beliefs is that they look mainly at the *similarities* between New Age and Christian beliefs. These are numerous: both believe in God, Christ, prayer, life after death, and many moral values. They also use terms such as revelation, cross, redemption, resurrection, and second coming.

However, like counterfeit currency, counterfeit religions are not detected by noting their similarities to the genuine, but by taking note of their *differences*. After all, a counterfeit $10 bill has many similarities to a real one. Hence it behooves believers to "test the spirits" (1 John 4:1), knowing that many false prophets have gone out into the world.

The following chart contrasts major teachings of biblical Christianity and New Age pantheism.

	Biblical Christianity	*New Age Pantheism*
God	Father	Force
	Personal	Impersonal
	Only Good	Good and Evil
	Created all things	Is all things
Man	Made like God	Is God
	Is evil	Is good
	Spirit/ Body	Spirit only
	Resurrection	Reincarnation
Jesus Christ	Same Person	Different persons ("Jesus" and "Christ")
	God-Man	
		God Spirit in man
	Death/resurrection	Death/reincarnation
Salvation	From moral guilt	From disharmony
	By grace	By human effort
	Victory over sin	Victory over fear
Faith	In divine power	In human potential
	Objective focus	Subjective focus
	To see God's will done	To see man's will done
Miracle	Done at God's command	Done at man's command
	Supernatural power (of the Creator)	Supranormal power (of creatures)
	Associated with good	Associated with evil

Failure to make such crucial differences led the well-known author of *The Gospel According to Peanuts*, Robert Short, to claim mistakenly that the God of the Bible and of "Star Wars" are one and the same God.[113]

Careful examination reveals that the Christian theistic view and New Age pantheistic view of God are diametrically opposed. The

The true God is not a combination of good and evil; He is absolutely perfect (Matt. 5:48); He is so holy that He cannot look approvingly on evil (Hab. 1:13). Furthermore He is not identical with all things; He created all things (Gen. 1:1; Col. 1:15–16). These contrasts show the difference between the true, living God and the false god of the New Age religions. The same kind of stark contrast exists between the God-incarnate Lord Jesus Christ of Scripture and the reincarnate occult master known as "Christ" in New Age thought.

Books Evaluating New Age Thinking

Space does not allow for a critique of pantheistic New Age thought. This is provided for, however, in the following books.

Bobgan, Martin and Diedre. *Hypnosis and the Christian.* Minneapolis: Bethany House Publishers, 1984.

Bowen, William, Jr. *Globalism—America's Demise.* Shreveport: Huntington House, 1984.

Clark, David K. *The Pantheism of Alan Watts.* Downers Grove, IL: InterVarsity Press, 1978.

Crouse, Bill. *A Primer on Occult Philosophy.* Dallas: Probe Insight Paper, 1983.

Cumbey, Constance E. *The Hidden Dangers of the Rainbow.* Shreveport: Huntington House, 1983.

_____. *A Planned Deception: The Staging of a New Age Messiah.* East Detroit, MI: Pointe Publishers, 1985.

Geisler, Norman. *False Gods of Our Time.* Eugene, OR: Harvest House Publishers, 1985.

_____, and Amano, J. Yutaka. *Religion of the Force.* Dallas, TX: Quest Publications, 1983.

_____. *The Reincarnation Sensation.* Wheaton, IL: Tyndale House Publishers, 1986.

_____, and Watkins, William. *Perspectives: Understanding and Evaluating Today's World Views.* San Bernardino, CA: Here's Life Publishers, 1984, chap. 4.

Groothuis, Douglas R. *Unmasking the New Age.* Downers Grove, IL: InterVarsity Press, 1973.

Hunt, Dave. *The Cult Explosion: An Exposé of Today's Cults and Why They Prosper.* Eugene, OR: Harvest House Publishers, 1980.

_____. *Peace, Prosperity and the Coming Holocaust.* Eugene, OR: Harvest House Publishers, 1983.

_____, and McMahon, T. A. *The Seduction of Christianity*.
Eugene, OR: Harvest House Publishers, 1985.

Johnson, David L. *A Reasoned Look at Asian Religions*.
Minneapolis: Bethany House Publishers, 1985.

Maharaj, Rabindranath R. *Escape into the Light*. Eugene, OR:
Harvest House Publishers, 1984.

Matrisciana, Caryl. *Gods of the New Age*. Eugene, OR: Harvest
House Publishers, 1985.

Raschke, Carl A. *The Interruption of Eternity: Modern Gnosticism
and the Origins of the New Religious Consciousness*. Chicago:
Nelson-Hall, 1980.

Reisser, Paul C. *The Holistic Healers*. Downers Grove, IL:
InterVarsity Press, 1983.

Rhodes, Ronald. "An Examination and Evaluation of the New
Age Christology of David Spangler." ThD diss., Dallas
Theological Seminary, 1986.

Sire, James W. *The Universe Next Door*. Downers Grove, IL:
InterVarsity Press, 1976.

Vitz, Paul. *Psychology as Religion*. Grand Rapids: Wm. B.
Eerdmans Publishing Co., 1977.

Wilson, Clifford, and Weldon, John. *Occult Shock and Psychic
Forces*. San Diego: Master Books, 1980.

In addition to articles in the *SCP* [Spiritual Counterfeits Project] *Journal* (e.g., August 1978 and Winter 1981–82), articles critiquing New Age thought appear regularly in *Forward* (San Juan Capistrano, CA) and *Cornerstone* magazine (Chicago), and from time to time in other evangelical magazines such as *Christianity Today* (e.g., May 16, 1986), *Eternity* (e.g., October 1984), and *Moody Monthly* (e.g., February 1985).

A critique of the basic pantheistic world view of New Age religions is found in the author's *Perspectives: Understanding and Evaluating Today's World Views*, chapter 4. The best general evaluation of the New Age movement to date is Douglas Groothuis's work, *Unmasking the New Age*.

Chapter Notes

Chapter 1

1. C. S. Lewis, *The Abolition of Man* (New York: Macmillan, 1947) and some of his essays in *Christian Reflections*, ed. Walter Hooper (Grand Rapids: Eerdmans, 1967).
2. Lewis, *The Abolition of Man*, pp. 56–57.
3. Edward J. Carnell, *An Introduction to Christian Apologetics* (Grand Rapids: Eerdmans, 1948), pp. 316–18.
4. Henry B. Veatch, *Two Logics* (Evanston, IL: Northwestern University Press, 1969), p. 252.
5. Carnell, *An Introduction to Christian Apologetics*, p. 326.
6. Francis A. Schaeffer, *He Is There and He Is Not Silent* (Wheaton, IL: Tyndale, 1972), p. 9.
7. See Barbara Branden, *Who Is Ayn Rand?* (New York: Random, 1962), p. 162. In her philosophy of objectivism, Rand sought to replace altruism with "creative selfishness" (Charles F. Schroder, "Ayn Rand: Far Right Prophetess," *Christian Century*, December 13, 1916, p. 1943).
8. Lewis, *Christian Reflections*, pp. 69–70.
9. Joseph Fletcher, Bishop John Robinson, and others have attempted to arrive at a morality that replaces an absolute standard with the word "love." Fletcher's *Situation Ethics* (Philadelphia: Westminster, 1966) uses a number of Christian terms, but his system is far removed from biblical Christianity. The Scriptures also emphasize love, but not to the exclusion of God's moral law. Though Fletcher claims that love is the fundamental principle that should determine one's behavior, he is blatantly inconsistent in his definition of this crucial word. Sometimes it means a motive, sometimes an action, and sometimes a formal principle. He is also inconsistent in his analysis of what makes an act moral; is it the act itself, the intentions behind the act, or the consequences of the act? The three cannot be reconciled and yet Fletcher suggests each of them at one point or another. Because of this confusion about the meaning of love and the meaning of morality, situationism is of no practical use as an ethical system. It leads directly to personal preferences and ethical subjectivity. The word "love" is given no real content, and situationism offers

no workable rules for loving actions. Both ends and means are relative, and situation ethics has no basis for elevating love from a relative to an absolute plane. A system founded on relativism cannot logically appeal to an unchanging absolute.

Chapter 2

1. See Roy L. Aldrich, *Holding Fast to Grace* (Findlay, OH: Dunham, n.d.).
2. When the oneness of God's love shines through the prism of finite experience, it forms a whole spectrum of His characteristics, some of which come into conflict with others in present human experience.
3. This is the view advanced by Joseph Fletcher in his book, *Situation Ethics: The New Morality* (Philadelphia: Westminster, 1966).
4. See John Murray, *Principles of Conduct* (Grand Rapids: Eerdmans, 1957).
5. See Erwin Lutzer, *The Morality Gap* (Chicago: Moody, 1972).
6. This contradiction in John Montgomery's view was pointed out a couple of times in *Situation Ethics: True or False* (Minneapolis: 1972).
7. See Norman L. Geisler, *The Christian Ethic of Love* (Grand Rapids: Zondervan, 1973) for further elaboration.
8. For a separate treatment of each of these views see Norman L. Geisler, *Ethics: Alternatives and Issues* (Grand Rapids: Zondervan, 1971).
9. Hodge held that there is a hierarchy in God's commands (Charles Hodge, *Systematic Theology* [New York: Scribner, 1906], 3:437–38). Even some of the Ten Commandments take priority over others.
10. This does not mean that dispensational commands based on God's *will* for a given people and/or period do not change. Only commands based on God's *nature* apply to all persons in all periods of time.

Chapter 3

1. Merrill McLoughlin, "America's New Civil War," *U.S. News and World Report* (October 3, 1988), p. 24.
2. This figure is based on statistics published for Guttmacher Institute for the years 1973–1988. The figures for 1989 to present are estimates based on trends from previous years.
3. Bill Horlacher, "Abortion: What Does the Bible Say?" *Worldwide Challenge* (July 1978), p. 6.
4. Susan T. Foh, "Abortion and Women's Lib," in *Thou Shalt Not Kill*, ed. Richard L. Ganz (New Rochelle, NY: Arlington House, 1978), p. 51.

5. *New Practical Standard Dictionary*, ed. Charles Earle Funk, 1964 ed., s. v. "Abortion," p. 5.
6. John Lippis, *The Challenge to Be "Pro Life"* (Santa Barbara, CA: Santa Barbara Pro Life Education, 1978), pp. 5–7; C. Everett Koop, "A Physician Looks at Abortion," in *Thou Shalt Not Kill*, pp. 10–12.
7. "Facts about RU 486," *Life in Oregon* (June 1993), p. 3.
8. David Neff, "The Human Pesticide," *Christianity Today* (December 9, 1988), p. 17.
9. "Clinton Strikes Abortion Rulings," *The Oregonian*, January 23, 1993.
10. J. C. Willke, *Abortion: How It Is* (Cincinnati: Hayes, 1972), pp. 6–7.
11. _____, *Handbook on Abortion* (Cincinnati: Hayes, 1975), p. 83. One reason for the great range in figures reported is that the majority of abortion-caused deaths do not occur during the procedure, but only afterward due to complications.
12. Lippis, *The Challenge to Be "Pro Life,"* p. 7.
13. Ibid., p. 8. See also C. Everett Koop, "A Physician Looks at Abortion," pp. 12–18, for a full disclosure.
14. Harold O. J. Brown, *Death before Life* (Nashville: Nelson, 1977), p. 74.
15. Ibid., pp. 83–84.
16. Meredith G. Kline, "Lex Talionis and the Human Fetus," *Journal of the Evangelical Theological Society* 20 (September 1977): 193.
17. Ibid., 200–201.
18. Cf. Bruce K. Waltke, "Old Testament Texts Bearing on Abortion," *Christianity Today* (November 8, 1968), pp. 99–105; and idem, "Old Testament Texts Bearing on the Issues," in *Birth Control and the Christian*, ed. W. O. Spitzer and Carlyle L. Saylor (Wheaton, IL: Tyndale, 1969), pp. 10–11. Waltke has since conceded that the support for this position is less than conclusive.
19. Bernard S. Jackson, "The Problem of Ex. XXI:22.5 (Lex Talionis)," *Vetus Testamentum* 23 (1973): 292.
20. C. F. Keil and F. Delitzsch, "Exodus," in vol. 2: *The Pentateuch*, 3 vols., trans. James Martin, *Commentary on the Old Testament* (reprints Grand Rapids: Eerdmans, 1949), pp. 134–35.
21. Jack W. Cottrell, "Abortion and the Mosaic Law," *Christianity Today* (March 16, 1973), p. 8.
22. Umberto Cassuto, *Commentary on the Book of Exodus*, trans. Israel Abrahams (Jerusalem: Magnes, 1967), p. 275.
23. John M. Frame, "Abortion from a Biblical Perspective," in *Thou Shalt Not Kill*, p. 56
24. Brown, *Death before Life*, p. 126.

25. *Theological Word Book of the Old Testament*, ed. R. Laird Harris, Gleason L. Archer, and Bruce K. Waltke, 2 vols., s.v. "צָרַר," by T. E. McComiskey, 1:396.

26. Ronald Barclay Allen, *In Celebrating Love of Life* (Portland, OR: Western Conservative Baptist Seminary, 1977), p. 6.

27. This translation of verse 13 is provided by Allen, *Love of Life*. His accurate and forceful translation of Psalm 139 is used throughout this consideration of the psalm.

28. A. Cohen suggests that this is possibly an allusion to the veins and arteries that are woven through the body like colored threads (*The Psalms*, Soncino Books of the Bible [London: Soncino 1945]), p. 453.

29. Francis Brown, S. R. Driver, and Charles A. Briggs, *A Hebrew and English Lexicon of the Old Testament* (Oxford: Clarendon, 1967), s.v. "גֹּלֶם," p. 166.

30. *The American Heritage Dictionary of the English Language*, ed. Wilham Morris, 1969 ed., s.v. "embryo," p. 426.

31. Charles C. Ryrie, *You Mean the Bible Teaches That?* (Chicago: Moody, 1974), p. 89.

32. For a well-illustrated presentation of the week-by-week development of the womb, see Axel Ingelman-Sundberg, *A Child Is Born: The Drama of Life before Birth* (New York: Dell, 1966), pp. 11–156.

33. Bruce K. Waltke, "Reflections from the Old Testament on Abortion," *Journal of the Evangelical Theological Society* 19 (Winter 1976): 10–13.

34. *Baker's Dictionary of Theology*, ed. Everett F. Harrison, 1960 ed., s.v. "Man," by Carl F. H. Henry, p. 340.

35. H. C. Leupold, *Exposition of the Psalms* (Grand Rapids: Baker, 1959), p. 403.

36. Frame, "*Abortion from a Biblical Perspective*," pp. 50–51.

37. Lucina Cisler, "Unfinished Business: Birth Control and Women's Liberation" in *Sisterhood Is Powerful*, ed. Robin Morgan (New York: Vintage 1970), p. 299.

38. C. Everett Koop, "Deception-on-Demand," *Moody Monthly* (May 1980), p. 24.

39. Lippis, *The Challenge to Be "Pro Life,"* p. 9.

40. Koop, "Deception-on-Demand," p. 24.

41. Ibid., p. 26.

42. Ectopic pregnancy refers to the implantation of the fertilized ovum somewhere other than in the uterus. Tubal pregnancy is the most frequent of all ectopic pregnancies. This condition is usually detected by hemorrhaging and requires immediate medical attention. Major

abdominal surgery is mandatory to remove the embryo before it ruptures the fallopian tube; neglecting treatment will allow the tube to burst, resulting in uncontrollable hemorrhaging and usually the death of the mother. This surgery is not considered "abortion" for its purpose is to prevent the death of the mother, not to prevent the birth of the child. Perhaps with medical advances, physicians will eventually be able to relocate and preserve the living embryo (cf. Brown, *Death before Life*, pp. 22–23.

Chapter 4

1. Virginia Ramey Mollenkott, "Reproductive Choice: Basic to Justice for Women," *Christian Scholar's Review* 17 (March 1988): 291.
2. For greater detail and defense of the biblical case against abortion rights, see John Jefferson Davis, *Abortion and the Christian* (Phillipsburg, NJ: Presbyterian and Reformed, 1984), pp. 35–62; and Norman L. Geisler, *Christian Ethics: Options and Issues* (Grand Rapids: Baker, 1989), pp. 142–46, 148.
3. Davis, *Abortion and the Christian*, p. 40.
4. Ibid., p. 41.
5. Ibid. The references above use the verse numbers of the English translations.
6. Robert N. Wennberg, *Life in the Balance: Exploring the Abortion Controversy* (Grand Rapids: Eerdmans, 1985), pp. 60–63.
7. Ibid., p. 62.
8. Ibid., p. 63.
9. James Sire, *Scripture Twisting* (Downers Grove, IL: InterVarsity, 1980), pp. 23–30, 127–44.
10. Ibid., p. 26.
11. Mollenkott, "Reproductive Choice," pp. 288–89.
12. Ibid., p. 293.
13. In a footnote in his important article on the Old Testament and abortion, Bruce K. Waltke makes a similar observation when he writes that "it does not necessarily follow that because the law did not apply the principle of *lex talionis*, that is 'person for person,' when the fetus was aborted through fighting that therefore the fetus is less than a human being." For "in the preceding case, the judgment did not apply the principle of *lex talionis* in the case of a debatable death of a servant at the hands of his master. But it does not follow that since 'life for life' was not exacted here that therefore the slave was less than a fully human life" (Bruce K. Waltke, "Reflections from the Old Testament on Abortion," *Journal of the Evangelical Theological Society* 19 [1976]: 3). Though appearing to accept the pro-choice interpretation of the Exodus

passage, Waltke takes a strong pro-life position and denies the pro-choicer's inference that this passage somehow supports legalized abortion on demand.

14. John Warwick Montgomery, "The Christian View of the Fetus," in *Jurisprudence: A Book of Readings*, ed. John Warwick Montgomery (Strasbourg: International Scholarly Publishers, 1974), p. 585.
15. Ibid.
16. For example see Ronald E. Clements, *Exodus*, Cambridge Commentaries on the New English Bible (Cambridge: Cambridge University Press, 1972), p. 138; J. Philip Hyatt, *Exodus*, New Century Bible (London: Oliphants. 1971), p. 233; Martin Noth, *Exodus: A Commentary*, trans. J. S. Dowden (Philadelphia: Westminster, 1962), p. 181; J. Coert Rylaarsdam, "Exodus," in *The Interpreter's Bible*, ed. George Arthur Buttrick et al., 12 vols. (New York: Cokesbury-Abingdon Press, 1951–57), 1:999; and Bruce K. Waltke, "Old Testament Texts Bearing on Abortion," *Christianity Today* (November 8,1968), pp. 99–105.
17. For example see Gleason Archer, *Encyclopedia of Bible Difficulties* (Grand Rapids: Zondervan, 1982), pp. 246–49; Umberto Cassuto, *A Commentary on the Book of Exodus*, trans. Israel Abrahams (Jerusalem: Magnes, 1967), p. 275; C. F. Keil and F. Delitzsch, "The Second Book of Moses: Exodus," in *The Pentateuch*, vol. 1 of *Commentary on the Old Testament* (reprint, Grand Rapids: Eerdmans, 1980), p. 135; Meredith G. Kline, "*Lex Talionis* & the Human Fetus," *Simon Greenleaf Law Review* 5 (1985–86): 73–89; and Montgomery, "The Christian View of the Fetus," pp. 585–87.
18. Cassuto, *A Commentary on the Book of Exodus*, p. 275.
19. Archer, *Encyclopedia of Bible Difficulties*, p. 247.
20. There is a third interpretation of this verse, defended by both Davis (*Abortion and the Christian*) and Kline ("*Lex Talionis* & the Human Fetus"), two pro-life theologians. Since, however, the focus of this article is simply to call into question the so-called "pro-choice" interpretation of Exodus 21:22–25, it is not necessary at this point to discuss yet another view that undermines the pro-choice position.
21. A portion of Wennberg's work on abortion (*Life in the Balance*) was instrumental in this writer's discovery of the differing views on Exodus 21:22–25.
22. "A Pro-Choice Bible Study" (Seattle: Episcopalians for Religious Freedom, 1989).
23. Ibid.

24. Other translations read as follows: "she will then be free to conceive children" (NASB); "she will bear children" (JB); "and shall conceive seed" (KJV); "and will be able to bear children" (TEV).
25. For more detailed critiques of this argument, see Harold O. J. Brown, *Death before Birth* (Nashville: Nelson, 1977), pp. 123–24; and Davis, *Abortion and the Christian*, pp. 101–2.
26. Davis, *Abortion and the Christian*, p. 101.
27. Brown, *Death before Birth*, p. 124.
28. Geisler, *Christian Ethics: Options and Issues*, p. 145.
29. Ibid.
30. "A Pro-Choice Bible Study," n.p.
31. Ibid.
32. Ibid.
33. Ibid.
34. Ibid.
35. See this writer's four-part series, "Answering the Arguments for Abortion Rights," *Christian Research Journal* 13 (Fall 1990): 20–26; (Winter 1991): 27–32; 14 (Spring 1991): 9–13; 14 (Summer 1991): 28–33. Also see Francis J. Beckwith, "Personal Bodily Rights, Abortion, and Unplugging the Violinist," *International Philosophical Quarterly* (March 1992).
36. Michael Gorman, *Abortion and the Early Church* (Downers Grove, IL: InterVarsity, 1982); and Nigel M. de S. Cameron and Pamela F. Sims, *Abortion: The Crisis in Morals and Medicine* (Leicester: Inter-Varsity, 1986), chaps. 1 and 2.
37. Concerning the church's historical view of abortion, one study concludes: "For the whole of Christian history until appreciably after 1900, so far as we can trace it, there was virtual unanimity amongst Christians, evangelical, catholic, orthodox, that, unless at the direct command of God, it was in all cases wrong directly to take innocent human life. Abortion and infanticide were grouped together as early as the writing called the *Didache* which comes from the first century after the crucifixion. These deeds were grouped with murder in that those committing or cooperating in them were, when penitent, still excluded from Communion for ten years by early Councils. . . . The absolute war was against the deliberate taking of *innocent* life, not in the sense of sinless life, but in the sense of life which was *innocent* (not harming). . . . We may note that this strictness constituted one of the most dramatic identifiable differences between Christian morality and pagan, Greek or Roman, morality." (David Braine, *Medical Ethics and Human Life* [Aberdeen, 1982], cited in Cameron and Sims, *Abortion*, p. 29).

Chapter 5

1. *Webster's Third New International Dictionary of the English Language,* 1971 ed., s.v. "euthanasia," p. 786.
2. A further discussion of the care and counseling of dying patients can be found in J. Kerby Anderson's book, *Life, Death, and Beyond* (Grand Rapids: Zondervan, 1980).
3. Perhaps the most famous case illustrating this form of euthanasia involved Roswell Gilbert, a 76–year-old retired electronics engineer living in Fort Lauderdale, Florida. His wife Emily had Alzheimer's disease and advancing osteoporosis. He shot her two times in what he said was a mercy-killing. But he was sentenced to 25 years in prison with no chance of parole.
4. "Commission Upholds Right to Choose to Die," *Moody Monthly* (June 1983), p. 108.
5. Interview with Former Surgeon General C. Everett Koop in a "Focus on the Family" radio broadcast, aired in 1986.
6. Former President Ronald Reagan ordered the Department of Health and Human Services to act under Section 504 of the 1973 Rehabilitation Act to protect the lives of handicapped infants. The regulations issued by then Secretary Richard Schwieker were overturned in a United States District Court in 1983 and upheld by the Supreme Court in 1986.
7. Interview with Koop, "Focus on the Family" radio broadcast.
8. Yale Kamisar, "Some Non-Religious Views against Proposed Mercy Killing Legislation," *Minnesota Law Review* 22 (May 1958):1031.
9. Joni Eareckson, *Joni* (Grand Rapids: Zondervan, 1976).
10. Joni Eareckson, *A Step Further* (Grand Rapids: Zondervan, 1978).

Chapter 6

1. Tom L. Beauchamp and James F. Childress, *Principles of Biomedical Ethics,* 2d ed. (New York: Oxford University Press, 1983), pp. 93–95.
2. Stanley Hauerwas, *Suffering Presence: Theological Reflections on Medicine, the Mentally Handicapped, and the Church* (Notre Dame: University of Notre Dame Press, 1986), pp. 103–5.
3. Tom L. Beauchamp, "Suicide," in *Matters of Life and Death*, ed. Tom Regan (Philadelphia: Temple University Press, 1980), pp. 75–77.
4. Some add the qualification that death must occur fairly quickly after the action or omission. See *Life-Sustaining Technology and the Elderly* (Washington, DC: U.S. Government Printing Office, 1987), p. 150. But the time factor is extremely controversial and

an act could be suicidal even if death did not occur for some time.

5. Richard B. Brandt, "The Morality and Rationality of Suicide," reprinted in *Biomedical Ethics,* ed. Thomas A. Mappes and Jane S. Zembaty, 2d ed. (New York: McGraw-Hill, 1986), pp. 337–43. See also, Beauchamp, "Suicide," pp. 78–96.

6. Beauchamp and Childress, *Principles of Biomedical Ethics,* pp. 93–101.

7. Hauerwas, *Suffering Presence: Theological Reflections on Medicine, the Mentally Handicapped, and the Church,* pp. 100–113.

8. This type of argument is offered by Albert Camus, "An Absurd Reasoning," in *The Myth of Sisyphus and Other Essays* (New York: Vintage, 1955), pp. 3–48.

9. For further distinctions regarding paternalism, see James Childress, *Who Should Decide? Paternalism in Health Care* (New York: Oxford University Press, 1982), pp. 12–21.

10. H. Tristram Engelhardt, Jr., *The Foundations of Bioethics* (New York: Oxford University Press, 1986), esp. chaps. 1–3 and pp. 301–20.

11. A less extreme libertarian view is expressed by Childress, *Who Should Decide?* esp. pp. 28–76, 157–85. Childress grounds his argument against paternalism not in the principle of autonomy, but in the principle of respect for persons. Thus respect for a person may require nonintervention if that honors a person's wishes, choices, and actions. Childress holds that paternalism is altruistic beneficence and generally ranks beneficence below autonomy because the latter may more clearly express respect for persons. However, it could be argued that in an act of suicide, a person actually disrespects himself or herself, and while allowing a suicide may in one sense respect a person, yet because of the finality of suicide, such an act shows overriding disrespect for the individual. Thus it shows more respect for persons to interfere with an autonomous suicide than to allow it.

12. Daniel Callahan, "Minimalistic Ethics," *Hastings Center Report* 11 (October 1983): 19–25.

13. Ibid. For more on the contrast between liberal and conservative approaches to abortion, infanticide, euthanasia, war, and capital punishment, see J. P. Moreland and Norman Geisler, *The Life and Death Debate: Moral Issues of Our Time* (Westport, CT: Praeger Books, 1990).

14. Edmund D. Pellegrino and David C. Thomasma, *For The Patient's Good: The Restoration of Beneficence in Health Care* (New York: Oxford University Press, 1988).

Chapter 7

1. M. Kent Millard, "Model for Thinking about Homosexuality," and James C. Logan, "Theological/Ethical Perspectives on Homosexuality," in *Homosexuality: In Search of a Christian Understanding,* ed. Leon Smith (Nashville: Discipleship Resources, 1981), pp. 25, 53.
2. John R. W. Stott, *Homosexual Partnerships: Why Same-Sex Relationships Are Not a Christian Option* (Downers Grove, IL: InterVarsity, 1985), p. 5.
3. Logan, "Theological/Ethical Perspectives on Homosexuality," p. 24.
4. Charles W. Socarides, "Homosexuality Is Not Just a Life Style," in *Male and Female: Christian Approaches to Sexuality,* ed. Ruth Tiffany Barnhouse and Urban T. Holmes III (New York: Seabury, 1976), p. 149.
5. Stott notes that there is now a division between what is sin and what is a crime: "Adultery has always been a sin, but in most countries it is not an offense punishable by the state. Rape, by contrast, is both a sin and a crime." This leads to confusion and ultimately to a question as to whether something which is not a crime (one's experience) should be considered a sin (one's morality) (Stott, *Homosexual Partnerships,* p. 5).
6. Wilham Norman Pittenger, "Theological Approach to Understanding Homosexuality," in *Male and Female: Christian Approaches to Sexuality,* pp. 159–63.
7. Ibid., pp. 161–62.
8. Ibid., p. 164.
9. Ibid., p. 165, and idem, *Time for Consent* (London: SCM, 1970). Also Thielicke seeks to decide the question of homosexuality on sociological and psychological grounds (Helmut Thielicke, "Erwägungen der Evangelisch-Theologischen Ethik zum Problem der Homosexualität und ihre Strafrechtlichen Relevanz," *Zeitschrift für Evangelische Ethik* 6 [May 1962]: 150–66).
10. Some of the major proponents of homosexuality as a valid practice for Christians are John Boswell, *Christianity, Social Tolerance, and Homosexuality: Gay People in Western Europe from the Beginning of the Christian Era to the Fourteenth Century* (Chicago: University of Chicago Press, 1980); Victor P. Furnish, "Homosexuality," in *The Moral Teaching of Paul: Selected Issues* (Nashville: Abingdon, 1979), pp. 52–83; John J. McNeill, *The Church and the Homosexual* (Kansas City: Sheed Andrews and McMeel, 1976); Letha Scanzoni and Virginia Ramey Mollenkott, *Is the Homosexual My Neighbor?* (San Francisco: Harper & Row, 1978); and Robin Scroggs, *The New Testament and Homosexuality:*

Contextual Background for Contemporary Debate (Philadelphia: Fortress, 1983).

11. Scanzoni and Mollenkott, *Is the Homosexual My Neighbor?* p. 64.

12. Scroggs, *The New Testament and Homosexuality: Contextual Background for Contemporary Debate,* p. 43.

13. Though not undisputed by present writers, the primary passages include Genesis 19 (cf. Ezek. 16:49–50 and Jude 7); Leviticus 18:22; 20:13; and Judges 19.

14. In discussing Genesis 19, Josephus pointed out that if Lot had offered the men of Sodom his own daughers, "not even this would content them" (*The Antiquities of the Jews* 1. 11. 13). Also the Babylonian Talmud deals with female homosexuality by stating, "Samuel's father did not permit his daughters to . . . sleep together" (Shabbath 65a). Also Rabbi Huna believed that "women that commit lewdness with one another are unfit for the priesthood" (Shabbath 65b). Other than these cases little is said about homosexuality in rabbinical literature. As Strickland notes, "Perhaps one plausible suggestion might be that the issue was straightforward. There were no situations which allowed homosexual practices. Under no condition was this practice condoned" (Wayne G. Strickland, "The Unnaturalness of Homosexuality" [ThM thesis, Dallas Theological Seminary, 1980], p. 20).

15. Tarsus "became the Athens of the eastern Mediterranean, the ancient equivalent of a university city, the resort of men of learning, the home town of Athenodorus (74 B.C.–A.D. 7), the respected teacher of Augustus himself, the seat of a school of Stoic philosophers, a place of learning and disputation, and the very climate in which a brilliant mind might grow up in the midst of stimulus and challenge and learn to think and to contend" (*Zondervan Pictorial Encyclopedia of the Bible,* s.v. "Tarsus," by E. M. Blaiklock, 5:602). Also see P. Michael Ukleja, "The Bible and Homosexuality; Part 2: Homosexuality in the New Testament," *Bibliotheca Sacra* 140 (October–December 1983): 354.

16. Ibid.

17. See Strickland, "The Unnaturalness of Homosexuality," pp. 4–23, for a more complete discussion of the various cultural influences on Paul's understanding of homosexuality.

18. This is contrary to some affirmations that "Paul's argument from nature is linked neither to theories of 'natural law' (a concept which developed later) nor to the Genesis creation stories" (Mark Olson, "Untangling the Web: A Look at What Scripture Does and Does Not Say about Homosexual Behavior," *The Other Side* [April 1984], p. 27). He is in error on both accounts. Creation will be

addressed below, but even Plato had a sense of "natural law" as
seen in these words: "When male unites with female for procreation
the pleasure experienced is held to be due to nature, but contrary
to nature when male mates with male or female with female"
(Plato, Laws 636C).

Going even further, Boswell proclaims that "'nature' is not a moral
force for Paul: men may be evil or good by nature, depending on
their own disposition." Therefore he concludes, "'Nature' in
Romans 1:26, then, should be understood as the personal nature of
the pagans in question" (Boswell, *Christianity, Social Tolerance,
and Homosexuality*, pp. 110–11).

However, after a rather thorough study of φύσις DeYoung
concludes that the term never has the sense of "what is natural to
me" (James B. DeYoung, "The Meaning of 'Nature' in Romans 1
and Its Implications for Biblical Proscriptions of Homosexual
Behavior," *Journal of the Evangelical Theological Society* 31
[December 1988]: 430). Likewise Köster says, "Φύσις is then
used for a man's character or nature, without reference to his birth
or descent, in so far as this nature is given and [is] not dependent
on conscious direction or education" (*Theological Dictionary of
the New Testament,* s.v. "φύσις, φυσικος, φυσικῶς," by Helmut
Köster, 9:253).

19. Walter Bauer, Wilham F. Arndt, and F. Wilbur Gingrich, *A Greek-
    English Lexicon of the New Testament and Other Early Christian
    Literature,* 2d ed., rev. F. Wilbur Gingrich and Frederick W. Danker
    (Chicago: University of Chicago Press, 1979), p. 869. DeYoung
    says, "Note how the Creator and creation immediately precede in
    the context (Rom. 1:19–23)" ("The Meaning of 'Nature' in Romans
    1 and Its Implications for Biblical Proscriptions of Homosexual
    Behavior," *Journal of the Evangelical Theological Society* 31
    [December 1988]: 439).
20. "Those who are uncircumcised from nature" are in contrast to
    Jews who become heathen by violating the Law.
21. "Οὐδὲ ἡ φύσις αὐτή διδάσκει ὑμᾶς."
22. Παρά has the sense of "beside" something in that it is "contrary
    to" it (Bauer, Arndt, and Gingrich, *A Greek-English Lexicon of
    the New Testament and Other Early Christian Literature,* p. 869).
    Also see H. E. Dana and Julius R. Mantey, *A Manual Grammar of
    the Greek New Testament* (New York: Macmillan, 1927), 108,
    116, where this same sense is affirmed.
23. C. E. B. Cranfield, *A Critical and Exegetical Commentary on the
    Epistle to Romans,* 2 vols., International Critical Commentary
    (Edinburgh: Clark, 1975), 1:125.

24. Ibid., p. 126.
25. S. Lewis Johnson, Jr., "God Gave Them Up: A Study in Divine Retribution," *Bibliotheca Sacra* 129 (April–June 1972): 132.
26. Ibid. For an in-depth discussion of the correlations of Genesis 1 and 2 with Romans 1 see Richard B. Hays, "Relations Natural and Unnatural: A Response to J. Boswell's Exegesis of Romans 1," *Journal of Religious Ethics* 14 (Spring 1986): 191, 212, n. 6.
27. David L. Bartlett, "Biblical Perspective on Homosexuality," *Foundations* 20 (April–June 1977): 139.
28. Ibid., p. 140.
29. Hays rightly says, "The genius of Paul's analysis, of course, lies in his refusal to posit a catalogue of sins as the cause of human alienation from God. Instead, he delves to the root: all other depravities follow from the radical rebellion of the creature against the creator" ("Relations Natural and Unnatural: A Response to J. Boswell's Exegesis of Romans 1," p. 189; cf. pp. 190–91).

    Käsemann writes, "For the apostle, history is governed by the primal sin of rebellion against the Creator, which finds repeated and universal expression. It is thus governed by the wrath of God, which throws the creature back on itself, corresponding to its own will, and abandons it to the world. . . . Paul paradoxically reverses the cause and consequence: Moral perversion is the result of God's wrath, not the reason for it" (Ernst Käsemann, *Commentary on Romans*, trans. and ed. Geoffrey W. Bromiley [Grand Rapids: Eerdmans, 1980], p. 47).
30. Johnson describes this word as a "terrifying refrain" ("God Gave Them Up: A Study in Divine Retribution," p. 126).
31. Ibid., p. 127.
32. Ibid., pp. 127–28.
33. Ibid., p. 128.
34. Hays, "Relations Natural and Unnatural: A Response to J. Boswell's Exegesis of Romans 1," p. 190.
35. See verses 23 (ἤλλαξαν), 25 (μετήλλαξαν), and 26 (μετήλλαξαν).
36. See similar discussions by Hays, "Relations Natural and Unnatural: A Response to J. Boswell's Exegesis of Romans 1," p. 200; Käsemann, *Commentary on Romans,* p. 33; and Johnson, "God Gave Them Up: A Study in Divine Retribution," pp. 125, 131–32. Concerning the exact time of this retribution toward mankind Johnson notes that the allusions to the Genesis creation account, as well as Paul's later mention of the entrance of sin in Eden, intimate that Paul had the Garden of Eden in mind. "There, then, man fell into sin, judgment, and the retributive justice of immorality, crime, and all manner of evil" (ibid., p. 132).

37. Boswell, *Christianity, Social Tolerance, and Homosexuality*, p. 109.
38. Ibid. Also see a similar discussion by McNeil, *The Church and the Homosexual*, pp. 10, 66. Surprisingly even Stott wrote that "although Paul knew nothing of the modern distinction between 'inverts' (who have a homosexual disposition) and 'perverts' (who, though hetero-sexually inclined, indulge in homosexual practices), nevertheless it is the latter he is condemning, not the former. This must be so, because they are described as having 'abandoned' natural relations with women, whereas no exclusively homosexual male would ever have had them" (Stott, *Homosexual Partnerships*, p. 11).
39. Scroggs, *The New Testament and Homosexuality: Contextual Background for Contemporary Debate*.
40. Ibid., p. 60.
41. Greger Walve, "A Critique of Some Contemporary Theologians" (ThM thesis, Dallas Theological Seminary, 1983), p. 23.
42. Boswell, *Christianity, Social Tolerance, and Homosexuality*, p. 109.
43. Hays discusses this very point in reference to Boggs's view ("Relations Natural and Unnatural: A Response to J. Boswell's Exegesis of Romans 1," p. 201). Even Scroggs affirms that the cultural climate of male superiority and male sexuality makes it impossible to distinguish between categories of inversion and perversion. Scroggs therefore questions Boswell's assertion that in Romans 1:26–27 Paul was speaking only of perversion (*The New Testament and Homosexuality*, p. 28, n. 39).
44. Ibid., p. 101.
45. "The homosexuality the New Testament opposes is pederasty of the Greco-Roman culture" (ibid., p. 84). And yet, strangely, this conclusion runs counter to evidence he presents in his discussion of Palestinian Judaism, for example.
46. DeYoung says that to claim that Paul had pederasty in view is to miss the point that he was speaking of "nature" from a Jewish perspective based on creation and not from a Greek viewpoint. Therefore Paul was not limiting his discussion to Greek abuses ("The Meaning of 'Nature' in Romans 1 and Its Implications for Biblical Proscriptions of Homosexual Behavior," p. 439). Much of the following support is derived from DeYoung's excellent observations (ibid., pp. 439–40).
47. "Ἀρρένων καὶ νέων," Plato, *Laws Book* 3, 836C.
48. "When male unites with female for procreation the pleasure experienced is held to be due to nature, but contrary to nature when male mates with male or female with female" (ibid., 636C).
49. Olson, "Untangling the Web: A Look at What Scripture Does and Does Not Say about Homosexual Behavior," p. 28.

50. Ibid.
51. Ibid.
52. Once again Scroggs provides an example of this special pleading in spite of the facts when he acknowledges that "nature" refers to creation (a point which argues against the theory that Paul discussed only Greco-Roman abuses) but then glibly dismisses the admission with, "however creation was understood" (Scroggs, *The New Testament and Homosexuality,* p. 60). For a Jew like Paul, there could be no question as to how creation was understood in Genesis 1 and 2.

Chapter 8

1. Elizabeth Kübler-Ross, *AIDS: The Ultimate Challenge* (New York: Macmillan, 1987), p. 6.
2. Cited by Sasha Alyson, *You Can Do Something about AIDS* (Boston: Stop AIDS Project, 1988), p. 15.
3. Kübler-Ross, *AIDS: The Ultimate Challenge,* p. 13.
4. Ibid., p. 5.
5. *The World Almanac and Book of Facts 1992* (New York: Pharos, 1991), p. 198.
6. Cited by John Eldredge, "The AIDS Scare, 10 Years Later," *Focus on the Family Citizen* (December 17, 1990), p. 13.
7. International Statistical Classification of Diseases and Related Adult Problems, *World Almanac 1993* (New York: Pharos, 1992), p. 177.
8. Gene Antonio, a physician, lists these diseases: pneumocystis carinii pneumonia (PCP), Kapaosi' sarcoma (KS), candidiasis, cytomegalovirus (CMV), herpes simplex (HSV), herpes zoster, toxoplasmosis, cryptosporidiosis, and cryptococcosis (*The AIDS Cover-Up?* [San Francisco: Ignatius, 1986], pp. 15–18).
9. Paul Douglas and Laura Pinsky, *The Essential AIDS Fact Book* (New York: Pocket, 1987), p. 22.
10. C. Everett Koop, *The Surgeon General's Report on Acquired Immune Deficiency Syndrome* (Washington: U.S. Department of Health and Human Services, 1986), p. 13.
11. William Masters, Virginia Johnson, and Robert Kolodny, *Crisis: Heterosexual Behavior in the Age of AIDS* (New York: Grove, 1988), p. 34.
12. Theodore Hammett and Harold Jaffe, "The Cause, Transmission, and Incidence of AIDS," *National Institute of Justice AIDS Bulletin* (June 1987), p. 3.
13. Koop, *The Surgeon General's Report on Acquired Immune Deficiency Syndrome,* p. 12.
14. Kübler-Ross, *Aids: The Ultimate Challenge,* p. 318.

15. James Watkins, "AIDS Quarterly," PBS Special, Robert Wood Johnson Foundation, February 28, 1989.
16. Ibid.
17. Alyson, *You Can Do Something about AIDS*, p. 84.
18. Two books on AIDS written by Christians are these: Glenn C. Wood and John E. Dietrich, *The AIDS Epidemic: Valuing Compassion and Justice*, (Portland, OR: Multnomah, 1990), and Shepherd and Anita Moreland Smith, *Christians in the Age of AIDS*, (Wheaton, IL: Victor, 1990).
19. Terry Muck, "AIDS in Your Church," *Christianity Today* (February 5, 1988), p. 12.

Chapter 9

1. One of the more recent liberal expressions is found in John Hick, ed., *The Myth of Christian Uniqueness* (Maryknoll, NY: Orbis, 1987). See the critique in Gavin D'Costa, ed., *Christian Uniqueness Reconsidered: The Myth of a Pluralistic Theology of Religions* (Maryknoll, NY: Orbis, 1991), and discussion in S. Mark Heim's "Crisscrossing the Rubicon: Reconsidering Religious Pluralism," *Christian Century* (July 10–17, 1991), pp. 688–90. For a discussion of the assumptions of theological pluralism, see Alister McGrath, "The Christian Church's Response to Pluralism," *Journal of the Evangelical Theological Society* 35 (December 1992): 493.
2. Gary Phillips and William E. Brown, *Making Sense of Your World* (Chicago: Moody, 1991), pp. 160–61. Representative of universalism was the February 1991 assembly of the World Council of Churches, from which a statement affirming a "cosmic pneumatology" was issued, embracing the work of the Spirit to express redemptive truth in ways other than through Jesus Christ. This was not without dissension, notably from African evangelicals. See Jeffrey Gros, "Christian Confession in a Pluralistic World," *Christian Century* (June 26–July 3, 1991), pp. 645–46.
3. Gros, "Christian Confession in a Pluralistic World," p. 645.
4. *Sura* 4:154–59.
5. Of course if exclusivism were false, it could also be true. (The reader may surmise that absolutists have great fun with the logic of relativists.)
6. This is also called the law of contradiction. See Irving M. Copi, *Introduction to Logic*, 7th ed. (New York: Macmillan, 1986), pp. 306–8. Also see Alan Bloom, *The Closing of the American Mind* (New York: Simon and Schuster, 1987), p. 25.
7. Gordon Clark, *Logic* (Jefferson, MD: Trinity Foundation, 1985), p. vii.
8. McGrath, "The Christian Church's Response to Pluralism," p. 500.

9. Gros, "Christian Confession in a Pluralistic World," p. 645.
10. John E. Sanders, "Is Belief in Christ Necessary for Salvation?" *Evangelical Quarterly* 60 (1988): 241–59. See his historical survey, "The Perennial Debate," *Christianity Today* (May 14, 1990), pp. 20–21.
11. Evert D. Osburn, "Those Who Have Never Heard: Have They No Hope?" *Journal of the Evangelical Theological Society* 32 (1989): 367–72.
12. See Clark Pinnock's proposal, "The Finality of Jesus Christ in a World of Religions," in *Christian Faith and Practice in the Modern World*, ed. Mark Noll and David Wells (Grand Rapids: Baker, 1988), pp. 152–68. Pinnock then added another position statement: "Toward an Evangelical Theology of Religions," *Journal of the Evangelical Theological Society* 33 (1990): 359–68. His comprehensive statement is found in his book *A Wideness in God's Mercy* (Grand Rapids: Zondervan, 1992).
13. This statement, heard by this writer at the San Diego meeting, is cited in Terry C. Muck, "Many Mansions?" *Christianity Today* (May 14, 1990), p. 14.
14. W. Gary Phillips, "Evangelicals and Pluralism: Current Options," *Evangelical Quarterly* 64 (1992): 229–44. Because the essay was published only recently (due to a significant publishing time lag) it includes little of the current nuances of the debate.
15. See *Proceedings of the Annual Wheaton Theology Conference* (Spring 1992).
16. Exclusivists do not include those who lived before Pentecost in these categories. This point will be discussed later in this article.
17. The following material under this heading may also be found in the present writer's article, "Evangelicals and Pluralism: Current Options."
18. Rather than use the term "exclusivist" Sanders uses the happier term "restrictivist," perhaps to defuse pejorative connotations from a view with which he disagrees.
19. John 3:18 (if by Jesus); 14:6 (cf. 6:29).
20. John 3:18 (if by John); Acts 4:12 (see 10:43); 16:31; Romans 10:9–15; Galatians 1:8; 1 Timothy 2:5.
21. John 3:18 (?); 8:19, 24, 41–42, 44, 47.
22. John 3:18 (?); Acts 13:39; 17:22–31; 26:17–18; Roman, 10:9–15; 1 Corinthians 10:20; 1 Thessalonians 1:9; implication of Galatians 2:21 and many other passages.
23. Sanders, Osburn, and Pinnock would agree with the thrust (if not the details) of these two propositions. Some of the discussion of the Evangelical Theological Society in San Diego assumed that

Pinnock does not affirm Jesus Christ as the ontological basis for salvation, when in reality he does.

24. Many have adopted a "greater light" view: God will send greater light to those who respond to the light they have. For a critique of this position, see Pinnock, *A Wideness in God's Mercy*, p. 166; and Sanders, *No Other Name*, pp. 152–64.

25. See Pinnock, "The Finality of Jesus Christ in a World of Religions," pp. 161–62. It should be noted that Pinnock is not a universalist (ibid., pp. 154–57).

26. J. N. D. Anderson, *Christianity and Comparative Religion* (Downers Grove, IL: InterVarsity, 1970), pp. 94–109. He contends that a right attitude toward God is essential for salvation; for assurance, though, knowledge is essential (ibid., p. 104).

27. R. Purtill, *C. S. Lewis's Case for the Christian Faith* (New York: Harper, 1981), chap. 7.

28. See Clark Pinnock, "Why Is Jesus the Only Way?" *Eternity* (December 1976), pp. 13-15, and idem, "The Finality of Jesus Christ in a World of Religions," pp. 165–66.

29. Pinnock, "Toward an Evangelical Theology of Religions," 368.

30. Annihilationism has been proposed by E. Fudge, *The Fire That Consumes* (Houston: Providential, 1982). It has been adopted or tentatively embraced by notable evangelicals such as Clark Pinnock, John Wenham, David Wenham, and John Stott. For a critique of annihilationism, see Kenneth L. Kantzer, ed., "Universalism: Will Everyone Be Saved?" *Christianity Today Institute* (March 20, 1987).
A similar view is called "conditional immortality," in which death for the unredeemed ends all (there is no final judgment). Eternal life is contingent on receiving Christ; it is a gift received at the moment of salvation. However, Luke 12:5 ("fear the One who after He has killed has authority to cast into hell") makes little sense unless the unbeliever's physical death and final judgment are distinct.
Those who cannot embrace annihilationism or conditional immortality may take some comfort in the probability that there are levels of accountability (and hence punishment) in hell (Matt. 11:22; Mark 12:40; Luke 12:47–48; 20:47; 2 Cor. 11:15; Heb. 10:29; Rev. 20:12–15; see also Mark 14:21; Rom. 2:5; Jude 15; Rev. 22:12). Still, the problem remains. See the interesting discussion in Kathleen Boone, *The Bible Tells Them So: The Discourse of Protestant Fundamentalism* (New York: SUNY, 1989), chap. 7.

31. See Pinnock's "Fire, Then Nothing," *Christianity Today* (March

20, 1987), pp. 40–41. One may hold to annihilationism without any accompanying posture regarding the untold; the views are not logically or theologically entwined (though they are psychologically compatible). For a more extended critique of both forms of eschatological solution, see Phillips, "Evangelicals and Pluralism: Current Options."

32. Though Pinnock and Sanders disagree with this "middle knowledge" view, they do acknowledge its possibilities. See Sanders, *No Other Name*, p. 111, note, pp. 173–75, 216; Pinnock, *A Wideness in God's Mercy*, pp. 160–61. Also see John R. W. Stott, "Response," in *Evangelical Essentials: A Liberal-Evangelical Dialogue*, by David L. Edwards (Downers Grove, IL: InterVarsity, 1988), pp. 325–26. This solution is not an exegetical insight derived from any biblical text. Rather, it is theological behaviorism and negates the clear meaning of many passages that anchor faith to this life (e.g., John 3:18; 1 John 2:23). Also it is doubtful that the word group for "election" can be enlarged to accommodate this redefinition. Such a position is questionable because it bypasses any need for actual faith on the part of the redeemed; and while this argument is put forth to support a limited inclusivism, it seems that it leads to absolute universalism, since God knows an infinite number of possible worlds.

33. Of course some may argue that all who die before placing explicit faith in Christ—including infants—are lost. Many maintain that some children are elect, but others are lost. See the *Westminster Confession of Faith*, 12.3, 73. Calling this view "foreseen potential," Gleason L. Archer says, "God knows in advance what each child will do and how he will respond when he reaches the age of moral decision" and so God elects accordingly (*The Encyclopedia of Bible Difficulties* [Grand Rapids: Zondervan, 1982], pp. 388–90). The view put forth in this article is that all in the category are redeemed. Regeneration for them takes place at the moment of death, because all (including infants) partake of original sin. See the *Westminster Confession of Faith*, 12.3, 73, and the extended discussion in *The Works of Benjamin B. Warfield* (reprint, Grand Rapids: Baker, 1981), 9:411–44. For the differences between those who have not heard and those who cannot hear, see the discussion below.

34. Faith itself does not save; it has no intrinsic value except what God chooses to ascribe to it (Eph. 2:8).

35. Sanders, *No Other Name*, pp. 287–305.

36. Clark Pinnock, "Acts 4:12—No Other Name under Heaven," in Crockett and Sigountos, *Through No Fault of Their Own?* p. 113.

37. Pinnock, *A Wideness in God's Mercy*, p. 26.
38. Bruce A. Demarest and Richard J. Harpel, "Don Richardson's 'Redemptive Analogies' and the Biblical Idea of Revelation," *Bibliotheca Sacra* 146 (July-September 1989): 336. While it is possible that God may use oral traditions, dreams, miracles, and/ or visions, to bring the untold to repentance, the motivating point of Romans 10:13–14 seems to be that God has limited Himself to human agencies in the preaching of the gospel of Christ, at least by the time of the writing of Romans. See C. K. Barrett, *The Epistle to the Romans* (New York: Harper, 1957), pp. 204–6. Also Hebrews 1:1–2 indicates that special revelation in the past—given in many forms and various ways—has at present narrowed to incarnational Christology.
39. Sanders, *No Other Name*, p. 208.
40. Copi, *Introduction to Logic*, pp. 397–402.
41. Sanders, *No Other Name*, p. 208 (italics his).
42. One would hope that God sends greater light to enlighten those who seek Him (Heb. 11:6). Often case studies (beginning with Cornelius in Acts 11:1) are cited by missiologists such as Don Richardson, *Eternity in Their Hearts*, rev. ed. (Ventura, CA: Regal, 1984). But this perspective must be balanced by (a) verses like Romans 3:11, (b) the consideration that Cornelius (if used as a case study) was actually a "God-fearer," and (c) the history of missions (which did not begin in earnest until recent centuries; had so few sought God until recently?).
43. Sanders's response to this view is unconvincing (*No Other Name*, pp. 64–66).
44. Pinnock, *A Wideness in God's Mercy*, p. 154. See also his comments on Revelation 1:7 (ibid., p. 153).
45. One wonders if the same narrow hermeneutic would be applied to the rest of the Sermon on the Mount—limiting application numerically and chronologically to that time and to those few.
46. Sanders, *No Other Name*, p. 254.
47. Ibid., p. 3. They also "indiscriminately damn" the unevangelized (ibid., p. 7).
48. Pinnock, *A Wideness in God's Mercy*, p. 154, cf. p. 19.
49. Donald Bloesch, *Essentials of Evangelical Theology I* (New York: Harper, 1978), pp. 245–47.
50. Phillips, "Evangelicals and Pluralism: Current Options," p. 234. See Robert H. Gundry, "Salvation According to Scripture: No Middle Ground," *Christianity Today* (December 9, 1977), p. 16.
51. Pinnock, *A Wideness in God's Mercy*, p. 171.
52. Ibid., p. 174.

53. Ibid., pp. 170–71.
54. Though couched by Sanders (*No Other Name*, pp. 230–32) in quotations of statements by Stuart Hackett and Charles Kraft, apparently this suggestion is cited with approval. Pinnock is more explicit (*A Wideness in God's Mercy*, pp. 98, 111, 158, 172–76). "The issue God cares about is the direction of the heart, not the content of theology" (ibid., p. 158).
55. Pinnock cites this teaching with favor (ibid., p. 98). Matthew 25:40 is reinterpreted to mean "deeds of love done to needy people will be regarded at the last judgment as having been done to Christ," by which he clearly means redemption. Why? Because "good works manifest one's basic attitude to God and . . . noncognitive responses to God count as much as cognitive responses do" (ibid., p. 164).
56. Ibid., p. 141.
57. "The Bible views religious activities on a spectrum which runs all the way from truth to error, from nobility to vileness" (ibid., p. 14; also see chap. 3).
58. "If God did not accept people whose religious faith was deficient, who among us could stand before Him?" (ibid., p. 101). Pinnock's meaning is that all religion—with regard to the faith principle—are on a continuum. However, Paul wrote that a similar gospel is an altogether different gospel (Gal. 1)—not a[lla("other") but e{ter("different").
59. See Pinnock, *A Wideness in God's Mercy*, chap. 4.
60. Yet Sanders notes Pinnock's recent shift toward even greater wideness (*No Other Name*, p. 259, note). Sanders himself seems to have moved beyond the view he expressed in 1988 in his article "Is Belief in Christ Necessary for Salvation?"
61. Pinnock, *A Wideness in God's Mercy*, p. 77.
62. Ibid., pp. 103–4.
63. For a thorough critique, see James Bradley, "Logos Christology and Religious Pluralism: A New Evangelical Proposal," in *Proceedings of the Annual Wheaton Theology Conference*, 1992 (forthcoming).
64. Pinnock, *A Wideness in God's Mercy*, pp. 176–80, and idem, "Acts 4:12—*No Other Name under Heaven*," pp. 114–15. Also see Sanders, *No Other Name*, pp. 48–50, 283.
65. Boone, *The Bible Tells Them So*, pp. 99–106.
66. James Davison Hunter, *Evangelicalism: The Coming Generation* (Chicago: University of Chicago Press, 1987), pp. 34, 47.
67. Sanders, *No Other Name*, xvii, 3, 6.
68. Ibid., p. 18.
69. Lesslie Newbegin, *The Gospel in a Pluralist Society* (Grand Rapids:

Eerdmans, 1989), p. 159. Newbegin's point was applied to world views, not "current options" regarding the unevangelized. Sanders says his "heart longs that the doctrine [of universalism] be proven correct" (*No Other Name*, p. 107).

70. Pinnock, *A Wideness in God's Mercy*, pp. 150–51.
71. Sanders, *No Other Name*, p. 18.
72. Logically, other than for the purposes of satisfying one's curiosity (and perhaps increasing the believer's apologetic comfort), there would be no point for God to reveal His plans for the untold and then add, as it were, "By the way, this message applies only to those who—through no fault of their own—will not or cannot hear this message." The problem (lack of exposure to the message, or lack of cognitive capacity to respond to the message) is not solved by enhancing the message.
73. Roger Nicole, in Kenneth L. Kantzer, ed., "Universalism: Will Everyone Be Saved?" *Christianity Today Institute* (March 20, 1987), p. 38.

Chapter 10

1. Richard Schaull, *Encounter with Revolution* (New York: Association, 1955).
2. See Robert McAfee Brown, *Theology in a New Key: Responding to Liberation Themes* (Philadelphia: Westminster, 1978).
3. Carlos Fuentes, in *Latin America: Yesterday and Today,* ed. John Rothchild (New York: Bantam, 1973), p. 370.
4. W. Stanley Mooneyham, *What Do You Say to a Hungry World?* (Waco, TX: Word, 1975), p. 45.
5. Richard Gott, *The Guardian* (London: Nelson, 1977), p. 8.
6. Mooneyham, *What Do You Say to a Hungry World?* pp. 117–18.
7. Alan B. Mountjoy, ed., *The Third World: Problems and Perspectives* (New York: St. Martin's, 1978), p. 81.
8. Arthur F. McGovern, *Marxism: An American Christian Perspective* (Maryknoll, NY: Orbis, 1980), p. 173.
9. Richard J. Barnet and Ronald E. Muller, *Global Reach: The Power of Multinational Corporations* (New York: Simon and Schuster, 1974), p. 179.
10. "1988 World Population Data Sheet" (Washington, DC: Population Reference Bureau, 1988).
11. Ibid.
12. Lester R. Brown, *World Population Trends: Signs of Hope, Signs of Stress* (Washington, DC: Worldwatch Institute, 1976), p. 10.
13. Gustavo Gutiérrez, *A Theology of Liberation,* trans. Caridad Inda and John Eagleson (Maryknoll, NY: Orbis, 1973), p. 88.

14. Emilio A. Núñez, *Liberation Theology* (Chicago: Moody, 1986), p. 47.
15. Lester DeKoster, "Is Liberation Theology Christian?" *Outlook* 10 (May 1984): 11.
16. Walter M. Abbott, ed., *The Documents of Vatican II*, trans. Joseph Gallagher (New York: American, 1966), p. 226.
17. Thomas G. Sanders, "The Theology of Liberation: Christian Utopianism," *Christianity and Crisis*, September 17, 1973, p. 168.
18. Gutiérrez, *A Theology of Liberation*, p. 46. See also Juan Luís Segundo, *Función de la iglesia en la realidad rioplantense* (Montevideo: Barrerro y Ramos, 1962), p. 41.
19. Ibid., pp. 190–91.
20. Julio de Santa Ana, "Notas para una ética de la liberación: A partir de la Bibha," *Cristianismo y Sociedad* 8 (1970): 55.
21. Abbott, *The Documents of Vatican II*, p. 303.
22. Gutiérrez, *A Theology of Liberation*, p. 88.
23. Gustavo Gutiérrez, *The Power of the Poor in History* (Maryknoll, NY: Orbis, 1983), p. 18.
24. Reinhold Niebuhr, *Faith and Politics* (New York: Braziller, 1968), p. 143.
25. Gordon Chutter, "Riches and Poverty in the Book of Proverbs," *Together* 3 (April–June 1984): 31.
26. Gutiérrez, *A Theology of Liberation*, p. 216.
27. Ibid.
28. Thomas More, *Utopia* (London: Van Nostrand, 1947).
29. Gutiérrez, *A Theology of Liberation*, p. 109. Gutierrez here quotes a statement of 300 Brazilian priests, "Brazilian Realities and the Church."
30. José P. Miranda, *Marx and the Bible: A Critique of the Philosophy of Oppression*, trans. John Eagleson (Maryknoll, NY: Orbis, 1974), p. 182.
31. Waldron Scott, *Bring Forth Justice* (Grand Rapids: Eerdmans, 1980), p. 263.
32. Edward Schillebeeckx, *World and Church*, trans. N. D. Smith (New York: Sheed and Ward, 1971), pp. 115–39.
33. Gutiérrez, *A Theology of Liberation*, p. 308.

Chapter 11

1. C. Peter Wagner refers to the "opening of an increasing number of traditional evangelical churches and institutions to the supernatural working of the Holy Spirit, even though they were not, nor did they wish to become, either Pentecostal or charismatic" ("The Third Wave Goes Public," *Christian Life* [January 1986], p. 67).

2. George Mallone, *Those Controversial Gifts* (Downers Grove, IL: InterVarsity, 1983), p. 11.

3. In his article "Supernatural Power in World Missions," *Evangelical Missions Quarterly* 20 (1984): 399, Peter Wagner cites John Wimber as one of the decisive influences on his thinking about the Holy Spirit. Likewise, in his book *Power Evangelism* (San Francisco: Harper & Row, 1986), p. 47, John Wimber names Peter Wagner as one who helped him understand how power evangelism works.

4. Wimber, *Power Evangelism,* p. 39.

5. C. Peter Wagner, "Healing without Hassle," *Leadership* 6 (Spring 1985): 114.

6. C. Peter Wagner, "What Happens When You See Jesus," *Christian Life* (April 1986), p. 73.

7. C. Peter Wagner, foreword to *Power Evangelism,* p. ix.

8. C. Peter Wagner, "A Third Wave?" *Pastoral Renewal* (July–August 1983), p. 1.

9. Tim Stafford, "Testing the Wine from John Wimber's Vineyard," *Christianity Today* (August 8, 1986), p. 18.

10. Ibid.

11. Wimber, *Power Evangelism,* p. xv.

12. John Wimber, *Power Healing* (San Francisco: Harper & Row, 1987), p. 23.

13. Wimber, *Power Evangelism,* p. xix.

14. Stafford, "Testing the Wine from John Wimber's Vineyard," p. 18.

15. Wimber, *Power Healing,* p. 31.

16. Ibid., p. 43.

17. Stafford, "Testing the Wine from John Wimber's Vineyard," p. 19. For a fuller account of how the Vineyard church began, see Wimber, *Power Healing,* pp. 44–45, and Carol Wimber, "A Hunger for God: A Reflective Look at the Vineyard's Beginnings," *Vineyard Newsletter* 2 (Fall 1987): 1–3, 7.

18. Stafford, "Testing the Wine from John Wimber's Vineyard," p. 18.

19. Ibid.

20. Wimber, "A Hunger for God," p. 3.

21. Wagner, foreword to *Power Evangelism,* p. x.

22. According to Wacker, the movement boasts 135 congregations and 50,000 followers nationwide (Grant Wacker, "Wimber and Wonders—What about Miracles Today?" *Reformed Journal* 37 [April 1987]: 16). EDITOR'S NOTE: In 1993 the Vineyard movement reportedly had 500 churches with about 100,000 members (Wayne Grudem, *Power and Truth: A Response to* Power Religion [Anaheim, CA: Association of Vineyard Churches, 1993], p. 65).

23. Stafford, "Testing the Wine from John Wimber's Vineyard," p. 18.
24. David Allan Hubbard, foreword to *Ministry and the Miraculous,* ed. Lewis B. Smedes (Pasadena, CA: Fuller Theological Seminary, 1987), p. 15.
25. "For example, C. Peter Wagner (who is a member of another church) is very effective in lengthening legs. Frequently people ask him to pray for their short legs and related back problems. He is almost a hundred percent successful in his prayers" (Wimber, *Power Healing,* p. 196).
26. C. Peter Wagner, "Raising the Dead," *Christian Life* (March 1986), p. 77.
27. Ben Patterson, "Cause for Concern," *Christianity Today* (August 8, 1986), p. 20. Patterson's brief article lists several problems enumerated by certain Fuller Seminary faculty, including an unbiblical dualism, exclusivity of views, a magical approach to the miraculous, the privatization of experience, and failures to heal.
28. Hubbard, foreword to *Ministry and the Miraculous,* p. 16. This publication is the report of the Fuller Seminary faculty task force.
29. Wacker, "Wimber and Wonders," pp. 16–17.
30. Wagner, "Healing without Hassle," p. 114.
31. The labels "third wave" and "Signs and Wonders movement" are synonymous. Both labels are more comprehensive than the term "Vineyard Movement," since they encompass those who affirm the continuation of all the miraculous gifts but who are not associated in any way with John Wimber's ministry. In other words Vineyard people are a subset of Signs and Wonders or third-wave people.
32. Charles Kraft, *Christianity and Culture* (Maryknoll, NY: Orbis, 1979), p. 53.
33. Wimber's argument is developed in chapter 5 of *Power Evangelism,* entitled "Signs, Wonders, and Worldviews."
34. Harry Blamires, *The Christian Mind* (Ann Arbor, MI: Servant, 1978), p. 44, cited in Wimber, *Power Evangelism,* p. 70.
35. Wimber, *Power Evangelism,* p. 70.
36. Ibid., p. 71.
37. Ibid., p. 70.
38. Smedes, ed., *Ministry and the Miraculous,* p. 41.
39. Paul G. Hiebert, "The Flaw of the Excluded Middle," *Missiology: An International Review* 10 (January 1982): 41.
40. Ibid., p. 43.
41. Ibid., p. 45.
42. Ibid., pp. 45–46. Here Hiebert develops the notion of a "holistic

theology" which incorporates power encounters in the middle level of reality.

43. "We see according to our expectations. Many times our expectations come from conditioning. . . . Our expectations are affected by our worldview, our assumptions about the nature of reality" (Wimber, *Power Evangelism,* pp. 86–87).

44. Francis Schaeffer has detailed the decline of the Western world view in such works as *Escape from Reason* (Downers Grove, IL: InterVarsity, 1968); *The God Who Is There* (Downers Grove, IL: InterVarsity, 1968); and *A Christian Manifesto* (Westchester, IL: Crossway, 1981). Other evangelical authors who have written from a similar perspective include Colin Brown, *Philosophy and the Christian Faith* (Downers Grove, IL: InterVarsity, 1968); Os Guinness, *The Dust of Death* (Downers Grove, IL: InterVarsity, 1973); H. R. Rookmaaker, *Modern Art and the Death of a Culture* (Downers Grove, IL: InterVarsity, 1970); and C. Gregg Singer, *From Rationalism to Irrationality: The Decline of the Western Mind from the Renaissance to the Present* (Phillipsburg, NJ: Presbyterian and Reformed, 1979).

45. It must be remembered that any discussion of world view must be couched in the broadest possible categories. To discuss the influence of a world view on a group of people is rather problematic to begin with. One example of the exceeding complexity of the issue is the fact that Miguel de Molinos, a 17th-century Spanish Catholic mystic and proponent of the "inner light," and Karl Marx, a 19th-century German dialectical materialist, are both included in the "Western world view."

46. Wimber, *Power Evangelism,* p. 84.

47. Rationalism may be defined as "a method, or very broadly, a theory of philosophy, in which the criterion of truth is not sensory but intellectual and deductive" (*Dictionary of Philosophy,* 1982 ed., s.v. "Rationalism," p. 280).

48. Walter Chantry, "Powerfully Misleading," *Eternity* (July–August 1987), p. 28.

49. Ibid.

50. Wimber, *Power Evangelism,* p. 89 (italics his).

51. No attempt will be made here to explore the new hermeneutics or to determine how many "horizons" exist in biblical interpretation. Needless to say the interpreter approaches the text with certain preconceived notions, some of which are based on his experience. Clearly there is a heuristic relationship between interpretation and experience. Nevertheless there is an objective meaning resident within the text, existing apart from the experience of the interpreter,

which can be used in validating the interpreter's experience. *How* that is done is a different subject.

52. Wimber's two major books, *Power Evangelism* and *Power Healing,* are filled with stories, anecdotes, and illustrations. At times the stories themselves become the basis of what is taught. There are numerous Scripture references, but invariably they are explained through an illustration.

53. Wimber, *Power Evangelism,* p. 85.

54. Ibid., pp. 51–54.

55. For a further elaboration of this interpretation, see Stanley D. Toussaint, *Behold the King: A Study of Matthew* (Portland, OR: Multnomah, 1980), pp. 168–85.

56. Louis A. Barbieri, "Matthew," in *The Bible Knowledge Commentary, New Testament,* ed. John F. Walvoord and Roy B. Zuck (Wheaton, IL: Victor, 1983), p. 49.

57. "But all the reprobate are deprived of the light of life, by God either withdrawing His Word from them or keeping their eyes and ears blocked up so that they may not hear and see" (John Calvin, *Calvin's New Testament Commentaries,* ed. David W. Torrance and Thomas F. Torrance [Grand Rapids: Eerdmans, 1960–1972], vol. 2: *A Harmony of the Gospels, Matthew, Mark and Luke* [1972], trans. J. H. L. Parker, p. 67). See also John F. Walvoord, *Matthew: Thy Kingdom Come* (Chicago: Moody, 1974), p. 99.

58. Wimber, *Power Evangelism,* p. 5.

59. In Wimber's *Power Evangelism,* the brief chapter on the kingdom of God includes eight quotations from or references to Ladd's writings.

60. In *The Blessed Hope* (Grand Rapids: Eerdmans, 1956), George Ladd affirms premillennialism (p. 13) but spends an entire chapter refuting dispensationalism. Cf. John F. Walvoord, *The Blessed Hope and the Tribulation* (Grand Rapids: Zondervan, 1976), pp. 40–59.

61. George Eldon Ladd, *The Gospel of the Kingdom* (Grand Rapids: Eerdmans, 1975), p. 42.

62. Wimber, *Power Evangelism,* pp. 5–6.

63. Ibid., p. 11.

64. Ibid., p. 13.

65. Ibid., p. 6.

66. John Wimber, "The Words and Works of Jesus: Is the Message the Same or Different?" *First Fruits* (May–June 1986), p. 6 (italics his).

67. Wimber, *Power Healing,* p. 208.

68. Smedes, ed., *Ministry and the Miraculous,* p. 29.

69. Ibid., pp. 29–30.

70. Ibid., p. 30. This is a rather remarkable concession for Fuller Seminary faculty to make in light of their nondispensational orientation.

71. The following dispensational theologians have advocated in one form or another the temporary nature of New Testament signs and wonders: Lewis Sperry Chafer, *Systematic Theology;* 8 vols., vol. 6: *Pneumatology* (Dallas, TX: Dallas Theological Seminary, 1948; reprint [8 vols. in 4] Grand Rapids: Kregel, 1992), p. 215; Thomas R. Edgar, *Miraculous Gifts: Are They for Today?* (Neptune, NJ: Loizeaux, 1983), pp. 266–78; Robert G. Gromacki, *The Modern Tongues Movement* (Grand Rapids: Baker, 1967), pp. 118–19; Zane C. Hodges, "The Purpose of Tongues," *Bibliotheca Sacra* 120 (July–September, 1963): 227; Charles C. Ryrie, *The Holy Spirit* (Chicago: Moody, 1965), pp. 84–85; Cyrus I. Scofield, *The New Scofield Reference Bible* (New York: Oxford University Press, 1967), note on 1 Corinthians 14:1; Merrill F. Unger, *The Baptism and Gifts of the Holy Spirit* (Chicago: Moody, 1974), pp. 138–40; and John F. Walvoord, *The Holy Spirit* (Grand Rapids: Zondervan, 1965), pp. 173–88.

72. The classic expression of the cessationist view of the miraculous gifts is found in Benjamin B. Warfield, *Counterfeit Miracles* (reprint, Carlisle, PA: Banner of Truth, 1972). Cf. Augustine *Ten Homilies on the First Epistle of John* 6. 10, in *Nicene and Post-Nicene Fathers,* ed. Philip Schaff, 14 vols. (Grand Rapids: Eerdmans, 1978), 7:497–98; John Chrysostom, *Homilies on the First Epistle of St. Paul the Apostle to the Corinthians* 29. 1, in *Nicene and Post-Nicene Fathers,* 12:168; John Calvin, *Institutes of the Christian Religion,* ed. John J. McNeill, trans. Ford Lewis Battles, 2 vols. (Philadelphia: Westminster, 1960), 1:14–18.

73. Unger, *The Baptism and Gifts of the Holy Spirit,* pp. 138–39.

74. Edgar, *Miraculous Gifts,* p. 268; and Ryrie, *The Holy Spirit,* p. 84.

75. Edgar, *Miraculous Gifts,* p. 269.

76. Hodges, "The Purpose of Tongues," p. 227 (italics his).

77. Alan R. Tippett, *People Movements in Southern Polynesia* (Chicago: Moody, 1971), cited by Wimber, *Power Evangelism,* p. 16.

78. Wimber, *Power Evangelism,* p. 16 (italics his).

79. C. Peter Wagner, "Special Kinds of Church Growth" (unpublished class notes, Fuller Theological Seminary, 1984), cited by Wimber, *Power Evangelism,* p. 16.

80. Stafford, "Testing the Wine from John Wimber's Vineyard," p. 18. Also see Wimber, *Power Evangelism,* pp. 17–18.

81. Wimber, *Power Evangelism,* p. 18.
82. Wagner, "What Happens When You See Jesus," p. 73.
83. Wimber, *Power Evangelism,* p. 31.
84. Ibid., p. 35.
85. Ibid., p. 37.
86. Ibid., p. 41.
87. Ibid., p. 45.
88. Ibid., p. 46.
89. Ibid., p. 47.
90. Ibid., p. 44.
91. Stafford, "Testing the Wine from John Wimber's Vineyard," p. 18.
92. The coming of the Messiah, the ministry of the Holy Spirit, and the progress of revelation, to name just a few.
93. Wimber, *Power Evangelism,* p. 24.
94. It should be added that the Spirit of God always works consistently with what He has revealed about Himself in Scripture.
95. Charles Grandison Finney (1792–1875), the famous ante-bellum revivalist, popularized many of the methods that now characterize programmatic evangelism.
96. J. I. Packer cited in Stafford, "Testing the Wine from John Wimber's Vineyard," p. 22.
97. Ibid.
98. Ibid.

Chapter 12

1. Walter J. Hollenweger, "After Twenty Years Research on Pentecostalism," *Theology* (November 1984): 403.
2. Ibid.
3. Though those in the Signs and Wonders movement and power evangelism claim they are not charismatic, they are, according to any normal definition of the term. Their disclaimer does not alter the fact.
4. Chrysostom, *Homilies on the First Epistle of St. Paul the Apostle to the Corinthians,* Homily 29, in *Nicene and Post-Nicene Fathers,* ed. Philip Schaff, 14 vols. (New York: Christian Literature), 12:168.
5. For a more complete discussion and analysis of the issues in this article see this writer's *Miraculous Gifts* (Neptune, NJ: Loizeaux, 1983). For this specific issue see pages 223–59.
6. Frank Stagg, E. Glenn Hinson, and Wayne E. Oates, *Glossolalia* (Nashville: Abingdon, 1967), pp. 45–46.
7. To argue on the basis of the few questionable assertions produced by George Mallone, (*Those Controversial Gifts* [Downers Grove, IL: InterVarsity, 1983], p. 22), that the gifts merely declined rather

than ceased is contrary to the evidence and is an unrealistic exercise in semantics.

8. Donald Dayton, *Theological Roots of Pentecostalism* (Grand Rapids: Zondervan, 1987), pp. 26–28.
9. Mallone, *Those Controversial Gifts,* p. 25.
10. See Edgar, *Miraculous Gifts,* pp. 19–222, for specific evidence and exegetical arguments for the characteristics of the miraculous gifts.
11. See the discussion by a medical doctor in Peter Masters, *The Healing Epidemic* (London: Wakeman, 1988), pp. 202–27. This book shows the significance as well as the error of charismatic healing.
12. "True Believer," *Dallas Life Magazine* (April 17, 1988), pp. 11–14, 22–26.
13. John Wimber, *Power Evangelism* (San Francisco: Harper & Row, 1986), pp. 104–6.
14. Edgar, *Miraculous Gifts,* pp. 108–259.
15. Dayton, *Theological Roots of Pentecostalism,* p. 23.
16. Mallone, *Those Controversial Gifts,* p. 19.
17. Edgar, *Miraculous Gifts,* pp. 46–85.
18. Ken L. Sarles gives examples of the charismatics' poor use of Scripture ("An Appraisal of the Signs and Wonders Movement," *Bibliotheca Sacra* 145 [January–March 1988]: 70).
19. Edgar, *Miraculous Gifts,* pp. 60–62.
20. The Greek genitive is appositional, and the context is definitely the church universal rather than a local assembly (cf. Edgar, *Miraculous Gifts,* pp. 58–60).
21. Frederic Dale Bruner, *A Theology of the Holy Spirit* (Grand Rapids: Eerdmans, 1970), pp. 56–224; and Edgar, *Miraculous Gifts,* pp. 207–11.
22. Bruner, *A Theology of the Holy Spirit,* pp. 243–45; and Kurt Koch, *The Strife of Tongues* (Grand Rapids: Kregel, 1969), pp. 44–47.
23. Gordon D. Fee, *First Epistle to the Corinthians,* The New International Commentary on the New Testament (Grand Rapids: Eerdmans, 1987), pp. 655–70. See by contrast Edgar, *Miraculous Gifts,* p. 152.
24. For a brief evaluation of this concept of the "excluded middle," see Sarles, "An Appraisal of the Signs and Wonders Movement," pp. 66–67.

Chapter 13

1. Contra Wayne Grudem, *The Gift of Prophecy in the New Testament and Today* (Westchester, IL: Crossway, 1988), pp. 14, 74, 76–80,

121. As Thomas notes, "Prophecy would have been an exercise in futility if recipients of its messages had the choice of accepting or not accepting its stipulations" (Robert L. Thomas, "Prophecy Rediscovered? A Review of *The Gift of Prophecy in the New Testament and Today*," *Bibliotheca Sacra* 149 [January–March 1992]: 92). Furthermore the relegation of prophecy to such an inferior status raises the question of how the early church would have protected itself against hopeless doctrinal confusion (cf. Eph. 3:5–10). The Spirit-mediated and miraculous nature of prophecy guaranteed the accuracy and full authority of the message and the messenger.

2. In the earliest occurrences of πρό, the prefix overwhelmingly assumes a local connotation. Since several other verbs (e.g., προλέγω, προφωνέω) are found with a local connotation, one may assume that προφήτης follows a similar pattern. Even with this original localized meaning of "forth," the verb eventually held the temporal meaning of "in advance" or "before," the temporal connotation of "foretelling" developing later in the evolution of the word's meaning. Hence in its original usage the specific or basic meaning of προφήτης was "herald" or "proclaimer" (*Theological Dictionary of the New Testament,* s.v. "προφήτης," by Helmut Krämer, 6 [1968]: 783; Theodore M. Crone, "Early Christian Prophecy: A Study of Its Origin and Function" [PhD diss., Tübingen University, 1973], p. 11; E. Fraenkel, *Geschichte der griechischen nomina agentis* [Strasbourg: Kärl J. Trübner, 1910], 1:34; Erich Fascher, *ΠΡΟΦΗΤΗΣ: Eine sprach- und Religionsgeschichtliche Untersuchung* [Giessen: Töpelmann, 1927], pp. 3–11). Fascher's work reflects the ideas of the *Religionsgeschichtliche Schule,* which assumes an evolutionary development between Greek or Hellenistic religions and Christianity. Reitzenstein, a leading proponent of this school, notes: "Kein Mensch behauptet, dass der Inhalt der frühchristlichen ἐνθουσιασμος dem Heidentum entlehnt sei; aber bestreiten sollte man nicht länger, dass seine Form und Auffassung tatsächlich übernommen ist" (Richard Reitzenstein, *Die hellenistichen Mysterienreligionen nach ihren Grundgedanken und Wirkungen* [Leipzig: Trübner, 1927], p. 240).
However, such assertions by the history-of-religions school of an evolutionary development between Christianity and Hellenistic religions has been called into serious question, nor is such a scheme assumed by the present writer. What is merely being asserted here is that the Bible did not develop in a vacuum and that the Greek language forms an important exploratory background to the use of

the term in the New Testament. For further information on the
discrediting of many of the assertions of the *Religionsgeschichtliche
Schule,* see Gerhard Hasel, *New Testament Theology: Basic Issues
in the Current Debate* (Grand Rapids: Eerdmans, 1978), pp. 51–
54, and Stephen Neill and Tom Wright, *The Interpretation of the
New Testament 1861–1986,* 2d ed. (Oxford: Oxford University,
1988), pp. 172–79.

3. Fascher notes that in its original usage, the term almost never has
   the sense of "predictor" or "foreteller," but must receive this
   meaning from other qualifying words in the context. It is the same
   with the cognate verb προφητεύω (Fascher, *ΠΡΟΦΗΤΗΣ,* pp. 51–
   52).

4. J. Lindblom, *Prophecy in Ancient Israel* (Philadelphia: Fortress,
   1973), p. 6. Aune notes regarding Christian prophets, "The prophet
   was unique among early Christian leaders in that, unlike other
   functionaries, he claimed no personal part in the communication
   which he conveyed. Prophets acted as leaders in many early
   Christian communities because they were regarded by themselves
   and others as inspired spokesmen for ultimate authority, God (or
   Jesus, or the Spirit of God, or even an angelic mediator)" (David
   Aune, *Prophecy in Early Christianity and the Mediterranean World*
   [Grand Rapids: Eerdmans, 1983], p. 204).

5. Boring describes a prophet in the following general terms: "A
   prophet is an immediately inspired spokesman for the (or a) deity
   of a particular community, who receives revelations which he is
   impelled to deliver to the community" (M. E. Boring, "What Are
   We Looking For? Toward a Definition of the Term 'Christian
   Prophet,'" *Society of Biblical Literature, Seminar Papers* 1 [1973]:
   152). Boring notes that a Christian prophet is "a Christian who
   functions within the Church as an immediately-inspired spokesman
   for the exalted Jesus, who receives intelligible revelation which he
   is impelled to deliver to the Christian community" (ibid., 44). Hill
   also notes that the prophet is "a divinely called and divinely inspired
   speaker who receives intelligible and authoritative revelations or
   messages which he is impelled to deliver publicly, in oral or written
   form, to Christian individuals and/or the Christian community"
   (David Hill, *New Testament Prophecy* [Atlanta: Knox, 1979], pp.
   8–9).

6. Krämer, "προφήτης," p.795; and *Theological Dictionary of the
   New Testament,* s.v. "κῆρυξ," by Gerhard Friedrich, 3:687. Friedrich
   defines the basic meaning of κῆρυξ as "herald" or "proclaimer"
   for the royal court or deity. Also see Fascher, *ΠΡΟΦΗΤΗΣ,* p. 51.

7. Krämer, "προφήτης," p. 795.

8. This also underscores why so much emphasis is placed in both Testaments on evaluating prophets (Deut. 13:1–5; 18:20–22; Matt. 7:15; 1 Cor. 14:29–31; 1 John 4:1–3; cf. *Didache* 11). False prophets could do much harm among believing communities through their false prophesying, which in turn could lead many astray. The woman named "Jezebel" at Thyatira is an example of this. As a self-styled "prophetess," she used her prophetic authority to mislead many in that local community (Rev. 2:20–23). The Montanist excesses are another example of false prophets who used their prophetic authority to lead some in the church astray. For further information see F. David Farnell, "The Current Debate about New Testament Prophecy," *Bibliotheca Sacra* 149 (July–September 1992): 277–303.

9. The conclusion that a prophetic "herald" somehow is to be equated with the modern "preacher" is a non sequitur. As will be demonstrated in the comparison of prophecy and other related gifts, the miraculous nature of the gift of prophecy, which involves the impartation of direct revelatory knowledge, sharply delineates prophet from preacher. While both the prophet and preacher proclaim truth, the evidence from the biblical data demonstrates that an equation of prophet with preacher is tenuous at best.

10. "Common to all representatives of the prophetic type here depicted is the consciousness of having access to information of the world above and experiences originating in the divine world, from which ordinary men are excluded" (Lindblom, *Prophecy in Ancient Israel*, pp. 32–33).

11. Even in "charismatic" exegesis, apostles who possessed the gift of prophecy demonstrate the miraculous nature of the gift. Paul illustrated this Spirit-guided supernatural element in his exegesis of Isaiah 59:20–21; 27:9 in Romans 11:25–26. Aune notes, "The remarkable thing about the quotation is that the phrase 'from Zion,' which apparently justifies the coming of Messiah from the Jews and his proclamation among the Gentiles, is found neither in the Hebrew original or in the LXX. . . . Through the medium of an interpretive alteration in the OT text, of the sort not found infrequently in the pesherim of Qumran, an insight into the destiny of both Israel and the Gentiles has been extrapolated. To Paul the OT text means that a redeemer (i.e., Jesus Christ) shall come *from* Zion (for the benefit of the Gentiles) and will banish ungodliness from Jacob (i.e., 'all Israel')" (Aune, *Prophecy in Early Christianity*, p. 252). Another example of this would be the use of Psalm 68:18 in Ephesians 4:8. Later, however, Aune asserts that someone with the gift of teaching could have produced such exegesis but this is

highly unlikely (ibid., pp. 345–46). After an extensive discussion
of the nature of New Testament exegesis, Longenecker correctly
asserts that when apostolic exegesis "is based upon a revelatory
stance" it cannot be reproduced on a merely human level (Richard
N. Longenecker, *Biblical Exegesis in the Apostolic Period* [Grand
Rapids: Eerdmans, 1975], pp. 219–20; cf. Robert L. Thomas, "The
Spiritual Gift of Prophecy in Revelation 22:18," *Journal of the
Evangelical Theological Society* 32 [June 1989]: 204, n. 16).

12. Saucy provides a definition of prophecy that is succinct and
consistent with the biblical data: "Prophecy in the biblical sense
[is] speech which is inspired by the Spirit and therefore totally
true and authoritative" (Robert L. Saucy, "Prophecy Today? An
Initial Response," *Sundoulos* [Spring 1990]: 5). Since the source
of genuine biblical prophecy is the Holy Spirit, attempts at arguing
for different levels of prophetic authority are tenuous. As Saucy
notes in response to Grudem's hypothesis, "we have seen nothing
sufficient to overturn the traditional understanding of all genuine
prophecy as speech directly inspired by the Spirit of God and
therefore fully authoritative" (ibid.).

13. "While prediction was not the major element in New Testament
prophecy, it was an indispensable part of it" (Thomas, "A Review
of *The Gift of Prophecy in the New Testament and Today,*" p. 94).

14. Edgar argues that a prophet "often predicts and, in fact, *must*
predict if he is to be recognized as a prophet" (Thomas R. Edgar,
Miraculous Gifts: Are They for Today? [Neptune, NJ: Loizeaux,
1983], p. 72 [italics his]). However, the role of προφήτης must
not be confused with the μάντις ("soothsayer"). The μάντις
belonged strictly to a secular setting and did not possess the
hortatory function of the prophet (Krämer, "προφήτης," p. 790,
and *The New International Dictionary of New Testament Theology,*
s.v. "Prophet," by C. H. Peisker and Colin Brown, 3:76).

15. Edgar aptly notes, "The prophet is representative of God. When
prophesying he often discerns and interprets God's will in a specific
situation. . . . His information is gained in a supernatural manner
directly from God. When he speaks apart from direct revelation,
his message is no more accurate than any ordinary spokesman for
God" (Edgar, *Miraculous Gifts: Are They for Today?* p. 72).

16. Just as ἑρμηνεία ("interpretation") was needed in conjunction with
the exercise of γλωσσῶν ("tongues"), διακρίσεις ("discernment")
was needed to accompany προφητεία ("prophecy"). Though this
correlation is not explicit in 1 Corinthians 14, it is strongly implicit
by virtue of the contextual flow of chapters 12–14 and the use of
cognate words in 12:10 and 14:29 to depict the gift and exercise

of discerning. Inspired spokesmen were in the best position to judge spontaneously whether a new utterance was in agreement with Paul's teaching (Gal. 1:8–9; 2 Thess. 2:1–3) and the generally accepted beliefs of the Christian community (1 Cor. 12:1–3). Cf. A. T. Robertson and Alfred Plummer, *A Critical and Exegetical Commentary on the First Epistle of St. Paul to the Corinthians*, International Critical Commentary, 2d ed. (Edinburgh: Clark, 1914), pp. 267, 321–22.

17. Also see Matthew 12:25; Mark 2:5–8; 9:33–41; 10:21; 12:15; Luke 6:8; 9:47; 11:17; 19:5; and John 2:24–25. Hill comments, "The ability to reveal the secret of man's heart was regarded by Paul as a distinctive mark of the effectiveness of prophesying (1 Cor. 14:24–25) and it seems to have been considered a mark of the prophetic phenomenon by Jesus' contemporaries" (Hill, *New Testament Prophecy*, p. 60).

18. This communication of divine revelation may assume a variety of forms, such as dreams (Deut. 13:1–5; Matt. 2:19–22; Acts 2:17), visions (Gen. 15:1; 2 Chron. 32:32; Isa. 1:1; Acts 10:10–16; 16:6–10), visitations by heavenly messengers (Zech. 1:11; 2 Kings 1:15; Acts 10:3; 27:21–25; Rev. 1:1), and the prophetic or ecstatic state of the prophet (1 Cor. 12:3; Rev. 1:10).

19. Edgar, *Miraculous Gifts: Are They for Today?* pp. 69–70.

20. Robert L. Thomas, *Understanding Spiritual Gifts* (Chicago: Moody, 1978), p. 121. "When Christians assembled together to hear the mind of God cogently declared in a language that they can understand, this promotes their upbuilding and encouragement and consolation" (F. F. Bruce, *1 and 2 Corinthians*, New Century Bible Commentary [Greenwood, SC: Attic, 1971], p. 130).

21. F. L. Godet, *The First Epistle to the Corinthians*, 2 vols. (Edinburgh: Clark, 1886; reprint, Grand Rapids: Zondervan, 1971), 2:267–68. In contrast, Ellis contends that the mere act of exhortation "is a form of prophecy" and constitutes a "specific ministry of a prophet." He contends that Judas and Silas in Acts 15:30–35 were prophets on the basis of their ministry of παράκλησις (E. Earle Ellis, "The Role of the Christian Prophet in Acts," in *Apostolic History and the Gospel*, ed. W. W. Gasque and Ralph Martin [Grand Rapids: Eerdmans, 1970], p. 55, n. 1; 56, n. 3; pp. 57–58). However, the verses cited do not actually support Ellis's contentions, for the content of the prophets' message of παράκλησις is not revealed. Acts 15:32 states only that the prophets Judas and Silas strengthened and encouraged the Antioch congregation "through many words" (διὰ λόγου πολλοῦ). This suggests that their message was the means through

which edification and strengthening of the congregation were accomplished. Furthermore Ellis's citation of Acts 11:23; 16:40; and 20:2 as examples of prophetic exhortation does not necessarily support his argument, for the verses merely state that Barnabas, Paul, and Silas exhorted believers and do not identify their activity directly with prophecy or with the missionaries' being prophets. In Acts, when the content of New Testament prophecy is revealed, the miraculous nature of that content is evident (e.g., Acts 11:28; 13:11; 20:23, 25; 21:10–11; 27:22). Furthermore Ellis, reflecting Conzelmann's view (H. Conzelmann, *Die Apostelgeschichte* [Tübingen: Mohr, 1963], p. 27) incorrectly suggests that tongues and the interpretation of tongues may possibly be equated with prophecy in Acts. Ellis cites Acts 2:4, 11, 17; 19:6 as examples where prophecy and tongues are closely associated. However, nothing in the context requires that the two spiritual gifts be equated. A variety of charismatic phenomena occurred on the day of Pentecost (Acts 2:17) with prophecy and tongues receiving prominence. In Acts 19:6 prophecy and tongues are best seen as separate phenomena experienced by John's disciples especially since distinct verbs are used to describe such activities and no attempt at equating them is seen in the passage. Also Scripture elsewhere distinguishes between tongues and prophecy as separate gifts (1 Cor. 14:1–33).

22. Several arguments add additional support to this assertion. (1) In Romans 12:8 edification is classified as a separate spiritual gift. Thus a distinction between speech which merely edifies and speech as prophecy must be intended. (2) Any believer could exhort, edify, or comfort without the activity of prophesying or being considered a prophet (Rom. 15:2; 1 Cor. 8:1; Eph. 4:29; Col. 4:8; 1 Thess. 3:2; 5:11). (3) In Ephesians 4:11–16 apostles, evangelists, pastors, and teachers are seen as gifted men given to the church, who along with prophets in the exercise of their functions caused the body of Christ to be edified and matured (Eph. 4:13). Therefore a distinction between the edifying nature of prophecy and the edifying effect of other spiritual gifts and gifted men given to the church must be considered. Most likely, this distinction centers in the fact that prophecy resulted from direct revelation from the Lord (1 Cor. 14:30), and the proclamation of that miraculous revelation resulted in edification, comfort, and encouragement of the hearers (14:3).

23. Ephesians 4:16 reinforces the idea that οἰκοδομήν ("building up," cf. v. 12) refers to the personal spiritual growth that came from the reception of prophetic truth (Charles J. Ellicott, *St. Paul's First*

Epistle to the Corinthians [London: Longmans, Green, 1887], p. 260).

24. Peisker and Brown, "Prophet," 88.

25. Four main schools of interpretation have existed regarding the Book of Revelation: praeterist, idealist, historicist, and futurist. The present writer holds to the futurist view of Revelation, the view held by dispensational premillennialists that most of the book (Rev. 4–22) depicts events that are yet future. The events of those chapters cover the time periods of the future Great Tribulation, the Second Advent, the millennium, and the new heavens and new earth. Only the futurist view gives due recognition to the prophetic nature of the book and points to the Second Advent as the central unifying theme of the book. Furthermore such a view is most consistent with the grammatical, historical hermeneutic with its emphasis on consistent literal interpretation, while allowing for figures of speech. See John F. Walvoord, *Revelation* (Chicago: Moody, 1966), p. 23; and D. Edmond Hiebert, *The Non-Pauline Epistles and Revelation,* vol. 3 of *An Introduction to the New Testament,* rev. ed. (Chicago: Moody, 1977), pp. 263–68.

26. The omniscience of Christ regarding the spiritual condition of the churches and the communication of that supernatural knowledge to the Prophet John is seen in such phrases as "I know" (οἶδα, 2:2, 9, 13, 19; 3:1, 8, 15). Supernatural communication is also reinforced by the recurring phrase "eyes like a flame of fire" with reference to Thyatira (1:14; 2:18). This phrase refers to the surpassing intelligence of the One so described (cf. Dan. 10:6, 14), particularly as He related the knowledge of the future to John (Robert L. Thomas, "The Glorified Christ on Patmos," *Bibliotheca Sacra* 122 [July–September 1965]: 244).

27. "New Testament prophets were . . . vehicles of divine revelation, some of which passed into written form and was included in Scripture (e.g., the Epistle to the Hebrews). The very words of their prophecies, being based on and inseparable from divine revelation (cf. 1 Cor. 14:29), were inspired and therefore authoritative. This was an indispensable element of prophecy. Without direct revelation from God someone who promoted edification through exhortation and comfort had to base his message on the inspired words of others and was exercising the gift of exhortation (cf. Rom. 12:8) or teaching (cf. 1 Cor. 12:28), not the gift of prophecy" (Thomas, "A Review of *The Gift of Prophecy in the New Testament and Today,*" pp. 93–94). Also see John F. Walvoord, *The Holy Spirit at Work Today* (Chicago: Moody, 1974), pp. 42–43; and Edgar, *Miraculous Gifts: Are They for Today?* p. 70.

28. The idea that biblical prophecy should be labeled as "ecstatic" is debated. Both the definition of ecstasy and the precise nature of the prophetic state of "ecstasy" have no consensus (T. Callan, "Prophecy and Ecstasy in Greco-Roman Religion in 1 Corinthians," *Novum Testamentum* 27 [1985]: 139). The term "ecstatic" connotes for some the idea that the biblical prophet was somehow irrational in the prophetic state. "The institutions of Israelite worship, its religious festivals, and sacrificial customs, appear to have been drawn largely from the practices of Canaan. . . . Even the prophets themselves . . . are genetically related to an older non-moral type Nebi'im, who are, perhaps, like the holy places and festivals, and the general details of sacrifice, a contribution of Canaan to Israel's development" (H. Wheeler Robinson, *The Religious Ideas of the Old Testament,* 2d ed. [London: Duckworth, 1956], pp. 17–18). Reflective of the *Religionsgeschichtliche Schule* approach, which posits an evolutionary development of religions, the assumption was that since other nations practiced various forms of irrational frenzy in the expression of their ecstatic state in the surrounding areas of Palestine (i.e., Asia Minor, Canaan, Greece, and Syria), the Hebrew prophets were influenced by such "prophetic" practices (for further information, see Theophile J. Meek, *Hebrew Origins* [New York: Harper, 1960], pp. 155–57; William O. Oesterley and Theodore H. Robinson, *Hebrew Religion: Its Origin and Development,* 2d ed. [London: S.P.C.K., 1944], p. 200; and idem, *An Introduction to the Books of the Old Testament* [Cleveland: World, 1962], p. 397).
However, in reply to such assertions, the "ecstatic" state of biblical prophets was qualitatively different from that of pagan prophetism, especially since the Holy Spirit was so intimately involved in the prophetic process of biblical prophets (Neh. 9:30; Mic. 3:8; Zech. 7:12; Ezek. 2:2; 3:12–14). Such a state prepared the prophet for receiving divine revelation, and at no time was he irrational. For a refutation of the concept of an irrational ecstatic state, consult Leon J. Wood, *The Prophets of Israel* (Grand Rapids: Baker, 1979), pp. 37–56; and idem, *The Holy Spirit in the Old Testament* (Grand Rapids: Zondervan, 1976), pp. 90–112.
29. In the Old Testament no single Hebrew word is used to describe the revelatory state. The Septuagint uses ἔκστασις 30 times to translate 11 Hebrew words, most of which mean "fear" (e.g., 2 Chron. 14:14; Ruth 3:8) or "trembling" (e.g., Gen. 27:33; Ex. 19:18). Furthermore the Septuagint uses ἐξιστάνω and ἐξίστημι for 29 Hebrew words that are synonyms for "fear" and "amazement."

30. Explicit statements are not made concerning some Old Testament prophets that they were empowered by the Spirit in the prophetic stapte (e.g., Joel, Amos, Obadiah, Nahum, and Malachi). However, Zechariah 7:12 and Nehemiah 9:30 all associate the ministry of such prophets directly with the enablement of the Holy Spirit. See Wood, *The Holy Spirit in the Old Testament*, pp. 46–47.

31. The context of 1 Corinthians 12:3 lends perspicuity to the situation addressed in 1 Corinthians 14:29. Apparently false prophets had preached that Jesus was "accursed" (12:3) even though they professed to be true prophets. The thrust of 12:1–3 is that genuine prophets are guarded by the Holy Spirit from making such starkly erroneous prophesyings. False prophesying becomes a signal that a false prophet is active. Paul later warned the congregation to evaluate each prophecy carefully to ensure that a genuine prophet was speaking (14:29–32).

32. This is in contrast to the secular prophet, whose experiences often were irrational. Expressions like μάντις ("soothsayer"), χρησμόλογος ("oracle-relater"), μαίνομαι ("to rave"), ἐνθουσιασμός ("god-possessed"), which convey an irrational ecstasy, are not used in the New Testament of biblical prophets. In the Septuagint μαντεύομαι and μάντις are almost always used of pagan soothsayers and false prophets. However, an exception in the Septuagint is in Proverbs 16:10—μαντεῖον ἐπὶ χείλεσιν βασιλέως (Friedrich, "προφήτης," p. 851, n. 430). In the New Testament μαντεύομαι is also used in a negative sense of soothsaying (Acts 16:16). In the Septuagint the word μαίνομαι is used in Jeremiah 32:16 (Heb., 25:16) and conveys a negative connotation of "going mad," while in Jeremiah 36:26 (Heb., 29:26) it is also used negatively to refer to madness. In the New Testament μαίνομαι has a negative connotation. In John 10:20 it is used by the Jews who asserted that Jesus was demonized and was thus "insane" (δαιμόνιον ἔχει καὶ μαίνεται). In Acts 12:15 the girl Rhoda was considered "mad" because she reported that Peter was standing at the door. When Paul gave his defense before King Herod Agrippa II, Festus used the word twice in referring to Paul as insane (Acts 26:24). Paul denied that he was "mad" (v. 25). Paul also used the term negatively in 1 Corinthians 14:23 where the word again has the idea of "insane" or "mad." In the Septuagint the verb χρησμολογέω occurs in Jeremiah 45:4 (Heb., 38:4), where government officials who opposed Jeremiah requested his death for not "giving oracular responses," or pronouncements, of peace (χρησμολεγεῖ εἰρήνην). Ἐνθουσιάζειν and its cognates do not appear in the Septuagint or the New Testament.

33. David Hill, "Prophets and Prophecy in the Revelation of St. John," *New Testament Studies* 18 (1971–72): 406.
34. Aune, *Prophecy in Early Christianity*, p. 202.
35. Friedrich, "προφήτης," p. 854.
36. "The teacher worked with material already known and made it relevant to his hearers' needs; the prophet's utterance cannot be dissociated from the impartation of knowledge which did not come there and then by rational thinking" (Ernest Best, "Prophets and Preachers," *Scottish Journal of Theology* 12 [1959]: 147). Cf. E. Schweizer, "Observance of Law and Charismatic Activity in Matthew," *New Testament Studies* 16 (1969–70): 228–29.
37. Grudem, *The Gift of Prophecy in 1 Corinthians*, p. 142. Grudem notes that these same considerations apply to the terms κατηχέω, παιδεύω, and παιδεία.
38. Ibid., p. 143.
39. Ibid.
40. Alan Redpath, *The Royal Route to Heaven* (Westwood, NJ: Revell, 1960), pp. 142–43. Robertson and Plummer comment that prophecy is "not necessarily predicting the future but preaching the word with power. . . . This gift implies special insight into revealed truths and great faculty for making them and their consequences known to others" (Robertson and Plummer, *A Critical and Exegetical Commentary on the First Epistle of St. Paul to the Corinthians*, p. 266). However, while prophets did perform this function, their "special insight" involved more than preaching. It also involved a revelatory communication directly from God to man.
41. John F. MacArthur, *Charismatic Chaos* (Grand Rapids: Zondervan, 1992), p. 231, n. 20. MacArthur agrees with Grudem's concept of two levels of prophecy. "Grudem . . . argues for two levels of New Testament prophecy. One is apostolic prophecy, which is infallible and on a par with both Old Testament prophecy and the inerrant written Word of God. The other is the gift of prophecy, which is meant to edify, encourage, and comfort. I would agree. But unlike Grudem I do not believe this second level of prophecy is revelatory" (ibid., p. 70, n. 12). Though the present writer disagrees strongly with Grudem on many points of his hypothesis, Grudem correctly recognizes the difficulty of separating the revelatory nature of prophecy from its proclamation. As will be demonstrated in this chapter, such a position of a second form of nonrevelatory "prophecy" synonymous with preaching is difficult to sustain in light of a close examination of the evidence. The concept of "preacher" should not be equated with the biblical

concept of "prophet."
42. Best, *"Prophets and Preachers,"* p. 145. Best observes that the close tie of New Testament prophets with their Old Testament counterpart, particularly in the element of prediction, sharply distinguishes the prophet from the preacher.
43. Ibid.
44. Friedrich, "profhvth"," p. 853.
45. Ibid., p. 854.
46. Ibid., pp. 854–55; also see *Theological Dictionary of the New Testament,* s.v. "eujaggelizomai," by Gerhard Friedrich, 2:736–37.
47. Thomas, *Understanding Spiritual Gifts,* pp. 105–6; Thomas C. Edwards, *A Commentary on the First Epistle to the Corinthians* (London: Hodder & Stoughton, 1903), p. 349.
48. The precise nature of the gifts of "wisdom" and "knowledge" is admittedly difficult. Commentators are divided on various aspects of this issue. Furthermore the precise relationship between "the word of wisdom" and "the word of knowledge" is also hotly debated. Some believe that the terms are virtually synonymous (e.g., Hans Conzelmann, *1 Corinthians* [Philadelphia: Fortress, 1975], p. 209; and C. K. Barrett, *The First Epistle to the Corinthians* [New York: Harper & Row, 1968], p. 285). Some see the gifts as revelatory (e.g., Thomas, *Understanding Spiritual Gifts,* p. 37; Charles Hodge, *Commentary on the First Epistle to the Corinthians* [Grand Rapids: Eerdmans, 1976), pp. 245–46; Leon Morris, *The First Epistle of Paul to the Corinthians,* Tyndale New Testament Commentaries [Grand Rapids: Eerdmans, 1958], p. 171). However, since teaching gifts may be involved in utterances of this type, the gift does not have to be revelatory (Friedrich, "προφήτης," p. 853).
49. For a detailed discussion of the cessationist implications of these and other verses, see such excellent works as Merrill F. Unger, *The Baptism and Gifts of the Holy Spirit* (Chicago: Moody, 1974), pp. 138–40; Edgar, *Miraculous Gifts: Are They for Today?* pp. 270–75; and Thomas, "The Spiritual Gift of Prophecy in Revelation 22:18," pp. 207–16.
50. Prominent cessationists have used these as central passages in their contention that the gift of prophecy is no longer in operation. Examples of dispensational theologians who have advocated the temporary nature of the prophetic gift are Lewis Sperry Chafer, *Systematic Theology,* 8 vols. (Dallas, TX: Dallas Theological Seminary, 1948; reprint [8 vols. in 4], Grand Rapids: Kregel, 1992), 6:215; John F. Walvoord, *The Holy Spirit* (Grand Rapids: Zondervan, 1965), pp. 173–88; idem, *The Holy Spirit at Work*

Today, pp. 1–54; Charles C. Ryrie, *The Holy Spirit* (Chicago: Moody, 1965), pp. 84–85; Robert L. Thomas, "Tongues . . . Will Cease," *Journal of the Evangelical Theological Society* 17 (Spring 1974): 81–89; idem, *Understanding Spiritual Gifts* (Chicago: Moody, 1978), pp. 105–13; Robert G. Gromacki, *The Modern Tongues Movement* (Philadelphia: Presbyterian and Reformed, 1967), pp. 118–19; Zane C. Hodges, "The Purpose of Tongues," *Bibliotheca Sacra* 120 (July–September 1963): 227; and Ken Sarles, "An Appraisal of the Signs and Wonders Movement," *Bibliotheca Sacra* 145 (January–March 1988): 75–76.
Examples of Reformed and covenant theologians who have advocated the cessation of the prophetic gift are Benjamin B. Warfield, *Counterfeit Miracles* (reprint, Carlisle, PA: Banner of Truth, 1972), pp. 1–32; Kenneth L. Gentry, *The Charismatic Gift of Prophecy* (Memphis: Footstool, 1989), p. 8; Robert L. Reymond, *What about Continuing Revelations and Miracles in the Presbyterian Church Today? A Study of the Doctrine of the Sufficiency of Scripture* (St. Louis: Presbyterian and Reformed, 1977), pp. 28–42; and Walter J. Chantry, *Signs of the Apostles: Observations on Pentecostalism Old and New,* 2d ed. (Carlisle, PA: Banner of Truth, 1976), pp. 22–37.

51. Edgar, *Miraculous Gifts: Are They for Today?* p. 268.
52. See Walter Bauer, William F. Arndt, and F. Wilbur Gingrich, *A Greek-English Lexicon of the New Testament and Other Early Christian Literature* 2d ed., rev. F. Wilbur Gingrich and Frederick W. Danker (Chicago: University of Chicago, 1979), p. 241; and *Theological Dictionary of the New Testament,* s.v. "ἐκκλησία," by Karl Ludwig Schmidt, 3:509–12.
53. Edgar, *Miraculous Gifts: Are They for Today?* p. 268; Ryrie, *The Holy Spirit,* p. 84; Reymond, *What about Continuing Revelations and Miracles in the Presbyterian Church Today?* p. 37.
54. "This mystery was revealed by the Spirit (cf. Eph. 2:22), and its recipients were God's holy apostles and prophets (cf. 2:20; 4:11)" (Harold W. Hoehner, "Ephesians," in *The Bible Knowledge Commentary, New Testament,* ed. John F. Walvoord and Roy B. Zuck [Wheaton, IL: Victor, 1983], p. 629). See also C. Leslie Mitton, *Ephesians,* New Century Bible Commentary (Grand Rapids: Eerdmans, 1981), p. 123.
55. George E. Ladd, *A Theology of the New Testament* (Grand Rapids: Eerdmans, 1974), p. 535.
56. Edgar, *Miraculous Gifts: Are They for Today?* p. 268.
57. However, contrary to Grudem, they are not to be equated but have a close association in their comprising the foundation of the church

and in their reception of revelatory doctrinal and canonical content. Though the New Testament apostles and prophets are not to be equated, the usage of the single article in Ephesians 2:20 (τῷ θεμελίῳ τῶν ἀποστόλων καὶ προφητῶν) emphasizes the close role these two groups had in doctrinal and canonical matters. As Robertson notes, the one article may indicate that "groups more or less distinct are treated as one for the purpose at hand" (A. T. Robertson, *A Grammar of the Greek New Testament in the Light of Historical Research* [Nashville: Broadman, 1934], p. 787; cf. Nigel Turner, *Syntax*, vol. 3 of *A Grammar of New Testament Greek,* by J. H. Moulton [Edinburgh: Clark, 1963], p. 181).

58. The *Didache* demonstrates the close association of apostles and New Testament prophets (*Didache* 11.3–6). Ignatius bore the same testimony and wrote that Christian prophets should be heard because they had "lived according to Jesus Christ" and were "inspired by his grace" (*To the Magnesians* 8.2). He said further that Christians should love not only the gospel and the apostles but also the prophets since they had announced the advent of Christ and had become His disciples (*To the Philippians* 5.2). The *Muratorian Fragment* also associates these gifts with one another as it declares the termination of apostleship and prophecy. In speaking of the *Shepherd of Hermas,* the *Fragment* says, "It cannot be read publicly to the people in the church either among the prophets, whose number is complete, nor among the apostles" (Harry Gamble, *The New Testament Canon: Its Making and Meaning* [Philadelphia: Fortress, 1985], p. 95). Gamble's work gives the full text of the Muratorian canon translated from the Latin.

59. According to Grudem, the gift of apostleship was temporary and ceased about the end of the first century A.D. so that "there are no apostles today" (see Grudem, *The Gift of Prophecy in the New Testament and Today,* pp. 275–76). However, Ephesians 2:20 not only shows the temporary nature of the gift of apostleship but it also shows that the gift of prophecy was also foundational and therefore temporary. With the completion of the New Testament, the gift of prophecy also became obsolete.

60. George Mallone, *Those Controversial Gifts* (Downers Grove, IL: InterVarsity, 1983), p. 18. Mallone cites John Stott as a confirmation of this position, but Stott himself is a cessationist who supports the temporary nature of such gifts as apostleship and prophecy. See John R. W. Stott, *Baptism and Fullness: The Work of the Holy Spirit Today* (Downers Grove, IL: InterVarsity, 1979), pp. 101–2. Stott notes that the gifts of apostle and prophet were

temporary and designed for the beginnings of the church in the first century A.D. ("they no longer exist in the church").

61. Reymond, *What about Continuing Revelations and Miracles in the Presbyterian Church Today?* p. 37.
62. Mallone, *Those Controversial Gifts,* p. 19.
63. Ryrie, *The Holy Spirit,* p. 85.
64. Ibid.
65. Regarding Ephesians 2:20, Stott notes, "Just as the foundation cannot be tampered with once it has been laid and the superstructure is being build upon it, so the New Testament foundation of the church is inviolable and cannot be changed by any additions, subtractions, or modifications offered by teachers who claim to be apostles or prophets today. The church stands or falls by its loyal dependence on the foundation truths which God revealed to his apostles and prophets, and which are now preserved in the New Testament Scriptures" (John R. W. Stott, *God's New Society: The Message of Ephesians* [Downers Grove, IL: InterVarsity, 1979], p. 107).
66. No less than five interpretive options for this verse have been formulated, making the issues surrounding these verses highly complex. Essentially all these arguments may be reduced to two views: τὸ τέλειον refers either to what is "perfect" or to "maturity." Three other options merit attention. They share the understanding that τὸ τέλειον signifies the idea of "perfect." (1) Edgar's view is that τὸ τέλειον refers to the death of the believer when the person is ushered into Christ's presence. He argues that (a) 1 Corinthians 13:11–12 has a personal emphasis in view, that (b) in verse 10 τὸ τέλειον "is stated as part of a general principle and not as a specific," and that (c) the time in which a believer has "perfect" knowledge is when he dies and goes to be with the Lord (Edgar, *Miraculous Gifts: Are They for Today?* pp. 340–44). However, the context argues against this view in that the passage focuses on the situation on earth, not in heaven. The emphasis is on the exercise of spiritual gifts and love in the Christian community. (2) MacArthur's view is that τὸ τέλειον refers to the eternal state. He gives two reasons for this. First, "in the millennial kingdom there will be prophesying and teaching resulting in knowledge" (Isa. 11:9; 30:20–21, 32:3–4; Jer. 3:14–15; 23:1–4; Joel 2:28–32; Rev. 11:1–12). Second, the phrase "face to face" (τότε δὲ πρόσωπον πρὸς πρόσωπον, 1 Cor. 13:12) must refer to being with God in the new creation or eternal state (John F. MacArthur, Jr., *The Charismatics: A Doctrinal Perspective* [Grand Rapids: Zondervan, 1978], pp. 165–71; idem, *Charismatic Chaos,* pp. 230–31, n. 20). A major problem with this view is that

the Pauline eschatological hope is not exclusively centered on events after the millennium (Rom. 8:22–23; 1 Cor. 1:7; 15:1–58; 1 Thess. 4:13–18). (3) Unger holds that the canon of the New Testament is identified with τὸ τέλειον. The argument is that the possession of the canonical Scriptures removes the partial or incomplete understanding and thus removes the need for prophesying. This view also finds support indirectly because of the role the gifts of prophecy and knowledge played in the completion of the New Testament canon (Merrill F. Unger, *The Baptism and Gifts of the Holy Spirit* [Chicago: Moody, 1974], pp. 141–42). However, no room for the Parousia (which is clearly in view in 1 Cor. 12:12) exists in such a view. Furthermore the concept of the New Testament canon is not directly involved in this context.

67. Commentators that support this view include Bruce, *1 and 2 Corinthians,* pp. 127–28; Robertson and Plummer, *A Critical and Exegetical Commentary on the First Epistle of St. Paul to the Corinthians,* p. 297; C. K. Barrett, *The First Epistle to the Corinthians* (New York: Harper & Row, 1968), p. 306; F. W. Grosheide, *The First Epistle to the Corinthians,* New International Commentary on the New Testament (Grand Rapids: Eerdmans, 1953), pp. 309–10; Gordon D. Fee, *The First Epistle to the Corinthians,* New International Commentary on the New Testament (Grand Rapids: Eerdmans, 1987), pp. 644–46; and H. Conzelmann, *A Commentary on the First Epistle to the Corinthians,* Hermeneia (Philadelphia: Fortress, 1975), p. 226.

68. For further information on this third argument, see Godet, *The First Epistle to the Corinthians,* 2:252.

69. This view has several major weaknesses. First, Paul's illustration of gradual development from childhood to adulthood does not really typify the immense transformation associated with the Lord's return (v. 11). Adulthood is not completely free of limitations as would be the Parousia. Second, the view fails to allow for the distinctive revelatory character of the gift of prophecy and the distinctive confirmatory character of tongues (v. 8; cf. 12:8–10, 28). Third, the contrast with ἐκ μέρους ("in part") requires a quantitative idea (i.e., "complete") rather than a qualitative idea ("perfect"). See Thomas, *Understanding Spiritual Gifts,* p. 203; and idem, *Exegetical Digest of 1 Corinthians 12–14* (n.p.: 1988), p. 96.

70. The major proponents of this meaning of τὸ τέλειον are Thomas, *Understanding Spiritual Gifts,* pp. 202–3; idem, *Exegetical Digest of 1 Corinthians 12–14,* pp. 95–98; Jody Dillow, *A Biblical Evaluation of the Twentieth-Century Tongues Movement (Seven*

Crucial Questions) (n.p.: 1972), pp. 35–36; and idem, *Speaking in Tongues* (Grand Rapids: Zondervan, 1979), pp. 88–90. Thomas and Dillow differ, however, on the ultimate significance of the idea of maturity or completeness. While Thomas places emphasis on a gradual development whereby the church is constantly entering new stages of maturity, Dillow places more stress on the close of the canon as the significance of the term. Both commentators, however, negate the idea of τὸ τέλειον as having an absolute sense of perfection.

71. The view adopted here is that of Thomas. While Dillow is correct in seeing the development of the New Testament canon as a significant stage in the maturation process, the close of the canon would represent only one stage in the body's progressive development and alone cannot satisfy the illustration of 13:12 (see Thomas, *Understanding Spiritual Gifts*, p. 108).

72. For further information on this point see *Theological Dictionary of the New Testament,* s.v. "τέλειος," by Gerhard Delling, 8:69–77; Thomas, "Tongues . . . Will Cease," p. 83; and idem, *Exegetical Digest of 1 Corinthians 12–14*, pp. 96–97. While classical Greek usage may convey the idea of "perfection" (Henry George Liddell and Robert Scott, *Greek-English Lexicon,* rev. Henry Stuart Jones, 9th ed. [Oxford: Clarendon, 1940], pp. 1769–70), Paul never used this word in that sense.

73. At least 11 striking similarities and parallels are seen between 1 Corinthians 13 and Ephesians 4 (Thomas, *Exegetical Digest on 1 Corinthians 12–14,* p. 97). (1) The νήπιος . . . τέλειος antithesis is found in both places. (2) The general subject of discussion in both is spiritual gifts. (3) Edification of the body of Christ is the stated objective in Ephesians 4 as well as in 1 Corinthians 12–14. (4) Both passages use the figure of the human body to represent the church. (5) Growth from childhood to maturity is emphasized in both cases. (6) Love is prominent in the growth process along with spiritual gifts in both passages. (7) Individual parts of Christ's body are depicted by the noun μέρος in both chapters (Eph. 4:16; 1 Cor. 12:27). (8) Whenever Paul discussed spiritual gifts, he had the body figure in view (Eph. 4:11–16; cf. Rom. 12:3–8). (9) An emphasis on unity is seen in Ephesians 4:1–6 (cf. 1 Cor. 12). (10) All seven unifying persons and features mentioned in Ephesians 4:4–6 are referred to in 1 Corinthians 12–14. (11) Ἀνήρ is used in both passages.

74. For further information on the place and date of writing, see Donald Guthrie, *New Testament Introduction,* rev. ed. (Downers Grove, IL: InterVarsity, 1990), pp. 457–59; and Hiebert, *The*

Pauline Epistles, vol. 2 of *An Introduction to the New Testament,* pp. 112–13.

75. Again, though the completion of the canon was a development in this maturation process, it was only one stage of that development.

76. Several criticisms are leveled against this view. First, this view, it is argued, does not do justice to the illustration of 1 Corinthians 13:12 which most likely refers to Christ's Second Coming. In reply, it may be noted that the view does see an absolute maturity (v. 12) represented along with a progressive maturity (v. 11) so that the view does do justice to the illustration in verse 12. Second, a gradual development does not suit the κατήργηκα of verse 11. However, if the transition is seen as a fading away until completely gone, the perfect could appropriately picture this. Third, this view does not give a good sense to the aorist ἔλθη. However, if the aorist is viewed as constantive, then an adequate sense may be supplied. Fourth, the question may be asked, Was the church ever mature enough not to need these gifts such as prophecy? In reply, it should be noted that when in the providence of God the church had a completed package of revelatory data (the New Testament canon) prophecy would have been rendered unnecessary. As will be seen, the analogy of the completion of the Old Testament canon and the cessation of prophecy in the Old Testament period would serve as paradigms for the cessation of New Testament prophecy. For further elaboration on arguments for and against this view, see Thomas, *Understanding Spiritual Gifts,* pp. 106–8; idem, *Exegetical Digest on 1 Corinthians 12–14,* pp. 95–98; and William McRae, *The Dynamics of Spiritual Gifts* (Grand Rapids: Zondervan, 1976), pp. 93–94.

77. Thomas, *Understanding Spiritual Gifts,* pp. 106–7, 207; and idem, *Exegetical Digest on First Corinthians 12–14,* p. 97.

78. Thomas, *Exegetical Digest on 1 Corinthians 12–14,* p. 98.

79. Geisler's comment is also important. "Although Paul does not specify when these gifts would cease, he does say that they will. Furthermore, he hints that this would occur as the church progressed toward 'maturity' (1 Corinthians 13:10; cf. Ephesians 4:12). Although this will not be complete till the Second Coming (v. 12), he does not say that all the gifts will last until then. Indeed, it is obvious from the contrasts above that the gifts petered out as the early church matured" (Geisler, *Signs and Wonders,* p. 137). Chrysostom wrote the following concerning the subject of spiritual gifts in 1 Corinthians 12:1–2 specifically, and chapters 12–14 in general: "This whole place is very obscure: but the obscurity is produced by our ignorance of the facts referred to and by their cessation, being such as then used to occur but now

no longer take place. And why do they not happen now? Why look now, the cause too of the obscurity has produced us again another question; namely, why did they then happen, and now do so no more?" (Chrysostom, *Homilies on the First Epistle of St. Paul the Apostle to the Corinthians,* Homily 29, in *Nicene and Post-Nicene Fathers* ed. Phillip Schaff, 14 vols. (New York: Christian Literature), 12:168; cf. Homily 36). Here is a clear statement by a leader of the church in the fourth century that miraculous gifts, like prophecy and tongues, ceased. Because Chrysostom was well traveled and would have most likely known the general status of practices in the church, he signaled the widespread absence of such gifts in his day. The Muratorian canon makes the explicit statement that the number of apostles and prophets "is complete," indicating an end to prophetic expression (Gamble, *The New Testament Canon: Its Making and Meaning,* p. 95). Thus Heine makes the following observation regarding the Muratorian canon list: "It should be noted that the Muratorian canon, which is to be dated at approximately this same time [as the Montanist Controversy] and located at Rome, rejected the *Shepherd of Hermas* for the same reason that Hippolytus advanced against the Montanist prophecy: it is a recent writing, and prophecy ceased with the apostles" (Ronald E. Heine, "The Role of the Gospel of John in the Montanist Controversy," *The Second Century* 6 [1987–88]: 12–13).

Many believe that this argument from church history constitutes one of the strongest arguments against the continuance of prophecy, and miraculous gifts in general. Constable terms this the "strongest evidence" for the cessation of revelation (Thomas L. Constable, "Review of 'The Spiritual Gift of Prophecy in Revelation 22:18,'" *Bibliotheca Sacra* 147 [April–June 1990]: 233). Also see Thomas R. Edgar, "The Cessation of the Sign Gifts," *Bibliotheca Sacra* 145 (April–June 1990): 372–75.

80. E.g., Justin Martyr, *Dialogue with Trypho* 82.
81. Contra Grudem, *Prophecy in the New Testament and Today,* pp. 110–12. Maudlin notes, "Grudem . . . argues that every prophet will make mistakes" and again, "According to Grudem—and the KCF [Kansas City Fellowship] and Vineyard leaders agree—there is a discontinuity between the canonical revelation found in the Bible, and the revelation received by modern-day prophets" (Michael Maudlin, "Seers in the Heartland," *Christianity Today* [January 14, 1991], p. 20).
82. This criterion is sometimes overlooked. For example an editorial in *Christianity Today* refers to five criteria given by Cecil M.

Robeck to test prophecy: the Christ Touchstone, the Apostolic Norm, the Unity Criterion, the Sanity Check, and the Messiah Check. The article ends with the following statements: "Such scrutiny is well in line with biblical teaching. . . . But believers who ignore the words of those genuinely gifted in speaking God's contemporary word to his contemporary people, do so at their own peril" (David Neff, "Testing the New Prophets," *Christianity Today* [January 14, 1991], p. 15). Sadly the article never mentions or alerts the reader to one of the most important tests for determining genuine biblical prophets from false prophets: Do any so-called prophets prophesy falsely (Deut. 13:1–3; 18:20–22)? Important also is the test that even if what a "prophet" says comes true, the prophet is not necessarily genuine (Deut. 13:2).

83. Exactly the opposite tactic from such scriptural warnings against false prophecy is sometimes evidenced. The desire for practicing the "prophetic gift" may be considered more important than the admonitions of Scripture. Tolerance of error by modern "prophets" is evidenced among many. "They [the KCF prophets] agreed that they had occasionally been proved wrong. Sometimes their revelation was right but their interpretation and application was wrong. According to Mike Bickle, who confirmed that they certainly could be wrong, the problem seemed to be that they were right too often to be ignored" (David Pytches, *Some Said It Thundered* [Nashville: Oliver Nelson, 1991], p. 109).

84. "In the Old Testament they would have been put to death for giving false prophecy (Deut. 18:20); but Mike [Bickle of the KCF of prophets—now known as the Metro Vineyard Church] pointed to the grace of God who had instructed simply, through New Testament revelation, that their visions and prophecies should be weighed by others (1 Cor. 14:29)" (Pytches, *Some Said It Thundered*, 109). In the afterword of Pytches's book, Jamie Buckingham also addresses the issue of "Discerning Prophecies." Buckingham mentions the subject of "the prophecy and fulfillment" but skirts the issue of "prophets" who prophesy falsely and places stress on signs and wonders as a means of giving credence to prophecies (Jamie Buckingham, "Afterword," in *Some Said It Thundered*, pp. 162–65, esp. 163). *However, a very dangerous situation exists when the desire for "prophesying" contributes to ignoring or glossing over basic scriptural warnings regarding false prophets.* Jeremiah's words come to mind: "An appalling and horrible thing has happened in the land. The prophets prophesy falsely . . . and my people love it so!" (Jer. 5:30–31).

85. For example Matthew's recording of Jesus' words regarding false

prophets employs the present tense in 7:15 (Προσέχετε ἀπὸ τῶν ψευδοπροφητῶν; cf. Acts 20:28).
86. Geisler, *Signs and Wonders*, pp. 138–39. Geisler cites David Wilkerson's prophetic "revelation" of April 1973 that "more than one-third of the United States will be designated a disaster area within the next few years." However, as Geisler demonstrates, such an event never happened. See David Wilkerson, *The Vision* (New York: Pillar, 1974), pp. 32–35.
87. See Victor Budgen, *The Charismatics and the Word of God* (Durham, England: Evangelical, 1989), p. 11; John W. Robbins, *Pat Robertson: A Warning to America* (Jefferson, MD: Trinity Foundation, 1988), pp. 31–38; MacArthur, *Charismatic Chaos*, 66–84; Geisler, *Signs and Wonders,* pp. 63–64, 138–39.
For a look at the attempts of Vineyard movement leaders to respond to current criticism of false prophecy leveled against them, see John Wimber, "A Response to Pastor Ernie Gruen's Controversy with Kansas City Fellowship," and Kevin Springer, "Paul Cain Answers Some Tough Questions about His Relationship with William Branham, Controversial Doctrines, and Occult Practices," and "Hearing God's Word," *Equipping the Saints* 4 (Fall 1990): 4–7, 8–14, 22, 27.
88. Another interesting article regarding the Vineyard "prophet" Paul Cain which has appeared in a Vineyard publication is by Nicky Gumbel. In the article the "accuracy" of Cain's prophecies are stressed with a "few examples from the evening" where these prophets "seemed to have information that was not available by natural means." Gumbel reports, "It appeared that people's names had been accurately revealed to him, often in riddles. For example, he said, 'Thomas, you are a chip off the old block' to a man named Thomas Chipper. To Philip, he said, "You have a pastor's heart and you are a noble man'; he was a pastor named Philip Noble. One of the more remarkable words was given to a man I know well: 'a real bishop . . . Richard the Lionhearted . . . Pontefax or something like that, Pontefract. . . . The Lord gave me an open vision of a field that is going to wake up. It is called 'Wakefield.' This was spoken to Richard Hare, Bishop of Pontefract in the diocese of Wakefield." Gumbel concludes, "As I read my Bible, I see we are to test prophecy . . . to me, all the evidence suggests that they are genuine men of God with an important message for the church" (Nicky Gumbel, "The Feedback Loop at London's HTB," *Equipping the Saints* 4 [Fall 1990]: 30–31).
Gumbel correctly recognizes that prophets are to be tested (1 John 4:1–3). However, besides wondering how revelation conveyed by

such "riddles" can be considered accurate, the manner and nature of these prophecies is qualitatively different from those in Scripture. For example in Acts 9:10–17, Ananias was sent to restore Paul's sight after his conversion. Through a vision God gave the man's precise name ("Saul of Tarsus") and location ("go to the street called Straight, and inquire at the house of Judas")—not in cryptic riddles—but in precision and accuracy. No such riddle–like messages are evidenced. The Holy Spirit not only conveyed the vision but also guaranteed the accuracy of the vision (cf. 1 Sam. 10:1–8; Matt. 17:27; John 1:48).

For an interesting explanation of such activities ("word of knowledge") from a skeptic's perspective, see James Randi, *The Faith Healers* (Buffalo, NY: Prometheus, 1987), pp. 30, 39–45, 99–181. Also see André Kole and Al Janssen, *Miracles or Magic?* (Eugene, OR: Harvest House, 1984), pp. 167–68. Recently *Christianity Today* reported the following concerning Cain's association with the Vineyard movement: "Prophet Paul Cain . . . has moved on from the Vineyard, where he previously affiliated. Cain joined Westminster Chapel in London, where Martin Lloyd-Jones once was pastor. Wimber said he and Cain realized their ministries were taking on different emphases" (*Christianity Today* [August 17, 1992], p. 49).

89. New Testament prophets spoke divinely inspired words which were guarded from error and fully authoritative through the ministry of the Holy Spirit. They did not speak mere human words that were sometimes correct and sometimes a mere hit-and-miss proposition. Contra Grudem, *The Gift of Prophecy in the New Testament and Today*, pp. 74, 76–80, 121, 167.

90. Grudem, *Prophecy in the New Testament*, p. 14. Other Vineyard movement proponents also admit that their prophecies can be wrong. Mallone, another Vineyard proponent, contends, "Prophecy today . . . is not in the category of revelation given to us in the Holy Spirit. . . . A person may hear the voice of the Lord and be compelled to speak, but there is no assurance that it is pollutant-free. There will be a mixture of flesh and spirit" (Mallone, *Those Controversial Gifts*, pp. 39–40).

91. "Either those who claim the gift of prophecy are uttering infallible truths on a par with those in the Bible or else the New Testament gift of prophecy does not exist today. For the 'prophecies' given today are not infallible, but are often false. Thus, we must conclude that the New Testament gift of prophecy does not exist today" (Geisler, *Signs and Wonders*, p. 162).

92. Grudem, *The Gift of Prophecy in the New Testament and Today*,

pp. 241–42. Grudem states that the suppression of prophecy in the church of the second century A.D. and beyond occurred because some "prophets" failed to distinguish between canonically authoritative prophecy of the apostles, which ceased, and edifying prophecy, which, he says, continued. The latter was not tolerated but rejected because such a form of prophecy "mistakenly" made claims to absolute authority. However, Grudem's hypothesis and his assertion here cannot stand in light of a close examination of the biblical and historical data.

Chapter 14

1. For an exposition and evaluation of secular humanism, see Norman L. Geisler, *Is Man the Measure? An Evaluation of Contemporary Humanism* (Grand Rapids: Baker, 1983).
2. This antisupernaturalism is examined in Norman L. Geisler, *Miracles and Modern Thought* (Grand Rapids: Zondervan, 1982).
3. Alice Bailey, *The Externalisation of the Hierarchy* (New York: Lucis, 1957), p. 551.
4. Benjamin Creme, *The Reappearance of the Christ and the Masters of Wisdom* (North Hollywood, CA: Tara Center, 1980), p. 47.
5. *The Golden Book of the Theosophical Society*, ed. C. Jinarajadasa (London: Theosophical, 1925), pp. 45–46.
6. See a critique of this in Norman L. Geisler and J. Yutaka Amano, *The Religion of the Force* (Dallas, TX: Quest, 1983).
7. In *Confluent Education* Beverly Galyean admits: "I think the whole purpose of life is to reown the Godlikeness within us; the perfect love, the perfect wisdom, the perfect understanding. . . . The system of confluent education as I work with it is totally dependent on that view" (quoted by *Christianity Today*, May 16, 1986, p. 20).
8. Reincarnation is evaluated in Norman L. Geisler and J. Yutaka Amano, *The Reincarnation Sensation* (Wheaton, IL: Tyndale, 1986).
9. There are some broad-based groups, such as The Unity-in-Diversity Council, World Trade Center, 350 South Figueroa Street, Suite 370, Los Angeles, CA 90071; and The International Cooperation Council, which publishes the Directory for a New World, Los Angeles, 1979.
10. Networking is done by "conferences, phone calls, air travel, books, phantom organizations, papers, pamphleteering, photocopying, lectures, workshops, parties, grapevine, mutual friends, summit meetings, coalitions, tapes, newsletters" (Marilyn Ferguson, *The Aquarian Conspiracy* [Los Angeles: Torcher, 1980], pp. 62–63).
11. See George Trevelyan, *A Vision of the Aquarian Age: The Emerging Spiritual World View* (Walpole, NH: Stillpoint, 1984), p. 171.

12. *The Aquarian Gospel* is a rewriting of the life of Jesus from a pantheistic perspective in which Jesus is presented as a pantheist who believes in reincarnation and is a master (occult) magician. See Levi Dowling, *The Aquarian Gospel of Jesus the Christ* (1907; reprint, Marina del Rey, CA: DeVorss, 1982).
13. *Visions and Findhorn: Anthology* (Farres, Scotland: Findhorn, 1978), p. 82.
14. Max Heindel, *Blavatsky and the Secret Doctrine* (1933; reprint, Marina del Rey, CA: DeVorss, 1979), pp. 61–64.
15. Alice Bailey, *The Reappearance of the Christ* (New York: Lucis, 1979), pp. 144–50.
16. Creme, *The Reappearance of the Christ*, p. 150.
17. Douglas R. Groothuis, *Unmasking the New Age* (Downers Grove, IL: InterVarsity, 1986), pp. 18–30.
18. Baha'u'llah, *Gleanings from the Writings of Baha'u'llah* (Wilmette, IL: Baha'i, 1952), p. 270.
19. Bailey, *The Reappearance of the Christ*, p. 126.
20. M. K. Gandhi, *The Message of Jesus Christ* (Bombay: Bharatiya Vidya Bhauan, 1963), p. 41.
21. Ibid., p. 55.
22. Dowling, *The Aquarian Gospel*, 7. 37. 19, p. 77.
23. Creme, *The Reappearance of the Christ*, p. 108.
24. David Spangler, *Revelation: The Birth of a New Age* (San Francisco: Rainbow Bridge, 1976), p. 77.
25. Ibid., p. 22.
26. Bailey, *The Reappearance of the Christ*, p. 147.
27. David Spangler, *Reflections on the Christ* (Farres, Scotland: Lecture series, 1978), p. 87.
28. *Time* (May 19, 1980), p. 73.
29. Creme, *The Reappearance of the Christ*, p. 115.
30. Spangler, *Revelation*, p. 60.
31. Creme, *The Reappearance of the Christ*, p. 122.
32. Ibid., p. 111.
33. P. Swami, *The Spiritual Heritage of India* (Hollywood, CA: Vedata, 1963), p. 45.
34. *Upanishads*, 6.7, quoted by Alan Watts, *The Way of Zen* (New York: Vintage, 1957), p. 34.
35. Spangler, *Revelation*, p. 60
36. Spangler, *Reflections on the Christ*, p. 82.
37. Bailey, *The Reappearance of the Christ*, p. 144.
38. George Lucas, *The Empire Strikes Back* (New York: Ballantine, 1980), p. 134.
39. Spangler, *Reflections of the Christ*, p. 40.

40. Benjamin Creme, *Messages from Maitreya the Christ*, vol. 1 (Los Angeles: Tara, 1980), no. 19, p. 46.
41. Creme, *The Reappearance of the Christ*, p. 115.
42. Dowling, *The Aquarian Gospel*, p. 36.
43. Creme, *The Reappearance of the Christ*, p. 120.
44. Ibid., p. 25.
45. Shirley MacLaine, *Out on a Limb* (New York: Bantam, 1983), p. 91.
46. Creme, *The Reappearance of the Christ*, p. 28.
47. Dowling, *The Aquarian Gospel*, p. 261.
48. Mary Baker Eddy, *Science and Health with Key to the Scriptures* (Boston: Allison V. Stewart, 1909), 44:20–30.
49. Dowling, *The Aquarian Gospel*, p. 255.
50. Ibid., p. 261.
51. Ibid., p. 184.
52. Ibid., p. 261.
53. Ibid., p. 18.
54. MacLaine, *Out on a Limb*, p. 326.
55. Dowling, *The Aquarian Gospel*, p. 57.
56. Trevelyan, *A Vision of the Aquarian Age*, p. 11.
57. Dowling, *The Aquarian Gospel*, p. 57.
58. MacLaine, *Out on a Limb*, p. 204.
59. Dowling, *The Aquarian Gospel*, p. 55.
60. Bailey, *The Externalisation of the Hierarchy*, p. 604.
61. Dowling, *The Aquarian Gospel*, p. 263.
62. Creme, *The Reappearance of the Christ*, p. 134.
63. Marilyn Ferguson, *The Aquarian Conspiracy: Personal and Social Transformation in the 1980's* (Los Angeles: Houghton Mifflin, 1980), p. 382.
64. Creme, *Messages from Maitreya the Christ*, no. 98, p. 204.
65. Ibid., no. 81, p. 170.
66. MacLaine, *Out on a Limb*, p. 347.
67. Creme, *The Reappearance of the Christ*, pp. 135–36.
68. See Groothuis, *Unmasking the New Age*, pp. 47–48.
69. See Plotinus *Enneads*, trans. Stephen MacKenna, 3d ed. (London: Faber and Faber, 1966), 5. 5. 6; 6.9.4.
70. Dowling, *The Aquarian Gospel*, p. 19.
71. Creme, *The Reappearance of the Christ*, p. 36.
72. Spangler, *Revelation*, p. 38.
73. Dowling, *The Aquarian Gospel*, p. 78.
74. Watts, *The Way of Zen*, p. 20.
75. Mark Satin, *New Age Politics*, rev. ed. (New York: Dell, 1979), p. 98.

76. Watts, *The Way of Zen*, p. 35.
77. Mary Baker Eddy, *Science and Health*, p. 584:1–16.
78. Spangler, *Revelation*, p. 13.
79. Watts, *The Way of Zen*, p. 52.
80. Satin, *New Age Politics*, p. 100.
81. Creme, *The Reappearance of the Christ*, p. 123.
82. Dowling, *The Aquarian Gospel*, p. 52.
83. Creme, *The Reappearance of the Christ*, p. 25.
84. Bailey, *The Reappearance of the Christ*, p. 143.
85. MacLaine, *Out on a Limb*, p. 45.
86. Spangler, *Reflections on the Christ*, p. 39.
87. Ibid., p. 29.
88. Ibid., p. 44.
89. Ibid., p. 41.
90. Ibid., p. 40.
91. Ibid., p. 41.
92. Bailey, *The Externalisation of the Hierarchy*, p. 593.
93. Robert Short, *The Gospel from Outer Space* (New York: Harper & Row, 1983), p. 55.
94. Satin, *New Age Politics*, p. 112.
95. Bailey, *The Reappearance of the Christ*, p. 59.
96. Ibid., p. 66.
97. Creme, *The Reappearance of the Christ*, p. 32.
98. Bailey, *The Externalisation of the Hierarchy*, p. 597.
99. Creme, *The Reappearance of the Christ*, p. 55.
100. Ibid., p. 37.
101. Ibid.
102. Bailey, *The Externalisation of the Hierarchy*, p. 612.
103. Creme, *The Reappearance of the Christ*, p. 115.
104. Ibid., p. 54.
105. Ibid., p. 46.
106. Bailey, *The Externalisation of the Hierarchy*, p. 612; cf. Creme, *The Reappearance of the Christ*, p. 169.
107. Creme, *The Reappearance of the Christ*, p. 37.
108. Ibid., p. 34.
109. Ibid., p. 37.
110. Ibid., p. 169.
111. Ibid., p. 31.
112. Ibid., p. 158.
113. Robert Short, *The Gospel from Outer Space*, p. 55.